MONONGAH

WEST VIRGINIA AND APPALACHIA

A SERIES EDITED BY RONALD L. LEWIS

VOLUME 6

MONONGAH

THE TRAGIC STORY
OF THE WORST
INDUSTRIAL ACCIDENT
IN US HISTORY

DAVITT McATEER

MORGANTOWN 2007

To Kathryn Grace
and to the memory of my Mother and Father

West Virginia University Press, Morgantown 26506

© 2007 West Virginia University Press

First edition 2007 by West Virginia University Press

10 09 08 07   8 7 6 5 4 3 2 1

ISBN-13 978-1-933202-29-7 [hardback]

ISBN-10 1-933202-29-7

Library of Congress Cataloguing-in-Publication Data

Monongah: The Tragic Story of the 1907 Monongah Mine Disaster, The Worst Industrial
Accident in US History (West Virginia and Appalachia; 6)

p.   cm.

1. Monongah Mine Disaster, Monongah, W. Va., 1907 2. Industrial accidents. 3. Industry—
West Virginia—History. 4. Coal mines and mining. 5. Coal mines and mining—West Virginia.
I. Title. II. McAteer, J. Davitt 1944 -.

IN PROCESS

Library of Congress Control Number: 2007940286

Cover and book design by Than Saffel

Printed in U.S.A. by BookMobile

CONTENTS

ACKNOWLEDGMENTS

THIRTY plus years ago, while looking into the history of mining in this country, I came upon the Monongah mine disaster and the fact that it had taken more lives than any mine accident in American history. Little was publicly known about the disaster and its victims, and although other events intervened in my life, I could not let go of this story. The odyssey that led to this book had begun.

The West Virginia and Regional History Collections at the West Virginia University Charles C. Wise, Jr., Library has perhaps the best mining collection in the country. Over two decades, the material and the people who steward it have been a great help: efficient, knowledgeable, and kind. Curators George Parkinson, Ken Fones-Wolf, and John Cuthbert have been generous with their thoughts and time. In addition, Dr. Ronald L. Lewis, of the West Virginia University Department of History, has inspired and encouraged my efforts.

Students at Fairmont State University and the staff of the Ruth Ann Musick Library have participated in research efforts; especially helpful were librarians Bill Grubb and Melody Bartlett, who, in conjunction with my research, developed "The Monongah Mine Disaster and its Social Setting, A Collage of Newspaper Accounts."

Mary Moore, the now-retired assistant librarian at Wheeling Jesuit University's Bishop Hodges Library, provided essential assistance, especially concerning the B&O Railroad accounts. Employees at the United States Department of Labor, Mine Safety and Health Academy Library—Merle Moore, Yvonne Farley, and Melody Bragg—were dedicated and helpful in the Bureau of Mines materials. And I am indebted to the Hagley Museum & Library in Wilmington, Delaware, for helping unravel the Fairmont Coal Company files.

Several of this book's most important chapters are made possible through the help given to me by the staff of the West Virginia Department of Culture & History, located at the West Virginia Archives & History in the State Capitol Complex in Charleston. The West Virginia Culture & History collection contains *The Report of Hearing Before the Select Committee of the Legislature of West Virginia to Investigate the Cause of Mine Explosions Within the State and to Recommend Remedial Legislation Relating Thereto*. That report, especially the "Transcript of Testimony Taken at an Inquisition Held at Fairmont, Marion County, West Virginia, Beginning January 6th and Concluding January 15th Before E. S. Amos, Coroner of Said County," is an invaluable window into that tragic day in 1907.

Thomas N. Bethell and John Colwell, old friends who have followed *Monongah*'s development, have continuously offered valuable suggestions.

The volunteer staff at the Marion County Historical Society, which is located on Main Street in Fairmont, were especially friendly and diligent in tracking down documents. Susan Robbins-Watson, archivist at the American Red Cross, Hazel Brough Records Center & Archives, in Lorton, Virginia, also helped enormously.

I owe a debt to Pat Conner, Geoffrey Fuller, Rachel Rosolina, and Than Saffel of West Virginia University Press, the publishers who constructively commented and edited to the end. Press interns Stephanie Grimm and Henry Johnson also contributed a great deal of time and attention to the book.

I wish to express particular appreciation to Debbie Roberts for her steadfast belief that this odyssey would be completed, and to Tricia Lollini, who supported our efforts.

When this book began, my children, Caitlin, Owen, Brigid, Kathleen, and Patrick were quite small and only mildly objected to visiting Monongah because it was—as the pictures showed—all black and white. Thanks to each of them. In addition, my brothers, Joseph and Timothy McAteer, helped in ways only brothers can.

Connie Kedward-Gorder of the Catholic Heritage Center, which is part of the Wheeling-Charleston Diocese, provided knowledgeable assistance in my search through the archives housed in Wheeling, West Virginia.

The families of Monongah victims have supported and provided help and information. Two were especially helpful. Bonnie Fleming Reese was a 10-year-old girl on the day of the explosion and had vivid memories of the events; Anne Vingle, Peter Urban's daughter, was interviewed at her home in Monongah at the age of 98. Both provided exceptional insights into events surrounding the disaster.

Authors frequently suggest in their acknowledgments that there are many whom they have left out. That is absolutely true in this case, especially as this project has stretched over nearly thirty years. My most humble apologies to those persons and institutions.

INTRODUCTION

Robert B. Reich

W HEN I heard Davitt McAteer was working on a book detailing the unparalleled disaster at the Monongah mines, I thought it promising news. I knew that when Davitt applied his considerable intelligence and insight to researching the true story, the results would take readers far beyond the official accounts to accurately convey the import and enormity of the worst industrial disaster in the history of the United States.

In 1993, Davitt McAteer began working for me at the Department of Labor, first as a consultant for about a year before he became the only assistant secretary of labor for Mine Safety and Health during the Clinton administration. In that capacity, Davitt served from 1994 to 2000, and I was much impressed with his knowledge of mining, as well as his energy and integrity during those seven years.

Sometime last year, I discovered that Davitt was extensively investigating the Monongah disaster and, in fact, had been for more than 20 years. He has combed through local, national, and international newspapers from the decades before and after the 1907 accident; read transcripts of the legal proceedings relating to the accident and the resulting legislation; and tracked down personal papers from company owners, charitable aid workers, and others who had a principal role in the events. Detailed inquiries like Davitt's are seldom purely professional undertakings; Davitt's search for the truth was a labor of love motivated by an intense will to reveal the unvarnished reality experienced in 1907 by the mining industry and the public.

In 1994, I swore Davitt into his new position with the Department of Labor in the town of Fairmont in Marion County, West Virginia, very near the site of the 1907 Monongah disaster. Nearly 300 people attended and, as I joked at the time and Davitt agreed, more than half of them were relatives of his. The hills of north-central West Virginia had well nourished the McAteer clan, which had grown from four or five immigrant McAteers in 1847 to well over 200 relatives living in the area 150 years later. Just prior to the swearing in, I visited an underground coal mine with Davitt and learned first hand the risks and dangers that miners continue to face today.

Indeed, the courtroom where the swearing-in took place is the very same courtroom where the coroner's inquest had been held barely a month after the massive 1907 explosions in the Monongah mines. That very room was where the first investigation of the disaster was presented and its possible causes were explored. The official death toll was variously cited by the Monongah Mining Company at the time as nearly 362 miners; in *Monongah*, readers learn from Davitt's research that the final toll was more probably well over 500 dead.

The mining industry has been a central force in the history and sociology of West Virginia for over a century, and West Virginia University Press, as the state's flagship university press, has the resources and connections to give the tragic events the treatment they so richly deserve. And no one is positioned better than Davitt McAteer to examine the Monongah mining disaster of 1907 from all the perspectives required: historical, sociological, legal, and economic.

Monongah is an important book, long overdue.

J. H. LEONARD,
OILER FOR THE No. 6 MINE

There is no other period in the nation's history when politics seems so complete-
ly dwarfed by economic changes, none in which the life of the country rests so
completely in the hands of the industrial entrepreneur. The industrialists of the
Gilded Age were . . . men of heroic audacity and magnificent exploitative tal-
ents—shrewd, energetic, aggressive, rapacious, domineering, insatiable. They
directed the proliferation of the country's wealth, they seized its opportunities,
they managed its corruption, and from them the era took its tone and color.
                    —*Richard Hofstadler, "The American Political Tradition"*

J.H. LEONARD was the oiler for the ventilation fan at the No. 6
mine. In Monongah for seventeen years, Leonard had been working as an
oiler for the last six. He had worked at the Monongah mine since it opened
and was one of the oldest men working there. As oiler, he cleaned fan belts
and lubricated the ventilation fan's motor and wheels. Using large oil cans
with long spouts, Leonard oiled the motor and wheels hourly and frequently
tightened the belt to keep it from slipping, which could reduce or eliminate
the flow of air into the mine.

The Monongah No. 6 mine fan measured 9 feet by 11 feet. Manufactured by the Clifford Company of Connellsville, Pennsylvania, the fan turned at 450 revolutions per minute and moved 350,000 cubic feet of air a minute through the mine tunnels. The exhaust fan pulled air through the mine to provide fresh air and to remove dangerous gasses from deep underground. In 1906, mine fan systems required constant attention; an oiler was required on each shift around the clock.

The mouth of the No. 6 Monongah mine was on the west side of the West Fork River. The tipple, the largest steel tipple in the country, spanned the river and carried the coal across to the preparation plant on the river's east side. The three-ton mine cars that had been hand-loaded underground were attached to a wire rope underground and pulled by a mechanical winch up the slope from the mine bottom, some 400 feet to the mouth of No. 6.

The coal then traveled up the length of the trestle, over the knuckle at the top, which was across the river, and then down the far side of the tipple into the preparation plant. There the coal was dumped onto a series of shakers or screens, called *picking tables*. The laborers, most of whom were disabled miners no longer able to work underground or boys aged eight or older, picked out the rocks and other impurities and separated the coal into sizes before it was loaded into waiting railroad cars for shipping to Chicago, Baltimore, and New York.

In the spring of 1907, Leonard had been assigned the additional duty of manning the derailing switch for coal cars coming out of the mine portal. The cars were pulled out of the mine and up over the steel tipple and then across the West Fork River. The derailing switch was located 25 feet above the entrance of the portal to No. 6 and had been installed because loaded cars would periodically break loose from the tipple as they were being pulled up and over the top. Early that spring, Charlie Dean, the surface foreman and Leonard's boss, decided that because Leonard's job as oiler was near the switch, he should be responsible for flipping the switch that would derail the cars should they break loose.[1]

The mine car pulley system, although one of the most advanced mine transportation systems in the country, had encountered problems in the past. Often, groups of cars would break loose at the top of the tipple and crash back into the mine, where they would tear down electrical wiring, knock out timber props, rip up track, and send sparks throughout the portal bottom and back into the mine entries. The derailing system had been installed earlier the same year in order to prevent that from happening.

In a coal mine, sparks are potentially disastrous. They can ignite whatever highly volatile methane gas and fine coal dust might be present. In the Monongah mines, small amounts of methane gas had been encountered, as well as large quantities of coal dust created by the mining process. Coal dust also formed as horses, mules, coal cars, and hundreds of miners passed through the mine tunnels.

Fourteen Three-ton Cars

At about 10:35 on the morning of December 6th, 1907, Leonard watched as fourteen loaded cars rose out of the mine and up the tipple toward the knuckle at the top. Bill Sloan, an underground foreman, was at the bottom of the slope some 900 feet down into the mine. Sloan had coupled the three-ton coal cars onto the wire rope and signaled Ed Fry, the preparation plant engineer, to start the winch. Fry pulled the winch engine arm, winding the wire rope onto the spindle, which pulled the cars out of the mine then up the 400-foot trestle that spanned the West Fork River. When the cars reached the knuckle at the top, they became stuck.

From his vantage point in the engine house, Fry could not see that the cars were stuck. There was, however, an electric light connected to the main current that acted as a warning light when the cars were moving, and Fry did see that light turn off. It was his practice to turn the winch engine off when he saw the light go dark. When the light went out, he could hear the winch engine increase in speed as it took up the slack in the rope; he turned off the winch engine.[2] Leonard, below the tipple near the derailing switch, described what happened next:

They stopped at the knuckle for some cause. They stop there frequently and especially when unloading box cars. They stopped this time and I waited a good bit for them to come back and they did not come back. . . . If I have to run to the engine to see if it is running, I just run in and right back; but this time when I run in, just as I got one step in the engine room I heard the trip. I run out and the two last cars were going by. I stood there looking down the slope a little bit and the explosion came.[3]

Leonard had watched as the cars stuck at the knuckle of the tipple, then, fearing the ventilation fan was stalling, he turned and ran toward the engine room to check the fan. In that split second, the fourteen three-ton cars rocketed back down the nearly 1,500-foot slope and back into the mine.

Pat McDonnell was on the mine haulage bridge facing the No. 6 mine entrance and glanced up as the cars broke loose. Remembering the explosion the previous year that had been caused by another group of runaway cars, he raced toward the derailing switch but was a moment too late and watched as the cars hurtled down the track.

THE NORTHERN COAL FIELDS
OF WEST VIRGINIA

This has been a century of mechanical invention rather than of social reconstruction—a period of rapidly increasing wealth production, rather than its just distribution.

— *"New York World" December 31, 1899*
Quoted in "After the Civil War," John S. Blay

THE Monongah mines were developed by the most powerful, wealthy West Virginian entrepreneurs and politicians and financed by some of the wealthiest men in America. West Virginia's ex-senators and ex-governors had organized and financed the companies, as did John D. Rockefeller, the Standard Oil Company, and banking interests in New York and Baltimore.

During the last quarter of the nineteenth century, the economy in the United States completed a transformation begun at the end of the Civil War, shifting from an agricultural to an industrial base. This transformation was fueled in large part by the rapid growth of the steel and rail industries, the explosive growth of the Midwest and Great Lakes regions, and the emergence of commercial generation of electricity.[1]

In the decade that closed the old century and opened the new—1895 to 1905—railroads, steamships, and the steel industry produced a nearly insatiable appetite for coal. Also, during that decade, more coal was mined in the United States than had been mined throughout its history.[2] Coal was not only the sole source of power for railroads and steamships, it was the sole source of fuel for the production of electricity, the use of which was increasing dramatically each year. Electricity was also critical in the production of iron and steel for the building of the cities of Chicago, Milwaukee, and the other cities along the Great Lakes. Coal was King.

The Lay of the Land

The Appalachian mountain range stretches 1,500 miles from Canada along the eastern half of the United States to central Alabama. Adjacent to this ancient mountain system is the richest deposit of coal the world has ever known. The Appalachian Coal Field stretches from northern Pennsylvania to central Alabama. It is the largest coal field in the United States and perhaps the world, stretching over 900 miles and covering 63,000 square miles. Within this field, one seam, the Pittsburgh seam, comprises 5,700 square miles of a large and persistent stratum of one kind of rock.[3]

Before the Civil War, the principal coal mining regions of the United States lay east of the Allegheny Mountains and included the Georges Creek Basin in western Maryland. The Georges Creek Basin is a canoe-shaped deposit 25 miles long and six miles wide under the western end of Allegany County, Maryland. In the valley between Savage Mountain and Dan Mountain, the Big Vein Seam is the site where numerous small companies were merged to form the Consolidation Coal Company, which began operation shortly after the conclusion of the Civil War. The Georges Creek coal basin had been mined since 1751 and had been somewhat depleted by the end of the Civil War. The search began for new deposits to the west.[4]

But earlier, in 1861, President Abraham Lincoln had encouraged a group of northwestern Virginians loyal to their union to carve out the Allegheny mountain region from the Confederate State of Virginia. The majority of these residents supported the effort because they felt little kinship with their eastern and southern neighbors. They were not slave owners and saw their economic interests tied more to the north or west than to the south. During the Civil War, the region was sympathetic to the North, and within its boundaries lay the Baltimore & Ohio tracks, the rail connection between the east coast and the Ohio River. Lincoln understood how vital that link would be to the war effort: control of the rail line through Cumberland, Maryland, and Harper's Ferry and Wheeling—both in what was then Virginia—would be critically important to the war's outcome. The mountainous western portion of Virginia eventually became, in 1865, West Virginia, the 35th state.

Consolidation Coal Company was chartered by the Maryland Legislature in 1860, but its organization was delayed by the Civil War. The small companies that composed Consol, as it came to be called, included the Cumberland Coal & Iron Company, the Ocean Steam Coal Company, Frostburg Coal Company, and the Mount Savage Iron Company. The Cumberland & Pennsylvania Railroad interests were behind the consolidation, and Cumberland & Pennsylvania stocks were the original payment accepted for the subscription bonds on April 19, 1864.[5] A second merger occurred just after the turn of the century when Consolidation Coal Company joined with the Fairmont Coal Company in 1903 and amassed large additional reserves in Maryland, West Virginia, Pennsylvania, and Kentucky.

By 1906, Consolidation Coal was operating more than sixty-five mines and employing tens of thousands of miners, and by 1907 it was one of the largest coal mining companies in the country.[6] From its inception, the merged company adopted an aggressive, combative philosophy toward unions and miners alike. Given its economic, political, and legal connections, especially in West Virginia, Consolidation Coal was able to exercise unlimited control over the workforce, especially at the Monongah mines, which had an unusually large number of immigrant miners.

In 1902, the United Mine Workers of America attempted to organize the Monongah miners. Company officials, with the help of a company police force that was secretly tied to the United States Marshal's Office, successfully obtained a legal but bogus injunction before a federal judge. Judge John J. Jackson was the same federal judge who had for years been receiving a free railcar of coal each winter for his personal use from the Fairmont Coal Company.

In 1852, the Baltimore & Ohio Railroad had become the first railroad in the country to open a track line from the Atlantic coast to the Ohio River.[7] Beginning in Baltimore, B&O laid a track first to Harpers Ferry, Virginia, then to Hagerstown and Cumberland, Maryland, then up and over the rugged Allegheny Mountains, passing back into what was then Virginia. It then stretched west, first to Fairmont and finally to Wheeling and the Ohio River. In what was a staggering engineering feat, the B&O had driven eleven tunnels and built 113 bridges, including one that was then the longest steel span in the nation. On Christmas Eve in 1852, the track reached Roseby's Rock, eighteen miles east of Wheeling. Here the rail going west met a track that had been laid from Wheeling east. Roseby's Rock, a massive sandstone formation some sixty-four feet long and twenty feet thick, served as a convenient landmark for the closing of the line between Baltimore and the Ohio River. Roseberry Carr, the rail system's superintendent, oversaw the joining of the lines, and his crew carved his name, albeit misspelled as Rosbby's Rock, in foot-high letters into the rock's surface.[8]

The B&O thus became the first and only railroad to stretch from the Atlantic coast to the Ohio River Valley. The rail construction had cost $15,628,963, a record for any railroad construction project at the time, and had required 5,000 men, mostly Irish immigrants, and 1,250 horses to complete.[9] To properly celebrate the completion, 500 citizens of Baltimore rode for eighteen hours to a temporary depot on the south bank of Wheeling Creek, where they crossed on a ferryboat to the center of Wheeling to join their Virginia counterparts. That evening, they attended an elaborate ball at the splendid Washington Hotel in Wheeling.

Many of the principal dignitaries spent the night at the McLure House, one of the region's newest and best hotels. In 1851, John McLure had built McLure House at the corner of 12th and Market streets. The ground floor was doughnut shaped with an opening to the street. The open center of McLure House included a watering trough and hitching posts for the carriages and stagecoaches traveling west from Cumberland, Maryland, along the Old National Road. The hotel's registration desk and lobby were located on the second floor in order to avoid the muddy conditions created by the horses and carriages at ground level. In concession to the dress code of the day, the 12th Street entrance had the word *Ladies* etched in the arch and was built with a wider door in order to accommodate the popular and fashionable wide hoop skirts.

The largest in the region, the hotel had been built in anticipation of the coming of the B&O, and formally opened on March 4, 1852. The night of the rail line completion, the party for B&O dignitaries who had chosen to make Wheeling the Ohio River terminus of the railroad, danced the "Tupsey Waltz," a song composed for and dedicated to Dr. John D. M. Carr who was a prominent physician and full-time resident of the McLure House.[10]

The completion of the rail line to Wheeling not only meant commerce from the Atlantic ports to the Ohio River Valley, it also opened up what was to become the country's—and the world's—greatest coal seam to development: the Pittsburgh seam, which now lay within easy reach of rail lines and, thus, within reach of markets both in the east and the west.

The Pittsburgh Seam

Discovered by James Burd, a colonel in the French and Indian War in 1759, the Pittsburgh seam of coal is perhaps the most valuable body of minerals ever discovered by man, certainly in the United States and perhaps in the world. It rivals the Comstock Lode in Nevada and Witwatersrand Gold Reef in South Africa, as well as the gold and silver deposits of California.

Coal is formed beneath the surface in "seams," which lay in *strata* or *beds*.[11] Within the Pittsburgh seam is the Monongahela formation, centered around northern West Virginia and southwestern Pennsylvania. The mines in the Fairmont region, including Monongah, exploit the Monongahela formation. The Pittsburgh seam runs northeast to southwest, stretching from Pennsylvania through West Virginia, Kentucky, and parts of Tennessee, then dipping and reappearing in Alabama. Remarkably uniform in both quality and pitch, in places it stands seven and a half feet high and has a gentle incline towards the northwest. The coal is of excellent thickness, consistency, and height, and—what is most significant—when burned produces a very high-energy output, averaging between 10,000 and 12,000 BTUs (British thermal units) of energy per ton of coal burned. It also produces excellent coke, a by-product critical to the production of iron and steel.[12]

Remarkably, the seam also offers some of the best geological conditions for mining ever encountered, in the United States or abroad. The coal bed itself is horizontal, with consistent grade, and the roof above the coal, for the most part, is extremely stable, typically consisting of sandstone or clays with 500 to 800 feet of cover between the seam and the earth's surface.

But the Pittsburgh seam has one serious disadvantage. Large quantities of methane gas occur naturally throughout the length of the bed, where the coal is found. Methane gas, also referred to as *firedamp*, is the pure form of natural gas. Extremely explosive, methane gas is carbureted hydrogen, or *marsh gas.* Like coal itself, methane is formed by the decomposition of organic matter. Odorless, colorless, and tasteless, methane is difficult to detect; it is also nonpoisonous when mixed with oxygen. An atmosphere of pure methane will not, however, support life.[13]

To make matters worse, *afterdamp*—gases that are formed as a result of a methane explosion, such as *blackdamp* (generally, 15 percent carbon dioxide and 85 percent nitrogen)—are fatal. Blackdamp is heavier than air and layers along the floor, suffocating its victims. Carbon monoxide is also produced by coal mine explosions. Miners who survive the initial explosion are sometimes asphyxiated by carbon monoxide, which combines with the hemoglobin of the blood more readily than oxygen, resulting in less oxygen being carried from the lungs to the body.[14]

Following the Civil War's end, coal mining efforts expanded to the north central West Virginia coalfields and the coalfields in western Pennsylvania. In the Connellsville area of Pennsylvania in the 1870s, a number of mines developed that exploited the same Pittsburgh seam outcroppings along the same Monongahela River. Closer to the iron and steel mills of Pittsburgh, and enjoying a better-developed water transportation system, as well as greater access to capital, the Connellsville mines prospered. The Connellsville coal also made excellent coking coal, and the region developed a reputation for high-quality coke.[15]

In 1875 the state of West Virginia was twelve years old, and for most of the state, the mountainous terrain had prevented large-scale economic development. Exploitation of the extensive natural resources—timber, oil, gas, and coal—was limited, in large part because of inadequate market access and difficult transportation.

For example, while the Fairmont field exploited the southerly end of the same coal formation as Connellsville, it lacked markets, adequate transportation, and most notably, capital. But in the years just prior to the turn of the century, all of that changed. West Virginia vaulted onto the coal-producing stage. In 1883 coal production in the entire state amounted to less than three million tons. Just twenty years later, in 1903, West Virginia mines produced over 22 million tons, most of which were clustered around Fairmont.

The Fairmont coal field was central to West Virginia's emergence as the nation's premier energy source of the early 1900s. Covering all or part of five northern West Virginia counties, the Fairmont fields were originally opened in 1852 when an entrepreneur, James O. Watson, developed the first coal mine west of the Allegheny Mountains in the town of Fairmont. By 1900 Fairmont had established itself as the leading production field in West Virginia and challenged established mining centers of Connellsville and Pittsburgh as well as Frostburg, Maryland.

Immigrant Wave

If America in the new century needed coal, it also needed miners to dig the coal. Following the Civil War, immigration increased rapidly, reaching its peak between 1903 and 1914, when a million immigrants a year entered the country.[16] During this period, immigrants came principally from central and southern Europe. In particular, immigrants came from Italy and the northern reaches of the Austro-Hungary Empire, especially the Kingdom of Poland, then under Russian control. Most came for jobs, and America in the century's first decades seemed to have a job for every one of them. The immigrants were also in demand because they were willing to take the jobs at lower pay, despite the dangerous conditions.

The immigrants were attractive to employers because they represented an abundant source of compliant labor. Immigrants proved to be more difficult for unions to organize, in part because of language differences but also because ancient suspicions between European cultures crossed the Atlantic. Many mine companies recognized this advantage, and immigrants were frequently used as a lever against the wage demands of "natural Americans," unions,[17] and other immigrants who were also easily pitted against one another.

At the time, America was experiencing one of its many waves of anti-immigrant sentiment. Anti-immigrant feelings had existed in the United States in previous decades, but they reached new heights in the early years of the 1900s. In few places were anti-immigrant sentiments stronger than in the coalfields of West Virginia.

In order to recruit these workers, employers—especially mining companies—sent labor agents to Europe to contract for laborers and arranged with steamship companies to pack large numbers of workers on board ships, many bound for a particular location and employer.

What the immigrants found, upon arrival, was a booming economy. Items were selling quickly, and prices were comparatively low: corned beef was 8 cents per pound, bowler-style felt hats were 89 cents, a suit sold for $10, and a shirt cost only 23 cents. Yet wages were also low. The immigrant making the shirt earned only $3.54 a week, or 5 cents an hour for over 70 hours a week. Wages were especially low in the basic industries of steel and coal mining.[18]

Nevertheless, the problems faced by the immigrants did not overshadow the overriding optimism that characterized the United States at the turn of the century. On the last day of the 19th century, the *New York Times*, after listing the inventions and developments of the 1800s—steam engines, railroads, the telegraph, ocean liners, telephones, electric lights, and the cash register—suggested that the new century would be even better: "We step upon the threshold of 1900 which leads to the new century . . . facing a still brighter dawn of civilization."[19] This optimism was based in part on the philosophy that unfettered capitalism would solve widespread economic and social problems. Nowhere were the challenges more profound and the realities more difficult than in the coalfields of West Virginia.

However, these years were considered by most to be good because whatever the trouble, whatever the problem, people believed that it could be fixed. Social ills caused by unrestrained capitalism could be addressed by the government. Theodore Roosevelt was in the White House and could handle any challenge. In the fall of 1906, baseball was well on its way to becoming the national pastime, for the immigrant miners as well as others. The World Series featured the powerful Chicago Cubs and the Detroit Tigers with a newly constructed press box on the first-base pavilion roof. The Tigers proved no match for the Cubs.[20] The newly arrived immigrants in the mining camps of West Virginia could learn the American game and root for the nearby Pittsburgh Pirates or Baltimore Orioles. They could also form their own local teams representing the mine or company they worked for, like the Fairmont Coal Company Skyscrapers.

But by 1907, much of the confidence had changed and an unsettled feeling began to permeate the country. In October of 1907, panic gripped Wall Street and the confidence of the nation was shaken. The stock market collapsed and a run on New York City banks sent shock waves throughout the country. The impact was felt as far away as the mining communities of West Virginia. Orders for coal were curtailed, work was sporadic, and the miners and their families faced an uncertain winter.

LESTER EMMITT TRADER:
ASSISTANT FIRE BOSS AT AGE 22

"Now one objective here, and that's to get it off my shoulders; I've nursed it for 65 years."

—*Lester E. Trader, 1972 Interview with Willis E. Cupp*

THURSDAY, December 5, 1907, was the eve of Saint Nicholas's Day, a holiday widely celebrated in Europe and especially important in Italy, the Austro-Hungarian Empire, and Russia. In Italy, St. Nicholas had been revered since the eleventh century, and the tradition of celebrating with food and drink crossed the Atlantic intact. In 1907, with the Monongah mines idle that Thursday for lack of coal orders, the holiday celebrations were more widespread than usual. In the evening, immigrant miners and their families gathered and told stories of the life of St. Nicholas, the third century Bishop of Myra and the protector of the poor against the rich. Traditional food and drink were shared, and cookies were passed around for all.[1] Following a tradition retained when St. Nicholas became Santa Claus, children's shoes were left by the fireplace with the hope that a coin would be placed inside.

Earlier that day, Anestis Stamboulis and several of his fellow Greek immigrants, all of whom worked in Monongah No. 6, had taken advantage of the idle workday and the mild weather by walking up into the hills above the town of Monongah. There they picked a large basket of mushrooms that, upon their return, were turned into a holiday dinner.

The Young Fire Boss

Even while the celebrations were getting underway around six o'clock that evening, Lester Emmitt Trader entered the No. 6 mine and began his rounds. 22-year-old Trader was the assistant fire boss and had worked in the mine for just over a year. Although the No. 6 had not worked that day, it was scheduled to start again Friday, December 6, and therefore needed to be fire-bossed—a specific pattern of inspection—before work resumed.

Over the course of the next twelve hours, Trader would *pre-shift* the mine by walking through the tunnels, entryways, and haul roads that made up the main roadways of the underground workings of the mine. As he checked for dangerous conditions, including the presence of methane gas and roof- or rib-falls, Trader led a horse-drawn water cart through the main entryway (headings) and sprinkled water in an effort to render the accumulated coal dust inert. The watering carts carried large wooden barrels filled with 300 gallons of water; perforated ends of the barrels were plugged by wooden combs that could be removed to allow water to sprinkle out. At the Monongah mines, the coal dust accumulation was left unwatered in the rooms off the main entries where the miners would actually shoot and load the coal. At nearby mines, including some Fairmont Coal Company operations, miners sprayed water into those rooms as well as the entryways, but the practice was not followed at Monongah No. 6 or No. 8.

Like other fire bosses, Trader worked alone but alternated shifts with his fellow fire boss, Andy H. Morris. Each week one of them would enter the mine at 5:00 or 6:00 P.M. and come out at 5:00 or 6:00 A.M., and the second man would begin around 1:00 A.M. and work until 1:00 P.M. The next week they would trade start times. If, during their inspections, either one of them detected dangerous conditions, he recorded his findings in the official fire boss book, noting the location and nature of the problem. Roof falls and elevated levels of methane gas were among the most common dangers. If the fire boss could not fix the problem immediately, he *dangered off* the area by writing the word *DANGER* with chalk on the rib or placing a wooden board with the word *DANGER* in front of any conditions that could endanger the lives of the men. Finally, on the way out of the mine, he noted the information on the mine chalkboard, kept at the entrance of each mine portal, and then dropped off his fire boss book at the office to alert incoming supervisors of the dangerous condition. The fire boss books were required to remain on mine property at all times, available for review by the state inspector.

The fire boss system of mine examination had begun in Europe during the 1700s. As the name implies, fire bosses were employed to detect fires or gases, especially accumulations of explosive methane gas, and to render them harmless before each shift. In French mines during the Napoleonic period, prisoners served as fire bosses; if they survived, they received shortened sentences for their service. The convicts would enter the mine with a lighted torch held high to burn off any accumulated methane gas. The prisoner-fire boss would be covered with a cloak soaked in water to protect against accidental ignition. Methane gas, which is lighter than air and layers on the roof of the mine, forms naturally in coal seams. It is highly explosive. Concentrations of methane between 5 and 15 percent will explode; concentrations above 15 percent do not explode because the gas density displaces the oxygen. By 1907, the fire boss system had evolved in the United States to the point where mining states required that fire boss or pre-shift examinations be made before the start of each shift.

Although Trader didn't know it, Libberato Delasandro had found methane gas the day before, Wednesday, December 4th. Delasandro, an Italian immigrant who had been digging coal at Monongah No. 6 for four years, had been working the G face second right when his foreman came in and said, "Get the light down, you have some gas." Delasandro answered, "All right," lowering his open flame to avoid an explosion. He had seen gas on previous occasions and had noticed that the gas would get "afire," sometimes "burning about twenty feet."

Earlier that day, while working the second right off D face, he had also noticed gas: "I blowed it out with my coat so as not to light." In what was common practice, the miners who noticed gas would take their coats and wave them in the air, causing air currents, which would move the gas out of the room where they were working. They hoped the gas would then be carried out the mine entries by ventilating air. Delasandro had also seen dust accumulations that same Wednesday.[2]

Early in the morning of December 6th, Trader made a note in his fire boss book of the locations of trace amounts of methane gas. He would later report his findings to Thomas Dolin, the mine foreman, who in turn would report the inspection results to A. J. Ruckman, the mine superintendent. However, Trader didn't actually see Dolin, who came to work after Trader had finished his shift and gone home. Instead he put the book in a drawer in the fire boss's shanty where the other fire boss, Andy Morris, collected it on his way home and delivered it to Ruckman's office, where Dolin worked.

Because of the importance of the fire boss to safety in the mines, by 1900 most coal mining states, including West Virginia, had adopted a fire boss certification system. Each fire boss was required to have worked a number of years as a miner or mine supervisor. In violation of the West Virginia Mining Law,[3] Lester E. Trader was not certified as a fire boss on December 5, 1907; he lacked the three years of mining experience required and had not taken the certification test.

In a 1972 interview, Trader explained,

The way I got to be Fire Boss was due to the fact that one of the fire bosses developed rheumatism and couldn't make his rounds and I helped him. Then when another fire boss quit, I took over the job. But because I was not certified . . . they kept me on the night shift so I wouldn't run into the mine inspector.[4]

Trader lacked not only the three years mining experience, but also the necessary training to qualify under state law.[5] However, because the West Virginia State Mine Inspector had agreed with Consolidation Coal Company in 1906 that Monongah mines No. 6 and 8 did not qualify as gassy mines, Trader and his fellow fire bosses would not need to be certified.

Even though Monongah No. 6 and No. 8 generated gas, and fire bosses were collecting samples and keeping records, the company was trying to keep the mines from being classified as gassy. At that time, West Virginia law permitted two classifications of mines, *gassy* or *nongassy*. The year before, in 1906, company superintendent J. C. Gaskill had written West Virginia State Mine Inspector E. V. Byner, the man in charge of the district that covered the Monongah mines, asking that they be exempted from the gassy classification. In a letter of reply, Byner had granted the nongassy status, thus eliminating the requirement of fire bosses for methane. Such an exemption was uncommon and illogical because trace levels of methane were being found and recorded, and because the Pittsburgh seam was well known for producing dangerous levels of methane. Most significant, it was well known that, as mines are driven deeper and farther into the earth, methane deposits are more likely to accumulate. As No. 6 mine had been in operation for eight years and No. 8 for two, both were now far enough and deep enough that it was increasingly likely that dangerous levels of methane would be found: fire-bossing should have been required. And as expected, methane was being found.

Safety Lamps and Methane Gas

Thursday night, December 5th, Trader checked for methane as he always did, with a flame safety lamp. The lamp had first been successfully demonstrated in 1813 by Dr. William R. Clanny, a British physician from Sunderland, England. The lamp's flame was encased in a wire gauze cone, or *chimney*, and thereby safely detected methane without igniting it. The increasing frequency of methane explosions in mines in England and throughout Europe in the late 1700s threatened to limit development of the coal industries; as mines were being driven deeper, more methane naturally occurred and was being ignited by the open flames used for illumination and gas detection.

The basic principle of the safety lamp is that the wire gauze will inhibit the lamp's flame, keeping it inside the lamp. The wire filaments of the gauze draw off the flames' heat and lower the temperature below combustion level. In other words, the mine safety lamp encloses the flame and retards its passage to the surrounding air. In the presence of methane, the flame inside the chamber will elongate and burn brighter, permitting methane detection while preventing an explosion of the ambient air. The fine wire gauze divides the flame into fine streamlets that are cooled and extinguished before they enter the mine atmosphere. In order to achieve the desired result, the mesh of the gauze must be 784 apertures per square inch, sufficient to cool the flame.

Dr. Clanny later added a glass cylinder and brass bonnet, the glass allowing the lamp to be used for illumination as well. The glass and bonnet also permitted the lamp's use in mines where ventilation systems, which pull large quantities of air down the shafts and tunnels, would otherwise extinguish unprotected flames. Two years later in 1815, Sir Humphrey Davy, a well known and highly regarded British scientist, refined the lamp and received much of the credit for the invention, despite the fact that he never claimed it.

Lester Trader carried a Wolf Lamp, the latest model manufactured by the Wolf Safety Lamp Company of America, located at 621 Broadway in New York City, which was a subsidiary of Friemann and Wolf Company of Zasicken, Germany. The Wolf Lamp was easily recognizable by its two conical gauze chimneys and distinctive corrugated bonnet. Its design permitted use in the strongest of air currents. It burned *naphtha*, a colorless hydrocarbon liquid, and gave off a strong light while detecting even small quantities of methane.

Flame safety lamps were designated to detect the presence of methane at any level. Especially important, however, was detection between 1 and 5 percent, the levels just under the 5 percent explosive level. In order to use the lamp, the flame was initially reduced to a point where the yellow flame disappeared entirely and only a small blue flame was visible. Then the lamp was slowly raised toward the roof of the mine, where the lighter-than-air methane typically accumulated, while the miner carefully observed the flame. If the flame elongated and burned brighter, methane was present. By judging the size of the elongation and the changing color of the flame, an experienced miner could not only detect the presence of methane but could also discern its approximate percentage in the air.

Use of the flame safety lamp was not without risks. If the flame elongated to the top of the wire gauze, it could heat the wire, allowing the flame to pass through the gauze, which could cause combustion or explosion. If the gauze was dented or if a hole occurred anywhere in the gauze chimney, the flame could escape and cause an explosion, not an uncommon occurrence, especially with earlier models.[6]

In theory, fire bosses were to check every part of the mine for methane. In practice, most bosses, including Trader, checked only those locations where gas would customarily accumulate. Voids or high spots in the mine roof were common collection points. Given the size of the mine, Trader would not have practically had time to check everywhere.

If methane was found, it would be recorded in the fire boss book and he would make efforts to change or increase the ventilation in order to remove the gas. If gas removal could not be done immediately, the fire boss marked a chalkboard or coal seam wall near where the sample was taken. This was done in order to warn miners of the risk. If the gas was elevated to a dangerous level, and the fire boss could not immediately render it harmless, he would danger off that section of the mine. By law no one would then be allowed to enter that section until steps had been taken to eliminate the accumulated gas or other danger.

The almost universal method of driving off or dissipating the gas was the use of a *brattice*, or partition, which was hung across the mine tunnels. Its purpose was to direct the ventilating air to the work areas or areas where methane had accumulated. Brattice is a heavy burlap or canvas cloth cut to the size of the mine tunnel and given a coating that made it somewhat impermeable to air. Brattice served to divert the air into the far reaches of the mines. Upon finding methane, the fire boss would hang brattice himself or notify a supervisor that it needed to be done.

As he left the mine, he would note any elevated gas levels on a chalkboard at the mine's entrance. The chalkboard for No. 8 hung on an oil house to the left of the portal about twenty feet away from the mine's mouth. No miner was allowed to enter the mine until the fire boss had completed his scheduled run and had recorded his findings on the chalkboard. At Monongah, the fire boss also controlled an iron gate that allowed miners to pass into the mine, and no miner was allowed to enter the mine until the fire boss had opened the gate. Miners would often congregate on the outside of the gate awaiting the fire boss.

The End of the Day

Shortly after midnight, during his lunch break, Trader sat down and continued writing a letter to his father in McKeesport, Pennsylvania, his home-town. He had started the letter earlier in the week but was completing it that Friday morning, December 6th. Among other things, Trader's thoughts were on mine safety, as news of the preceding week's mine disaster in Fayette City, Pennsylvania, some ninety miles north of Monongah, had spread through the coalfields. On Monday, December 2, methane gas had exploded there in the Naomi mine and thirty-four miners were killed. Trader's letter to his father was filled with unintentional portent. On Tuesday, December 3rd, he had written,

It used to make the shivers run through me to read the news accounts of mine hor-ror, but since I have been in the mines and see into all the little details . . . it has lost a great part of the horror for me, and the small, everyday accidents are more to be feared in my estimation than an extended explosion.

On Friday morning, December 6th, he continued in a prophetic passage in the dim light of the underground shanty:

The greater danger in a mine is not done so much by the flame of the explosion, ex-cept when a dust explosion happens immediately after the gas explosion, but by the concussion . . . where a dust explosion takes places; there is a quick flash throughout the mine or a series of flashes . . .[7]

We have been reading with much interest the news paper accounts of the Naomi Mine explosion. Our own mine being a mine laid out and worked on the same prin-cipal as it and having the same principal dangers to contend with namely gas, dust, and the poor class of foreign labor any one of which would be sufficient to cause a great deal of apprehension for the safety of the mine but coming as they do together it keeps us on the look out for the same fate of the Naomi Mine.

On his way out of the mine, after completing the letter, Trader passed his fellow fire bosses Lyden and Morris, who had come in after midnight, and marked his findings on the mine entry board. He opened the iron gate, allowing the waiting miners to go underground, into the No. 6 mine. He then dropped by the foreman's office and recorded his findings in the outside fire boss book. He cleaned up, stopped by the post office in the company store, and mailed his letter.

At home, his wife Mayme had prepared breakfast. After breakfast and after checking on their still-sleeping two-year-old daughter Elizabeth, Lester Emmitt Trader went to bed.

THE COMPANY MEN

"Clarence was always in control."

— *James O. Watson, II, referring to his son, Clarence W. Watson.*

The Monongah Coal & Coke Company: Johnson Newlon Camden

ON June 11, 1887, U.S. Senator Johnson Newlon Camden entered into an agreement with Aretas Brooks Fleming and Joseph H. Sands, the head cashier of the First National Bank of Fairmont, to form a syndicate for the purpose of "purchasing and controlling as large an amount of the coal territory of the upper Monongahela coal basin as could be got together and where might seem desirable."[1]

A week later, on June 18, a meeting was held at the McLure House in Wheeling. Here, in addition to Sands and Fleming, Camden met with William Hood to finalize the original scheme. The group entered into an agreement, known as the McLure House Agreement, to obtain contracts and options for the purchase of all available coal lands in the upper Monongahela

Coal basin. The region stretched from the West Virginia-Pennsylvania line above Morgantown, south to Clarksburg—some 33 miles along both sides of the Monongahela and West Fork rivers.

Sands, Hood, and Fleming already owned some coal properties in this area and, in accordance with the McLure House Agreement, would act as purchasing agents for the remainder. Camden, for his part, would form and finance a syndicate for the purchases of all these coal lands. In return for Sands, Hood, and Fleming turning over their current property to the syndicate and agreeing to act as purchasing agents, they were to be paid by Camden the sum of $50,000 in cash, with a $50,000 bonus upon meeting certain conditions, and granted membership and ownership in the syndicate.[2]

After the Wheeling meeting, Camden formed two companies, the Monongahela River Railroad Company and the Upper Monongahela Coal & Coke Company. The railroad company was established to construct a spur line from the B&O line terminus in Fairmont to Clarksburg where it would connect with the Parkersburg Branch of the B&O line, thus opening up the north central West Virginia coal basin.

On January 24, 1889, Camden, as president of the Monongahela River Railroad Company, and Charles F. Mays, president of the B&O Railroad Company, entered into an agreement to prorate fees and establish rates for transporting Monongah coal and coke. This agreement also provided for the B&O to guarantee the financing of the spur line.

The second company, the Upper Monongahela Coal and Coke Company, was not established until two years after the initial McLure House meeting. In May of 1889, Camden established the Upper Monongahela Coal & Coke Company with initial capitalization of 12 shares of $50,000 each. In choosing business partners, Camden followed the common practice of the day, relying upon friends and the existing partners; he also chose persons who would be helpful in and have an interest in seeing the business succeed.

The members included U. S. Senator Anthem P. Gorman and Governor Elihu E. Jackson of Maryland, both of whom were invested in and part of the B&O directorship; E. W. Clark of the financial firm of E. W. Clark and Company, Philadelphia; James Sloan, Jr., of the Farmers and Merchants National Bank of Baltimore; Samuel Sperrow of Drexel Morgan and Company of New York; Charles W. Harkens of the Standard Oil Company of Cleveland, Ohio, representing the Rockefeller interest; former U. S. Senator James G. Fair of Nevada; Judge A. B. Fleming of Fairmont; Joseph H. Sands, first cashier of the First National Bank of Fairmont; and J. N. Camden, Jr., who—with his father—had held back some additional shares. With this stock, they then brought in Charles F. Mayer, president, and C. K. Lord, third vice president of the B&O Railroad; Camden's son-in-law, Baldwin D. Spilman; and Camden's brothers-in-law G. W. Thompson and D. S. Thompson. Camden also brought in William P. Thompson to the company, who was another brother-in-law and a former colonel in the Confederate calvary as well as the Secretary of Standard Oil of Ohio.[3]

In 1890, the company was reorganized and the name changed to the Monongah Coal & Coke Company, with capital stock increasing to $2 million.[4] Some $600,000 was raised, about half of which was committed to purchase the mineral rights. The intention was to purchase 15,000 acres at an average price of no more than $25.50 per acre.[5] In fact, 12,000 acres were purchased at $22.50 per acre, each acre carried on the books at $100 per acre. The overall cost was $275,000 including $25,000 for surface acreage for use as company towns and plant locations.[6]

A. B. Fleming had previously worked with Camden and had become his legal advisor. Fleming also represented Standard Oil Company in West Virginia. In the spring of 1875, Camden and John D. Rockefeller entered into an agreement. As was Rockefeller's practice, absolute secrecy surrounded the deal. Essentially, Camden agreed to transfer to the Standard Oil Company the refining plant accessories and all real estate of the J. N. Camden Company in exchange for Standard Oil Company stock. In May of 1875, Camden renamed his company, which was now a subsidiary of Standard Oil Company, the Camden Consolidated Oil Company.

The agreement set out that Camden should continue to operate the company and that no mention was to be made that it had contractual obligation with Rockefeller's Standard Oil Company. But Camden and his management were also charged with the consolidation of the oil industry in the territory contiguous with the B&O Railroad. Camden went to great lengths to hide his association with Rockefeller and Standard Oil, keeping the fact hidden not only from the public, his suppliers, and his customers, but also from his employees.[7]

Camden had a business relationship with the B&O Railroad, which was then struggling to avoid the grasp of the Rockefeller monopoly. Rockefeller and the Standard Oil Company were known as The Combination because of his effort to monopolize the oil business. Camden was thorough in his deception of the B&O management, writing to O. H. Payne, treasurer of the Standard Oil Company, when a B&O official came to visit: "Mr. Garnett is coming to see us tomorrow. . . . I suppose he will encourage us to keep up our oil business and fight the 'combination.'"[8]

Even during this time, as Camden was negotiating the secret sale of his company to Rockefeller, he entered into what today would be known as an illegal freight rate kickback scheme with the B&O. It was a common practice in those days, but it had the result of causing the B&O to unknowingly give preferential rates to Rockefeller—whom they were out to defeat.[9] It was not unexpected that the Rockefeller interest would be represented, however, and in addition, the Secretary of Standard Oil of Ohio was Camden's brother-in-law, William P. Thompson.[10]

Shortly thereafter, Rockefeller authorized Camden to purchase three competing Parkersburg refineries, again without making known the identity of the three owners. With these purchases, Rockefeller completed his nearly total takeover of the West Virginia oil fields, a move that was essential to his monopolization of the entire United States oil refining business. Since no other country yet produced large-scale commercial oil, Rockefeller, in effect, controlled the world's entire oil production.[11]

In another coal-related venture, in 1886 Camden was invited by James O. Watson and nine other investors to become part of the ownership of the Montana mines, a mine property four miles northeast of Fairmont along the Monongahela River. This venture was unusual because it was the first mine opened along the recently completed B&O spur from Fairmont to Morgantown, which had been designed to ultimately reach Pittsburgh, Pennsylvania. Even more significant, the Montana mine coal was expected to have good coking qualities. If that proved true, the Fairmont coal fields would be capable of competing with the Connellsville field. Up until this effort, the Fairmont coals were considered unfit for coking purposes. Geologically, this was questionable because both the Fairmont and Connellsville fields were part of the larger Pittsburgh seam. By 1890, Camden had increased his initial modest investment in the Montana mine to a point where he owned the majority interest. Camden's interests here were not only to make a profit, but to study the commercial possibilities of coal and coke from the Monongahela Valley.[12]

Camden, with J. O. Watson and the others, had experiments conducted that established without question the coking capabilities of the coal. The success of the Montana venture laid open the prospects of an entire new field stretching from Morgantown to Clarksburg.[13]

Camden's plan had two aspects: first, that the Fairmont field mines could become the finest coking coal in the country, replacing Connellsville coke and others; second, that the Fairmont coal fields would become the standard for quality coal at least in the region and perhaps in the nation. Camden hoped to accomplish in the coal industry what John D. Rockefeller had recently accomplished in the oil business with Standard Oil.

Under real estate law, rights or interest in coal can be sold separately from the surface ownership rights. Beginning in 1885, Camden, through his associates, paid local farmers between $5 and $13 an acre for the mineral rights, which included the rights to mine the coal. Even then, the price was considered low. The rationale for such a low price was that the coal could not be mined because a way to transport it to market would not exist for ages, rendering the coal valueless. But Camden had already begun developing a railroad right-of-way and securing the access rights to the B&O, as well as development rights for the spur line between Fairmont and Monongah.

The Monongah Coal & Coke Company was chosen as the name for the mine operation company, and it included the real estate syndicate, operations of the company stores, rental houses, utilities, and so on. In 1890, the Monongah Coal & Coke Company began building the mining camp of Monongah and opened the first mines. By 1901 three mines had been opened, including Nos. 1, 2, and 6, and the No. 8 mine was added in 1904.[14]

At the same time, Camden started a second company: the Monongahela River Railroad Company.[15] This company was formed to build the railroad spur line from Fairmont to the mines in Monongah. Camden had extracted commitments from B&O Railroad management that they would provide adequate rail cars for shipping the coal, a reversal of its previous practice of ignoring the mining traffic.

In 1899, Camden separated his coal and railroad interests in order to focus his attention on his coal properties. He sold the Monongahela River Railroad Company to the B&O Railroad Company for $75.00 a share and an agreement to lease to Camden and his associates the coal holdings of the Monongahela Railroad Company for 999 years.

Camden then formed the Monongah Company with Spriggs D. Camden, J. A. Fickenger, Charles K. Lord, C. B. Alexander, and himself as incorporators. The new company consolidated all of Camden's interests in the Monongahela Valley. Camden himself described this as owning practically all the coal on the east side of the Monongahela River road and 5,000 acres on the west side, from Fairmont to Clarksburg. By January 1, 1900, no less than 15,000 acres belonging to the Monongah Company were under lease.

The commonly prevailing royalty rate was six cents per ton and the lessee was required to pay on a minimum of fifteen thousand tons for each one hundred acres of land under lease, whether or not that amount was mined.[16] Mines No. 6 and No. 8 were among those leased to the Fairmont Coal Company.

The Watsons

James Otis Watson was born in May of 1815, the first child of Thomas and Rebecca Haymond Watson. His grandfather, James Greene Watson, had come to what is now Marion County, West Virginia, from Port Tobacco, Maryland. He bought a 254-acre tract of land along the White Day Creek, which flowed into the Monongahela River.

In 1841, J. O. Watson married Matilda Lamb, whose father, Leonard, was prominent in the beginning of the iron industry. James and Matilda bought a farm from Alexander Fleming, who had been one of the founders of Fairmont and in the course of their marriage had ten children.

In 1852, J. O. Watson opened the first bituminous coal mine west of the Alleghenies in 1852. The Fairmont mine actually operated inside the city limits of Fairmont and sold coal to local markets, including blacksmiths and the like. Francis H. Pierpont was a lawyer and pioneer coal developer along with J. O. Watson. They opened one of the country's first mines to send coal shipments to eastern markets.[17] The following year, in 1853, the B&O

Railroad opened the first rail line over the mountains from Cumberland to Fairmont, and as a result, coal could be shipped east. Watson and his associates opened new mines and expanded production.

In 1885, at the age of 70, J. O. Watson turned over the mining operation to his fourth son, James Edwin, age 26, and an older son, Sylvanus, age 37. His youngest son, Clarence Wayland, age 21, was not interested in the actual mining operations, but was keenly interested in financial matters. James Edwin managed the mining operations for several years, but because of ill health, turned the operations over to Clarence, who would later also become a US Senator. Clarence had emerged as the person in charge of the family business and was known for an extravagant lifestyle. His father disapproved of his youngest son's lack of concern for money and standard of living.[18]

Clarence took over the family homestead, which was a three-story brick structure called LaGrange after his great-grandfather's home in Port Tobacco, Maryland. Clarence transformed the lavishly furnished home into a showplace, and in addition, he expanded the family's holdings and changed the name of the section to Fairmont Farms. LaGrange, built in Spanish-style architecture and situated on extensive grounds, was renovated and renamed The Homestead.

Multiple stables were needed in which Clarence and his family maintained a fine collection of world famous show horses. Expert trainer Frank Winterbotten was put in charge of the stables and prepared the horses for competition. Clarence and his wife, Minnie, were regulars on the riding circuit of New York, Baltimore, and up and down the east coast. The most famous of their horses, Lord Baltimore, was one of the leading show horses in the nation. Others included Lady Baltimore, My Maryland I, My Maryland II, Virginia, Ringing Bells, and Moonshine. In 1909, Clarence Watson and his wife boarded the RMS Mauretania and sailed to London where they competed in the Great International Horse Exhibition. Lead by the "four Sterling

Bays," Lord Baltimore, Lady Baltimore, My Maryland I, and Virginia, where they won fifty blue ribbons and the Berkeley Cup, the most prestigious equestrian trophy worldwide. Lord Baltimore returned to Fairmont with the title of World's Greatest Show Horse.[19]

Aretas Brooks Fleming

A. B. Fleming was a Fairmont lawyer married to J. O. Watson's oldest daughter, Caroline Margaret, or Carrie, as she was called. His father, Benjamin Fleming, had been associated with J. O. Watson, Francis H. Pierpont, and other mining operators and operations.[20] Fleming's grandfather had purchased some 400 acres of land along the West Fork in 1790, and the family added acreage through the succeeding generations. Fleming himself purchased a home on Jefferson Street from Colonel William Hood, a Fairmont financier. This home also served as the offices of the Gaston Coal Company, which Fleming and J. O. Watson opened in 1877.

During these early years, Fleming had worked with US Senator J. N. Camden and became his legal advisor. Camden, in turn, promoted Fleming's bid for the Governorship. In the controversial election of 1888, Fleming, a Democrat, lost by 106 votes to Nathan Goff, a Clarksburg Republican. He challenged some 2,000 votes in southern West Virginia's McDowell County. After a year of wrangling, the legislature voted along party lines 43 to 40, and Fleming was sworn in as the eighth governor of West Virginia in 1890, nearly one year after the election.[21]

THE MINING COMPANIES:
THE EARLY YEARS

ALTHOUGH not entirely completed, both the mining plant and the Monongahela Railroad from Fairmont began operation in the early months of 1890. In February, a contract agreement had been entered into with the Ohio Coal Exchange Company of Chicago and its subsidiary, Consolidation Coal & Mining Company, granting them the exclusive right to sell Monongah's coal west of the Ohio River for $.80 per ton. In March, the Monongah Coal & Coke Company began shipping coal.

In the early years, the Monongah mines faced problems common to start-up mining companies, wages principal among them. Camden had set the wage rate at $.17 per ton, counter to the prevailing rate of $.32 for cutting and blowing down and $.35 for breaking up and loading coal at Montana. The miners demanded $.25 of Camden, who claimed that the presence of the electric cutting machine had changed the nature of the work, making it less difficult and thus lowering the pay, neglecting to recognize that most of the work still had to be done by hand in the commonly practiced method.

This wage dispute led to a strike within days of opening. The strike cost between $4,000 and $5,000, according to B. D. Spilman, general manager of the Monongah Coal & Coke Company, who described the progress for the six months from November 1, 1890, to May 1, 1891, in his May 20 report to President Camden. He considered the strike a net gain for the company as it had lowered the cost of mining $.05 per ton by reducing the miners' wages. In addition, the contract with the Ohio Coal Exchange Company for 100,000 tons of coal allowed the company to mine and ship some 1,500 tons per day per mine, or 3,000 tons per day. Thirty percent, about one-third of the production, was going to the Monongah coke ovens before shipment. Although the company started the period with a $13,728.25 loss and had suffered a slow business period as well as a three-week strike, things were looking up.[1]

The general manager's main concern was the shortage of houses to rent to miners. The company had only 119 houses while the company employed more than 500 men. Spilman recommended that at least 50 additional houses be built and that they be built much cheaper. Spilman suggested that "[a] house costing $325.00 will answer all requirements and bring $4.00 per month rent." Basically, he was suggesting that in six years and nine months, the houses would pay for themselves.[2]

Finally, Spilman discussed the need for a bridge across the Monongahela River at Monongah. The river could not be forded for much of the year, and the ferry was too slow and tedious, which meant that the miners objected to living on the far side. A bridge would cost $15,000, and if the county would pay $10,000, it could be operated for free. If not, a toll bridge could be built and operated by the company.[3]

But almost immediately a railroad car shortage occurred, making efficient transportation of the mined coal difficult. The shortage was to be the single largest stumbling block to the company's development and a reflection of a longstanding disdain by the B&O for the coal shipping market, despite the B&O's executives' financial interest in the Monongah venture.

By the early 1890s Monongah Coal & Coke Company became profitable, and the Ohio Coal Exchange contract was extended. A new contract was signed with the Lehigh Coal & Iron Company, which also operated in the Great Lakes.[4]

Camden continued to receive financial support from Standard Oil during his campaign for the United States Senate in 1881, and while serving as U. S. Senator continued to work on Standard Oil's behalf. Henry Morrison Flagler, one of the original partners with Rockefeller in Standard Oil, was told by Camden in 1881, "Politics is dearer than it used to be—and my understood connection with the Standard Oil Co. don't tend to cheapen it—as we are all supposed to have bushels." That statement was followed by a request for "$10,000 in some turn-stocks or oil—Please keep an eye out and let me know." When Camden next wrote to advise Flagler of his election to the United States Senate, he said, "I also appreciate sincerely the substantial kindness of the Ex[ecutive] Com[mittee]—and used it without hesitation and I needed it temporarily."[5]

The Fairmont Coal Company

In 1899, the upper Monongahela coal field was coming into its own. Camden's mines, as well as other upper Monongahela coal mines, were making new sources of coal available for eastern, Great Lakes, and western markets. This coal availability homerun was complicated by the fact that the B&O Railroad was habitually short of coal cars to ship coal and played favorites among other regional producers, leading to concerns about competition both among local producers and with regions such as the Connellsville area.

To address this problem, Camden, Watson, and other large producers of the upper Monongahela field devised a plan to address the problem. Meeting in September of 1900, they formed the organization known as the Fairmont Miner's Coal Association and chose Clarence W. Watson as the founding president. Clarence, while lacking interest in the complexities of mining, was a brilliant strategist and promptly formed a syndicate to form the Fairmont Coal Company from the various interests who made up the association.

On June 20, 1901, the Fairmont Coal Company was incorporated in West Virginia under the Watson leadership. On June 26, 1901, the Monongah mines and all other Camden coal property interests were leased to the Fairmont Coal Company—more than 23,000 acres of the Pittsburgh coal seam.[6] Camden and the other principles now had an organization, albeit one that existed only on paper, with continuing interest in the mines at Monongah. On January 3, 1903, two short years later, Consolidation Coal Company officials met with Fairmont Coal Company officials in Baltimore to enter into a merger agreement; Consolidation Coal then acquired control of Fairmont Coal, whose 1902 output was 3.8 million tons from some 37 mines, including Monongah No. 2 and No. 6.

These rapid mergers reflected the opening up of the West Virginia coalfields and the struggles between competing New York financiers. In 1901, the Pennsylvania Railroad had acquired sizable holdings in the B&O Railroad, so much so that the Pennsylvania Railroad president, Leonor F. Loree, became a director of the B&O shortly thereafter.

Later that same year, fearing that George Gould, acting through the Wabash Railroad, was preparing to buy the Fairmont Coal Company, President Loree bought an additional block of shares of Consolidation Coal Company, effectively taking control with 53,532 of the 100,000 outstanding shares of Consolidation Coal.[7] By 1903, the Pennsylvania Railroad through the B&O, the Consolidation Coal Company, and the Fairmont Coal Company owned the largest acreage of unmined coal in the country. The mines at Monongah were the crown jewels.[8]

Camden was not left out. His company, the Monongah Company, received a variable minimum royalty based on a rising scale of annual production over a number of years and a fixed minimum royalty thereafter. If insufficient tonnage was produced, the Fairmont Coal Company had to make up the difference.[9]

On April 26, 1906, the Pennsylvania Railroad and the B&O Railroad sold its holdings of Consolidation stock to a Baltimore syndicate headed by Clarence W. Watson, president of the Fairmont Coal Company; Jere H. Wheelwright, Consolidation vice president; and H. Crawford Black, Consolidation Coal manager. The stock consisted of the same 53,532 shares or 52% of the total capitalization of $10,250,000. By this time, Consolidation was producing 10,000,000 tons annually, owned around 200,000 acres, and employed coal distribution companies around the country, operating in the east through Baltimore and in the west through the Northwestern Fuel Company.

The sale by B&O was not voluntary, it was made in anticipation of an antitrust investigation then being conducted by the Interstate Commerce Commission into the relations existing between the coal-carrying railroads and mining companies along their lines. The Supreme Court had ruled on February 19, 1906, that railroads could not deal in the commodities that they hauled. As a result of that decision and the ICC investigation, on June 29, 1906, the Hepburn Act was passed by Congress, which prohibited railroad companies from owning stock in producing companies.[10]

By the middle of 1903, Clarence W. Watson became president of Consolidation Coal Company. By 1906, Watson, A. B. Fleming, and S. L. Watson, all of whom were Fairmont Coal Company officials, became directors of the Consolidation Coal Company, headquartered at the Continental Building in Baltimore. In part, it was a case of the child consuming the parent, with Consolidation Coal being consumed by the smaller, younger Fairmont Coal Company. Camden remained heavily involved behind the scenes, providing both advice and the financial backstop to allow such a large purchase of the Pennsylvania Railroad/B&O stock.[11]

Consolidation Coal Company: The Merged Giant

By the beginning of 1906, Consolidation Coal Company had emerged as a dominant force in United States mining. Among its divisions, the Fairmont Coal Company owned 29, 447 acres of coal and leased another 22,000 acres in Marion, Taylor, Harrison, and Monongalia counties in West Virginia.[12]

Watson, with Camden and the B&O (which held a majority of Consolidation's stock), used their extensive financial resources and expanded rapidly, moving into the Somerset Field of Pennsylvania by January, 1906—the Somerset Coal Company owned 29,310 acres of coal—and then a second company, Pennmont, owned 24,700 for a total of nearly 55,000 acres of coal. Consolidation was also expanding into southern West Virginia and eastern Kentucky.

By 1906, Consolidation Coal Company owned or controlled 88,345 acres in northern West Virginia and 57,892 acres in Pennsylvania, 146,237 acres total, as well as coal land not yet in production in Kentucky.[13] By 1907, the Consolidation Coal Company produced 10,660,972 tons of coal annually, making it the largest producer in the country.

In addition, the company owned the Canal Towage Company, which operated 101 canal boats on the Chesapeake and Ohio Canal between Cumberland and Georgetown in Washington, DC. Through this canal begun by George Washington, boats carried 174,920 tons of coal in 1905. Consolidation also owned and operated the Hoboken Docks in Hoboken, New Jersey—conveniently located for coaling yachts, tugs, and so on in New York harbor—and the Metropolitan Coal Company, which had expensive facilities in Boston that handled 740,096 tons of coal in 1905 for both local consumption and ocean delivery. The company operated a fleet of steamers, tugs, and barges for transporting Consolidation coal between Baltimore, Washington, and New England points to provide storage and distribution to its midwestern markets. Consolidation owned the Northwestern Fuel

Company, which consisted of storage plants in Chicago and docks in Duluth, West Superior, Washburn, and Milwaukee. Another Consolidation division owned West Superior Coal yards at St. Paul, Minneapolis, and Chicago and a shipping office in Cleveland. By the fall of 1906, the Consolidation/ Fairmont Coal Company owned 64 mines alone in northern West Virginia, Maryland, and Pennsylvania.[14]

The merger between Fairmont Coal Company and the Camden interest had proved to be hugely profitable. Three years before this merger, Camden had sketched out a profit picture from a proposed merger of the Wheeling Coal interest and the Fairmont Coal Company. While that proposed merger never materialized, the projected profit would in one year have been in excess of the entire cash investment of $1.6 million.[15] The Fairmont and Consolidation Coal merger was twice the size of the earlier proposed merger and presumably more profitable. This merger also came about as a result of a looming battle between George Gould and his Wabash Railroad and the rival Pennsylvania Railroad, of which the smaller B&O Railroad was now a part. The B&O continued to own the largest share of Consolidation.

Gould had threatened to enter the northern West Virginia coalfields and build a line to compete with the B&O monopoly lines from Cumberland to Fairmont. At about the same time, the Pennsylvania Railroad purchased large shares of the B&O and installed Leonor F. Loree as B&O president. The B&O then increased its holding in the Consolidation Coal Company to 53,532 shares out of 100,000 outstanding, giving it controlling interest.

Then, to secure control of the mines and the coal being shipped through the Consolidation Coal Company, which it controlled, the B&O sought majority control of the Fairmont Coal Company and the Somerset Coal Company, also a Watson Fleming-controlled company.

When, in 1903, Consolidation Coal and Fairmont Coal officials entered into the merger agreement, the document they drafted was unusual in that it limited the majority stockholders rights, suggesting that the two parties' financial stakes were nearly the same. Consolidation was to have only one Board of Directors member more than the minority group, the Fairmont/Watson interest. In addition, it restricted the majority's ability to sell without the minority's provisions being protected. C. W. Watson, A. B. Fleming, J. H. Wheelwright, S. L. Watson, and J. E. Watson signed for the Fairmont Coal Company; Charles K. Lord, Chairman of Consolidation Coal Company and the president of the B&O, signed for Consolidation. Almost immediately, C. W. Watson replaced Lord as president of Consolidation.

Given the minority's control of the Board and the presidency, it appeared that the Watson interest had prevailed. The Fairmont interest—Watson's and Fleming's—would in fact lead the merged company for decades.[16]

THE CITY OF MINES

"One of the most important places in this country, considering size, is Monongah, and it is also one of the principal coal and coke centers of the state."

—*Fairmont Index, July 10, 1896*

Monongahela is a Delaware Indian name meaning "river of falling banks." The river is characterized by high banks that frequently break off and plummet into the river below. The Monongahela River is formed from the confluence of the Tygart Valley River and the West Fork River, which flows through the village of Monongah. From its formation near Fairmont, the Monongahela River flows 128 miles to Pittsburgh, where it joins with the Allegheny River to form the Ohio River.[1]

In 1778, Nathaniel Cochran took up a tomahawk right along the West Fork River where Booths Creek enters the River and where the town of Monongah would eventually stand. Cochran was from eastern Virginia, had fought in the Revolutionary War, and had been captured by the Shawnee Indians. He was sold to the British, who imprisoned him in Quebec until the end of the war.

Shortly afterward, he returned home to Winchester, Virginia, and married Elizabeth Ford, the daughter of a soldier who was a fifer with General George Washington. In April of 1789, the couple moved from Winchester to the West Fork River, seeking land. They built a log cabin and became the first white settlers of what would become known as Briar Town. During the next several years, they and a few other families farmed, trapped, and hunted to eke out a living in the wilderness.[2]

Around 1818, John Anderson built a mill on Booths Creek for grinding corn, wheat, and buckwheat; the mill was also used for sawing lumber, which was loaded on flatboats and transported to Pittsburgh. Some years later, mills were built by John Brown, Jacob Veach, James Watkins, and Leonard Lamb. Brown sold his mill to Leonard Lamb, who then turned the operation over to his son-in-law, James O. Watson.

On February 22, 1850, Watkins hired a surveyor, T. A. Little, to lay out plots for a settlement along the creek, which was to be called Pleasantville; but a local neighbor remarked that they were laying the town out in a briar patch, and it should be called Briar Town. The name stuck for 40 years.[3]

But in 1890 a post office opened inside the Monongahela Coal & Coke Company's recently built company store. The company's principal owner, J. N. Camden, directed D. S. Thompson, who was the mine superintendent, to have the name *Monongah, W. Va.*, printed on the stationary as the mine company's return address. Monongah became the official name.[4]

The village of Monongah sits along both the east and west banks of the West Fork River. On the west side, a bluff rises high above the river, while on the east side a flat stretch of ground gives way to gradual hills. Farming and hunting were the principal commercial activities of the community until the last decade of the nineteenth century. The only mining activity in the region had been in the town of Fairmont itself and in Montana, a community at the other end of Marion County.

These early coal mines were, for the most part, limited to selling coal locally to blacksmiths or for home consumption. Despite the presence of numerous coal outcroppings along the river, including locations near Monongah, little effort had been given to developing mining enterprises because no method existed for getting the mined coal to the market. The nearest railway line was located in Fairmont, eight miles away. The shallow West Fork River between Monongah and Fairmont provided limited transportation. The dirt roads connecting Monongah to Fairmont were of poor quality, inadequately maintained, and impassable for part of the year.

Despite these limitations, agents for J. N. Camden began in 1888 to purchase virtually all of the mineral rights along both sides of the river from the Pennsylvania line above Morgantown to below Clarksburg, a distance of roughly 33 miles. In addition, Camden agents bought up all available surface property in Monongah and the surrounding neighborhoods.[5]

Legally, land can be owned in a variety of ways. Land ownership or *interest* is called an estate. The most complete and inclusive estate of land ownership is the *fee simple* estate, which includes all rights to the property. But some rights and parts of a land estate can be severed from the fee simple ownership, most notably *mineral rights*. Mineral rights can be severed and sold off separately, creating a mineral ownership and surface ownership. Under this arrangement, the mineral owners own the minerals below the surface and have a right to tunnel or mine through the surface in order to reach the minerals and remove them.[6] At the time the mineral rights along the Monongahela were being sold, no means of transporting the coal existed. What was not known to most of the sellers was that Camden and a group of investors were planning to build a railroad spur line from the B&O's terminal in Fairmont to Monongah, where Camden planned to develop a mining center, unbeknownst to most of the mineral rights sellers.[7]

In 1889, agents representing Camden's interest hired the firm of Dickerson and Clayton to build a coal company camp on the Watkins and Davis farms in Monongah. In 1890, the Monongah Coal & Coke Company, controlled by Senator J. N. Camden, who had recently completed a term in the U.S. Senate, began building houses, stores, offices, and various outbuildings in Monongah and on the hills surrounding the town. Along the flat stretch of land on the east side of the river, a massive coal preparation plant four stories high was built, along with the mine offices, machine repair shops, and 320 beehive coking furnaces. The coking ovens would make Monongah one of the largest coking operations in the state. Mines No. 1, 2, 3, 6, and 8 were opened with entrances driven into the base of the bluff on the river's west side.

By the mid 1890s, the mines were producing large quantities of coal and the 320 coke ovens lit up the sky for miles around. The *Fairmont Index* said on July 10, 1896, that the lit coke ovens created, "an eerie sight in the hilly rural surrounding." The mines were connected across the river by steel tipples. The trestle for No. 6 was the largest steel trestle built in the United States up until that point. Straddling the river, the trestle to the tipple allowed mine rail cars to carry the coal from the underground workings of Mines Nos. 6 and 8 across the arched tipple to the preparation plant. There the coal would be separated according to size, cleaned, and either sent to the coking furnaces or loaded onto railroad cars to be shipped to markets. Mine No. 8, upstream from the town, was also connected to the east side by a second, smaller tipple.[8]

Senator J. N. Camden envisioned that these mines and the coal and coke from the Monongah mines would become the United State's coal industry's standard for high quality and they would become the leading producer in West Virginia. Camden, for the past decade, had secretly been part of the

John D. Rockefeller, Jr.'s, efforts to monopolize the oil industry and to establish Standard Oil Company as the dominant oil company in the country.[9]

About the same time, in the summer of 1890, Columbus Mason opened the first saloon in Monongah, anticipating the coming coal boom and catering to the thirst of the construction workers. Soon, others like Michael Kelly opened taverns catering to Irish immigrants among the railroad workers, construction crews, and miners. These taverns, when aided by bootleggers, assured that residents did not want for drink. In fact, over time, the town gained a reputation for roughness. One story reported that drinking alcohol was a popular form of amusement, and that the consumption of beer ran as high as two quarts a day per person, plus some whiskey. Indeed, news accounts speculated that such conduct led to frequent absences from work, especially following a payday or holiday.[10]

The only governmental law enforcement force in the county was the Marion County Sheriff's Office; the West Virginia state police force did not yet exist.[11] The town police force, which was hired and paid by the coal company, consisted of the town sergeant William Finley, who also served as the chief of the fire department, and policeman John Carwell.[12] But, as was the practice in coal company-owned towns, a private police force existed in Monongah. The company's own private security force was far more substantial both in size and authority than either of the town or county governmental bodies. It consisted of forty or more men who also served in other company capacities and was the real force in the community.[13]

In 1891, Monongah was incorporated and the first City Council meeting was held in the Monongah Coal & Coke Company office with company officials serving as council members. The mayor, J. A. Showalter, was also manager for the Fairmont Coal Company, and David Victor, a Fairmont Coal Company supervisor and safety director, served as a member of the Monongah City Council.

By 1889, the first building phase was completed: fifty houses plus a hotel and store. The principal street was Camden Avenue on the west side of town, atop the bluff. The first of the company houses were built along Camden Avenue. Rows of company houses, all painted one color, spread out from the river and up the hillsides. By 1892, the newly built company camp surrounded, and was larger than, the small village that had existed prior to that time. Monongah was the most extensively planned company town in West Virginia. It was not the classic company town, entirely controlled by the company; rather, it was grafted onto an existing community. The houses and streets were laid out in a grid spreading out from the mine facilities.

The town was divided into sections. Old Monongah was the section that existed before the company moved in; new sections were named Brookdale, Thorburne, Wahoo, Hill No. 3, Italy, Middleton, Africa, and so on. The houses were numbered, or in some instances, lettered. Lester Emmitt Trader lived in house 23 with his wife, Mayme, and four children, the oldest of whom was seven and the youngest just five weeks old. Trader, fire boss in mine No. 8, was a nephew of the company's safety director, David Victor.[14] In downtown Monongah on the east side of the river, two hotels, the Currey and the Eureka, and several restaurants, including the Coliseum Opera House Restaurant, provided food as well as entertainment. Miss Anne Watkins' Millinery Shop provided the latest in fashions for the ladies of Monongah and surrounding towns. The shop employed women in making hats and other items on site.[15] Two barber shops kept some of the citizens trimmed, while grocers William J. Talbott and William H. Moon provided alternatives to the company store. One of the immigrants, C. Salvait, opened a grocery along with a store operated by Ross Maruka at 210 Company Row.[16] People in particular ethnic groups—Italians, Polish, and so on—tended to rent and live near one another in the various sections of town, and some supported the grocers and store owners from their own countries.

In Brookdale, at house 232, Dominac Colarusso and his wife, Carmela, lived with their two children. In the fall of 1907 they were expecting their third child. They also rented space to six boarders: Felice Colasessano, Domenico Mainella, Juste Bitonti, Giuseppe Colarusso, Jim Bitonti, and Felice Colaneri. Dominac and all of the boarders worked at mine No. 8.[17]

In Old Monongah, in house 753, Mrs. Grace Snodgrass, her daughter, and her husband, G. Snodgrass, kept two boarders: Henry Burke and Sam Nolan. All three of the men worked at mine No. 8.

Peter Urban and his wife, Caroline, had arrived in the United States in April of 1891, with their three children, Anne (7), Stanley (4), and Andy (1) and lived in house 99. They had emigrated from their small village of Czmolas, near the town of Kolbuszowa in the province of Galitzia, Austria, which was part of the Austro-Hungarian Empire. Peter had come to join his brother Stanley, who had been in working in the Monongah mines for eight years. Stanley and his wife, Mary, had four children, Joe, Kate, John, and Nelle, and lived in house 83 in Middleton. Stanley and Peter both worked together in mine No. 8.

By the turn of the century, Monongah was a bustling town "boasting of six general stores, one of the best equipped shaving parlors in the state. . ." and two ice cream parlors.[18] A newspaper account described the town in 1896:

One of the most important places in this county, considering size, is Monongah and it is also one of the principal coal and coke centers of the state. A great many people of the county do not realize what great dimensions the former Briar Town has recently reached and would be surprised to know that the population is estimated at 3,000 in the summer and 2,000 in winter. . . . The population is an enterprising one and have great pride in their little city. At present the people are just recovering from the good time they enjoyed last Saturday at Cheswood Park, and are getting ready to cast their votes for their favorites at the primary election tomorrow.

By 1896, the town's environment was dominated by the mining and coking operators. To the residents, the dirt, dust, and smoke were signs that the mines were working and the miners were earning wages; and in the early years of the twentieth century when work was often erratic, the dust was welcomed.

By 1903, the *Fairmont Times* reported, "the sparsely populated valley of the West Fork afforded support for almost eleven hundred miners and their families." By 1907, Monongah had doubled in size to a population of over 2000. The *Fairmont Times* continued:

In visiting Monongah we are always reminded of Mr. Pickwick's description of a town in England. He says there is a great quantity of dirt, smoke, and dust to be found, but, to those who look upon this as a sign of commercial prosperity, the sight is truly gratifying.[19]

Company Housing

The Monongah Coal & Coke Company built three types of houses: a three-room unit for small families, a larger version with four or five rooms for larger families, and an eight-room house where a family and several boarders could be accommodated.[20] The houses were laid out on lots of 55 by 110 feet, and the tenants were required to "keep the premises tidy and in a healthy looking condition."[21] The miners' houses were built as near to the mine portal as possible so that the miners could change their clothes at home, and there would be no need for the construction of changing sheds at the mine. Close proximity also allowed the miners to get back and forth to and from work as quickly as possible.

The smaller houses were all on one level, with a living room, bedroom, kitchen, and a small porch. The larger units for boarders had a single second floor bedroom. The keeping of boarders was an essential part of the economic life of Monongah as well as other coal camps at the time. Seven out of ten south Italian and Ruthenian families did so. One study in nearby Western Pennsylvania reported, "Almost one-half of all immigrant families receive a part of their income from boarders and lodgers. These earnings accounted for as much as two-thirds of the overall income."[22]

Often the immigrant miners were single, or they were on their own in the U.S. with a wife and family living in the old country. In Monongah, boarding houses were common, and each had a *boss* or landlord who maintained order and collected the rent. Typically, the wife of the boss would be responsible for cooking, cleaning, and maintaining the boarding house. At house 233, Tony Mysella was the boss, while his wife fed and cleaned for three boarders: Pasquale Riccinto, Antonio Riccinto, and Dominic Richard. Pasquale Riccinto was married with two children living in Duronia del Sannio, Italy; his brother, Antonio Riccinto, also had a wife and three children who lived in Duronia del Sannio with Antonio's grandfather; Dominic Richard was a single 19-year-old.

The arrangement between the landlords and boarders varied. Some were from the same town in the old country or were related, while others were simply strangers living in rooms, paying cash at the end of the shift or week. Given this informal nature of the boarding arrangement, it was not uncommon that the boss or mistress of the house knew little about the boarders or their original hometowns.

In many houses the boss did not admit to keeping boarders, possibly for fear of having to share income with the mining company. The National Immigration Commission, set up by President Theodore Roosevelt, concluded in a study of mining and immigrant conditions that if all those keeping boarders were counted "there would be two boarders for each of the households whose members were immigrants." According to the study, the practice of keeping lodgers was highest among the Italian, Slovenian, and

Polish miners.[23] Among these groups, all of the rooms in a house were used for sleeping. Given the fact that neither the miners nor the landlords had any interest in their presence, it is safe to say that few records exist of miners who were boarders living in Monongah. There was no way to identify them other than the company payroll records, and as payment was usually in cash, those records were quite limited.

In addition to boarders, children also contributed to the overall income of the families by working in the mines or in the community. Frequently, an immigrant miner arrived without his wife and children, but after working for a period of time to establish himself and save sufficient funds, he would return to his homeland for his family.

The original company house at Monongah cost about $300 to construct, but as time passed, Camden's staff was able to reduce the amount and could have houses built for less, closer to $260. Rent from the small houses yielded $4.00 per month, the larger ones, $6.00 per month. The standard lease was month to month and was contingent on the miner's continued employment and good behavior. Should the employment terminate, whether voluntarily or because he was fired, the lease would end immediately and the miner and family would be required to surrender the premises. If the miner failed to do so, the operator could, according to the lease, reenter and seize the property, even without 'legal powers' (a court order). These leases favored the coal company in all matters. For example, the rent was deducted from the miner's pay, thus ensuring timely payment, but because a great many of the Monongah miners could not read or write, the one-sided nature of the lease hardly mattered.[24]

Coal stoves were used to heat the houses and coal had to be purchased by the miners from the company, sometimes at a reduced price of $2.00 per ton, but more often at $3.00 per ton. Water for roughly a dozen houses was available from hydrants at the end of the street. Outhouses were located at the back of the house lot, and the lots were large enough for small vegetable gardens.[25] In 1900, the *Fairmont Free Press* reported,

One of the greatest improvements that the company had recently made is the build-ing of a system of water works. Two large tanks have been erected and water is fur-nished to those who rent company houses, free. While not plumbed to the residences, there were numerous hydrants in convenient places.[26]

The residents' view was slightly different.

In her book, *Coal: A Memoir and Critique*, Duane Lockard reports that the lack of running water "was a special burden for the housewife but not for her alone." On page 92, Lockard, a political science professor *emeritus* at Princeton University, discusses her memories of growing up in Monongah in the 1940s, when families hauled water from fire hydrants, much as they had in 1907:

I recall that it was my job every Sunday evening to lug endless buckets of water from the street hydrant that served a dozen houses. This was in preparation for Monday—traditional laundry day—and it took a lot of water plus backbreaking labor over a washboard to free work clothes of grease, sweat, and coal dust. Then it fell to the children to use leftover wash water to scrub porches and wooden walkways.

In 1895, telephone and telegraph lines were installed to the company of-fice buildings, but not to the houses. In 1904, gas lines were added for com-pany stores and businesses, but these amenities were not available to the min-ers. By 1900, electricity was available to the coal company offices and mine facilities, but it was not until 1916 that power was made available to homes, when the company developed an electric distribution system.[27]

Typically, houses were furnished with two inexpensive but serviceable chairs, a table, a kitchen stove, and ordinary culinary utensils. Cots instead of beds were often used for sleeping, especially where several lodgers were kept. One local article commented that the floors in the houses of immigrants from southern and eastern Europeans were generally uncarpeted and sometimes scrubbed and clean; but more often they were allowed to become dirty. This was generally true where many boarders were kept.

The conditions confronting the women of the household were extremely difficult. The housewife had to keep house for the family as well as the boarders. She would cook the meals, make the beds, wash and mend the clothing for her family, as well as each boarding miner. In addition, women often washed and mended boarders' clothes for additional money. She also bought the food and carried—or had the children carry—all the water from the well or hydrant up to a hundred yards away. When the men returned from work wet, muddy, and covered with dirt and coal dust, she had to heat and prepare the water, scrub their backs, clean the tubs, and feed the boarders as well as her family. The next day, she had to prepare breakfast and lunch buckets for the men to carry back into the mines.

The rent paid by the boarders or lodgers depended on the supply and demand in each company town. In nearby western Pennsylvania, Italians paid 78 cents per month, Poles and Russians 93 and 84 cents, respectively. The cost of food ranged from $4 to $10 per month. A study of payroll, company store, and employee records describes several families' financial situations. An Irish family of four had a monthly income of $222.30, paid rent of $16.50, bought food and supplies from the company store for $73.27, and paid $2.70 for coal, for a total of $92.47. A Hungarian family of four had $217.42 income, paid rent of $18, spent $84.19 at the company store, and bought fuel for $1.20, for a total of $103.30. A Slovak family earned $136.65: rent, $18; store, $53.88; fuel $1.20; light, $3.30; for a total of $76.46.[28]

The economics in Monongah were even more difficult because from the very beginning, the Monongah mine company paid their miners less than the surrounding mines. The company's rationale was that since these newly arrived immigrants had less experience than other miners, they should be paid less. Clearly, the lower salaries at the Monongah mines were also a result of the fact that the newly arrived miners were less likely to organize into a union and strike. In fact, conditions in Monongah were so difficult that even the company superintendent complained to Camden that the miners were being underpaid.

In 1890, F. F. Lyon, the company superintendent, wrote to Camden, describing the miners' pay:

Looking at it from the miner's side of the subject, my opinion is the average miner will not blow down, clean and load more than 12 tons per day on the average, but say that we bring that average up to 15 cars, then the miner would make $2.55 per day. Deducting from this his powder and oil, which will cost him 1-1/4 cents per ton, he will have left $2.36 for his days work, saying nothing about the expense of keeping up his tools. My experience has been that the average miner will not work to exceed 20 to 22 days per month. Say 22 days. He will then earn $51.92. Deducting from this the average of $6 per month for rent, $2 for coal and $1 for his doctor bills, he will have left from $41 to $42 per month. Of which the store will get $9-10 if not the whole of it.

I understand that the men at Gaston and Montana are making considerable more money than this for their months work, and unless we pay our men nearly or quite as much as the men are paid at other mines in the neighborhood, they will sooner or later cause us trouble.[29]

Camden was unmoved, Superintendent Lyon soon retired, and the company continued to pay wages at levels below nearly all surrounding mines.

At the turn of the century, life in coal mining camps was extremely difficult. The camps were located in isolated regions in rural communities, and the living conditions depended on the good will of the corporate owners. Coal camps in general, and Monongah in particular, had open drainage systems. Street gutters were simply shallow ditches and where the hillsides sloped sharply; the gutters became deep gullies. Monongah and the nearby camps were typical of coal camps throughout the region:

Rubbish, household articles commonly litter the gutters, streets, and yards. . . . [T]he majority of the streets and yards are covered with coke ashes. . . . Living conditions as a rule are exceedingly unsanitary. Toilets are in all cases dry, with ground vaults, and are often located near the dwelling. . . . Wells or hydrants are placed about 200 yards apart, one for each ten or twelve families.[30]

Dirt streets with no sidewalks, as well as the dust and smoke from the preparation plant, railroad yard, and power plant, ensured that the camp was constantly dirty. Far worse was the impact of the coke furnaces. At Monongah, the 320 coke furnaces spread dust and fumes around the clock. "The smoke and gas from the ovens destroy all vegetation in and around the small mining communities."[31] Washing and drying of miners' work clothes, as well as all clothes, was done by hand. Clothes were hung on the line to dry, usually exposing every load to a fresh coat of dust. Attempting to keep porches and walkways free of dust was an exercise in futility.

Frequently, families farmed a garden plot at the house and many leased additional space or simply tended vacant fields away from the mine camp. Gardening and canning skills brought from the old country were essential and could be used to stockpile extra food for the winter, times of labor trouble, or unemployment. Wives and children frequently were expected to raise the garden, gather berries and nuts, and pick coal from the slate piles and along the railroad tracks.

The Company Store

The *company store* was opened at Monongah in 1889; five years later, in 1894, C. R. Bartlett became manager. As company store manager, Bartlett was important to the individual miner and his family, as he controlled much in their day-to-day lives. For the next 53 years, Bartlett was in charge of selling miners axes, shovels, black powder in 5-gallon buckets, and pretty much everything else they needed to do their jobs. The company store sold most household goods and food supplies, as well. So many company stores were notorious for charging inflated prices that they came to be called *pluck-me stores* by the miners and their families. The company controlled prices and credit, and discouraged competition. Miners who failed to buy at the company store risked being considered disloyal and frequently were among the first to suffer layoffs or given reduced work days. Additionally, the use of *company scrip* also forced miners to shop at the company store. The *Fairmont Free Press* of the time described the practice:

In some cases the store is the most profitable branch of a company's business. The relationship between a company store and a mining company is simple. When a workman or a member of his family desires to purchase goods at the store and has no cash or does not wish to use such cash as he has on hand, he asks the pay clerk of such amount as he may wish.

This check is a printed slip, which in form is an assignment to the store company of money owed by the mining company to the workman, with spaces left blank for the amount and the assignor's signature. If the mine employee's earnings to date, less previous checks, equal or exceed the amount desired, the check is made out, signed by the man, and received at the store in payment for the goods bought. On pay day the total amount of these checks is deducted from the man's earnings and turned over to the store in payment of his bills. [32]

Lester Trader's letter referred to certificates as well:

It is hard to tell what the result would have been if the foreigners had been paid in the certificates as they are so hard to make understand even more simple matters than that. Then again I talked with several of the store keepers and they told me they would not do business at all if they had to do it with the paper. This shows that the certificate does not stand high in Monongah in light of the fact that they are worth their face value in money.

At Monongah, most miners were not paid in cash. Scrip is credit slips or tickets issued by mining companies to employees before payday in lieu of cash; the scrip is charged against the employee's payout and is good at face value only at the company store.[33] At stores not owned by the company, company scrip was discounted between 10 and 15 percent because when the independent store owners redeemed the Monongah Company scrip with the company, the face value would be discounted by that amount or more. In addition to issuing scrip, the company at Monongah also kept books that were known as *the orders*, which tallied up the prices of items that the miner and his family purchased during the week. These totals were deducted from the amount the miner received as payment.

At the nearby Gaston and Montana mines, also operated by the Fairmont Coal Company, miners were paid in cash, which was considered better by the men.[34] In 1888, one of the Monongah mine owners, A. B. Fleming, was running for governor. Charges that he had operated pluck-me stores at

Monongah and elsewhere were aired. By 1907, the use of scrip to miners as their wages was outlawed in West Virginia. However, because scrip was often used by the miners as a way to receive pay advances, especially by immigrant miners because they more often lived paycheck to paycheck, the practice remained common. Fleming vehemently denied the charges. It was well known that the company's ownership of the land, the houses, the train cars, and the stores resulted in a stranglehold over the miners and their families, and it was a political liability to be openly associated with the practices.

In a study, similar circumstances were described in western Pennsylvania:

Theoretically the bituminous coal mineworker may make his purchases wherever he may wish. Practically he has to make the bulk of them at the company stores for the reason that many mining companies shut off competition through their ownership of the territory surrounding their operations, and as a consequence stores other than those conducted by the company are inaccessible. Hucksters and peddlers of fruits, vegetables, and meats are generally excluded from the villages so far as possible. The company also used other means to encourage shopping at its store, and failure to do so had several consequences: The offending workman is either discharged at the first opportunity or an unsatisfactory working place is assigned to him in the mine, which usually results in his voluntary withdrawal from the service of the company.[35]

When payday did arrive, pay statements showed deductions for the costs of food, household items, the house itself, smithing services, fuel (coal), all the tools miners purchased to work in the mine, black powder, oil and other charges. Smithing charges also included sharpening and repairing tools by the company blacksmith. In addition, doctors were hired and controlled by the company. Each miner had an amount deducted as a monthly fee to pay the doctor regardless of whether the miner used the doctor's services or not. Prior approval for such charges was not considered necessary. At Monongah, the doctor's deductions varied between 50 and 90 cents for single men and $1 for married miners. On average, 35 percent of the wages were deducted each month before the miner received his payment.[36]

Other than the company railroad, travel into and out of Monongah was by dirt road until 1903, when one of the most modern light-rail systems in the country opened. The Interurban Transit System was a trolley car system operated by the Fairmont and Clarksburg Traction Company. The company was a Watson and Fleming family venture, operated in two parts. The interurban served the Fairmont, Monongah, Clarksburg, and Weston mining camps, and all the camps in between. The interurban line connected with the city line at Traction Park in Fairmont; the city line carried passengers around town. *Big Yellow Cars*, or street trolley cars, provided the traveler with a ride for a fare of 55 cents between Fairmont and Clarksburg. The longest run, between Fairmont and Weston, took less than 36 minutes. Later, the Fairmont and Clarksburg Traction Company, which initially was a competing enterprise controlled by Camden interest, were merged and the Monongahela Valley Traction Company was formed and headquartered in Fairmont.[37]

Schools at Monongah for the miners' children began in mid-November and ended in early April.[38] Only a limited number of families could afford to send their children, as most relied upon child labor to provide additional income to support the family. In 1890, after the first month of school in November, it was reported that the Monongah grade school had an enrollment of 125. By the age of eight, many of the male children went to work in the mines. Entry-level work included picking rock and other impurities from the coal on tables located in the preparation plant, or working underground ,operating the wooden ventilation doors, which controlled the flow of air inside the mines.[39] These boys, called *trapper boys*, opened and closed the *traps*, or doors, which were used to create ventilating air currents to the working faces. These doors had to be opened manually, thus providing ventilation to the faces.

Other boys who worked in the mine were not reported or carried on the company payroll. The boys went to work with their fathers and uncles, helping to mine and load the coal itself and were therefore paid, if at all, through their guardians' wages, which were based upon the amount of coal the miner delivered to the surface at the end of the shift.[40]

Miners at Monongah were paid under a two-tier payment system common in the industry. The majority of miners, who actually dug the coal, were paid based upon the amount of coal that they dug each day. The coal was loaded into mine cars, which were pushed by the miner or pulled by wire rope along the mains out of the mine. The *weigh man* then weighed the coal, and the miner was paid based on that weight. Others performed specific jobs or support work and were paid at a fixed per-day rate.

For example, *bit boys*, who carried drill bits from the outside to replace the broken bits for the miners at the coal face, made 85 cents per day; *drillers* received $1.90 per day. *Gathering motorman*, who drove motors to gather the mine cars and take them outside, received the highest pay of $2.35 per day, while *coal car couplers* were paid $2.10. *Trapper boys* received 85 cents a day; *boilers* and *pumpers* got $1.90 each day. Timbering work was compensated at $1.90 per day. Cleaning up falls earned the miners $1.80 a day, while those working falls—loading the fallen coal and rock in cars—were paid at the rate of 24 cents per car.

Brattice work, which consisted of installing tarred burlap cloth curtains to direct the ventilation, received $2.25 a day. As discussed in chapter 2, brattice was an important element of the ventilation system. Drivers who hauled coal in carts from the face inside the mine to the outside were paid by the run at 12 cents per hour. Finally, some who actually dug coal worked under contract receiving between 25 cents and 50 cents per yard in headings and an allowance of 50 cents per place for cutting coal.[41]

The Mines

Monongah mine No. 6 opened in October 1899. Six years later, on May 12, 1905, ground was broken for mine No. 8. Both mines were driven into the base of the bluff on the west side of the Monongahela River, with the Fairmont & Clarksburg Traction Company interurban rail line running past the front of each mine entrance.

The No. 6 mine was almost directly across from the preparation plant near the town. It was a *slope mine* with a *double entry system*.[42] Slope mining uses a sloping entrance that is driven down an incline toward the coal bed, acting as the main entryway of the mine. In a double entry mine, two entries were driven simultaneously rather than just one. Double entries allowed more access for miners and materials, and provided easier access to the coal seam by increasing the number of coal faces being mined. Double entry mines allowed more miners access to more coal at a single time.

Mine No. 8 was also on the east side of the West Fork River and sat one half-mile south of Monongah. It was also a slope mine using a double entry system, with an ultimate production capacity of 6,330 tons per day by 1905.

In both mines, the coal seam was eight feet high in places. The No. 6 had two openings; No. 8 had just one opening and a prop hole, a hole to the surface that allowed access for materials. By the fall of 1907, these mines together encompassed a large underground area, and between the two mines there were 475 working places, or *rooms*, where coal had been or was being mined. The rooms were driven perpendicular from the entry ways, or *mains*, into the seam.[43]

To extract the coal, both mines used a *panel mining system* with *room-and-pillar workings*. A panel system is a method of coal extraction in which the ground is laid off in separate *districts* or *panels*, with a large pillar of coal left to separate other workings. The panel refers to a group of rooms or *breasts*, separated from the other workings by large pillars.

Within each panel, a room-and-pillar technique was followed. In the first phase, called *driving*, the miners created rooms by removing roughly half the coal from a section, leaving the remainder as pillar. This system creates a mine like a checker board: all the coal in the red squares, or rooms, is removed, and all the coal in the black squares, or pillars, is left. When mining is complete to the end of the panel, or the end of the checkerboard, the process is reversed; *retreat mining* begins, and the pillars are removed, or *pulled*, and the roof is allowed to fall.[44]

Mines No. 6 and 8 both employed the most up-to-date, sophisticated ventilation systems. Each mine was initially capable of producing more than 3,500 tons per day, but in the fall of 1907, No. 8 was producing more than No. 6. For this reason, more men and equipment were in No. 8. However, as both of these mines were projected to extract a large amount of coal over time, the ventilation systems, fans, and so on, were designed with the capacity to provide sufficient air to cover a large underground area. Both mines had projection plans calling for development covering 1,600 to 1,700 acres per mine.[45]

The actual mining was done in three phases. During the first phase, the coal was undercut: a miner would lie on his side and, with a short-handled miner's pick, remove a four- to six-inch slice from the bottom of the face just next to the floor. This space was created in order to allow the coal face to fall when the explosive charge was detonated.

In the second phase, the miner drilled three small holes, six to eight feet deep in the face of the seam of coal, about chest high. Using a six-foot, handheld auger drill, the miner leaned against the chest plate that was attached to the back of the auger and applied pressure. Three holes were drilled: one at the center and one to either side, in the shape of a fan.

In the third phase, black powder or other explosives were placed into each hole. The explosives were tamped or held in place with a clay plug or *dummy*. The dummy prevented the force of the explosion from coming out the hole and directed the energy from the explosion into the coal bed itself, causing the coal to be displaced into the void where the undercut was made, releasing the explosion energy harmlessly. Ideally, the coal broke loose from the wall and dropped to the floor in a mound. The coal would then be loaded into horse-drawn mine cars, pulled out, and transferred to the main line.

However, Monongah miners, like miners throughout the nation, often engaged in the practice of what was called *shooting-off-the-solid*. This shortcut could speed the mining cycle, thus allowing the miner to load more coal and increase his pay. Instead of undercutting the coal face, the miner would allow the face to remain solid. After drilling the three holes, the miner would add slightly more powder than usual and shoot the coal. The explosion would release the coal into the room, despite the absence of a void or undercut. Frequently, however, the overcharged explosive force would seek the path of least resistance and come out the hole drilled by the miner. The force would rush back into the mine room itself, sending sparks through the now-airborne coal dust and risking a methane or coal dust explosion.

According to the state inspectors' reports, shooting-off-the-solid was practiced in both mines on frequent occasions. In the previous year, mine No. 8 had reported three nonfatal accidents "caused by non-competent men handling explosives which caused a blowing out shot."[46]

Churches

St. Anthony's Irish Catholic Church was the first Catholic Church erected in Monongah in 1893. It primarily served the Irish immigrant community of railroad men, construction workers, and miners. As the immigrant population shifted to include more Polish and Italians, new churches were needed.

Each immigrant group maintained their own religious community and harbored suspicion toward all other groups. Immigrant groups and the existing church administration worked hard to find priests from the old country to immigrate in order to administer to their needs. Such was the case with the Italian and Slavic miners in Monongah.

In May of 1903, Bishop Patrick J. Donahue had arranged through Bishop Scharbrine for Father Joseph D'Andrea, C.S.B.C.,[47] an Italian priest, to come over in order to assist the Italian immigrant families. Under the Bishop's direction, a meeting was organized in Monongah to decide whether to build a church. Mine superintendent A. J. Ruckman addressed the group and said that the Fairmont Coal Company would do "all in its power to assist them to become good American citizens, and that [he] was glad to see a disposition on their part to build churches and schools."

Because of the large number of Italian immigrants who were living in the area, the Italian government had recently established a consul's office in Fairmont. The Royal Italian Consul, Mr. Joseph W. Marianni, was in attendance and provided translation. After a brief discussion, the group voted to build a church and elected officers.[48]

Later that year, on land leased from the Fairmont Coal Company, ground was broken in Monongah for the first Italian church in West Virginia. Two years later in 1905, Our Lady of the Most Holy Rosary of the Vale of Pompeii was completed at a cost of $4,068.79. Donations came primarily from the miners. One beautiful young parishioner, Virginia Loss, worked on the committee raising funds. She made three trips into the mines to collect donations from the miners while they were at work, fearing that some might spend their wages before they got home. Born around 1888, Miss Loss, who worked in the Fairmont Coal Company store, raised more money than anyone else for the church construction and as a result was given a small diamond ring by the miners when the church was completed.[49]

Our Lady of the Vale of Pompeii was a one-story wooden structure with small, handmade stained glass windows created by one of the parishioners. The church sat at the intersection of Church Street and Camden Avenue, which was Route 19, located on the east side of town.[50] Father D'Andrea had come from the village of Premia in the Administrative District of Novara in the Province of Piedmont in northern Italy. Several of the miners had come from there, too, including Father D'Andrea's brother. Victor D'Andrea and his wife, Maria Gattini, lived in Monongah with their three children while he worked in the Monongah mines. Father D'Andrea, a young spare man with a quick smile on his dark face, had come to Monongah in 1902. By 1906, he had baptized 170 Italian-American babies. He was actually the second pastor to serve Monongah, the first being Father Ricardo Lorenzoni who, like Father D'Andrea, was on loan from either Boston or Hartford Diocese.

Just one block down the hill from Our Lady of Pompeii, around the same time, the St. Stanislaus Catholic Church was built on Maple Avenue to provide services for the Polish and Serbian miners. Father Joseph Lekston, himself a Polish immigrant who fled the Russian-dominated portion of Poland, opened the church and became its first pastor in 1904. Father Lekston had completed his seminary studies in Italy when he was invited by Bishop Donahue of the West Virginia diocese, to come to Monongah and minister to the immigrant Polish miners. St. Stanislaus Church was a wooden frame structure, painted red. It sat halfway up the hill above the No. 6 mine entrance. The first floor was a low-ceilinged room while the second floor housed the chapel sanctuary where mass was held.[51]

Relations between the new Catholic communities and the predominately Protestant native population were strained. Protestant ministers sometimes received support from the mine company management in their efforts to convert the "papists." Tent revivals were held on Monongah mine company property in an attempt to bring these newly arrived immigrants into the prevailing fold. The *Fairmont Free Press* reported that a Reverend Helmick gained some fifteen converts at his 1890 revival meeting. It was common practice in some locations for the company to subsidize Protestant churches by paying for the church building and, occasionally, paying the minister's salary; in Monongah the company assisted but the immigrants leased the land from the company and paid to build their churches through donations.

But the Fairmont Coal Company, recognizing the importance of the immigrant religious affiliations, provided additional benefits for ministers and priests alike. Railway and interurban passes were provided to the clergy by the coal company, but these gratuities were not given without expectations of favors in return, especially in times of labor trouble. In 1894, H. G. Bowles, general superintendent of the Monongah Railroad, wrote to Camden:

My opinion is that we might afford to still issue Bishop Donahoe a pass for 1895, though since one or two preachers from other denominations took special notice of the annual held by Rev. O'Conner last year, I don't know whether it would be a good policy or not to re-issue the O'Conner pass. He uses it quite a good deal and last summer when he was called on to assist here in quelling the strike, I think he failed to materialize.[52]

Recreation

Because of the remote and rural settings of the mining operations, the Fairmont Coal Company developed a recreation area for the miners and their families. Traction Park was built at one of the interurban line stops, located between the two mines. The grounds included a dance hall, a baseball diamond with a grandstand, and a stage for concerts.

To provide for concerts, in the first years of the new century, popular music was provided by brass bands. Popular in Europe, brass bands had been imported by the immigrants and had adapted well to American influences. In Monongah, several brass bands provided entertainment at dances and parades. The Verdi Brass Band, under the direction of Professor Raymond Verdi, was associated with Our Lady of Pompeii Church and was made up almost entirely of Monongah's Italian miners. The Monongah Italian Band and the Coronet Band of Monongah were popular both in Fairmont and Monongah. In addition to concerts, other cultural events were held at the Monongah Coliseum, a restaurant on Main Street in Monongah, which provided live theater, including productions of "Isbam's Octorooms" and "Uncle Josh Spruceby."

However, American music was also gaining popularity among immigrants throughout the country and was played in Monongah homes and social halls. "School Days" and "Honey Boy" were in demand because, as the Fairmont newspaper pointed out, there were "probably five hundred phonographs in Fairmont so hundreds of people are familiar with the popular songs of the day."[53]

But in Monongah and Fairmont, relations were strained between the immigrants and the "native" people in the mining communities—not only because some of the immigrants had been brought in as strike breakers, but also because they were just different from the natives. Frequent references in newspapers and by other public organs poked fun at the newcomers and their cultural and religious beliefs. The *Fairmont Index* and others referred to the *foreigners* when describing new immigrant mine accident victims, while 'Americans' were referred to by name. When describing disturbances or arrests, news accounts would state that "five Italians" were held, rather than referring to them by name. For example, in its "Monongah Items" the *Fairmont Free Press* reported, "A fight took place in the Monongah Company Store Saturday evening in which a Slavish man threw a four pound weight at John Edwards. The latter trying to defend himself was put out of the store and the fight was kept up for several minutes. Both were beat bad and paid a big fine."[54] The *Free Press* also reported in the local news column, entitled "Monongah the City of Mines," "There was a slight scrap in 'Africa' last Saturday night in which Thos. Filkins stuck a pick in Ed. Cusin's face, (all colored) making an ugly wound, No arrests." The column continued, "Last Thursday night several of our boys filled up on speakeasy whiskey, and retired to Chas. Arpp's chicken roost taking sixteen chickens which they roasted and presumably ate."[55]

The same issue of the *Free Press* also editorialized on the front page about the Italian immigrants' violence:

When Louige Maryhan was stabbed in a drunken quarrel, Frank Goots was charged after being captured on the train trying to escape to Pittsburgh, the sheriff brought him back to town, a large crowd gathered and threatened to take matters into their own hands.

The aforementioned news article also suggested: "A hanging or two seems to be necessary in order to make rows, and occasionally murders, less numerous among the foreigners of this vicinity."

Tensions were also felt between the 'foreign' miners and the surrounding communities. In Worthington, a village next to Monongah, the local paper reported: "Of late a lot of Italians from Monongah have been committing depredations on the farms of the vicinity, and will pay no attention to the warnings, and those who have suffered from their petty thieving propose to resort to the shot gun in the future."[56]

Fairmont

If Monongah was a thriving coal camp and home to the immigrant miners, the town of Fairmont, eight miles to the north along the West Fork River, was the hub for north-central West Virginia and the center of the booming coalfields that had sprung up in the past fifteen years. Marion County had been created as a Virginia county in 1842 and named for Francis Marion, the Swamp Fox, hero of the American Revolution.[57] Fairmont, the county seat of Marion County, was described on pages 4 and 5 of Polk's 1902 city directory as

the leading commercial city of the B&O Railroad between Cumberland and Wheeling and it has and is having a phenomenal growth, 10,000 laborers are employed in the surrounding coal fields. Ten years ago Fairmont was a town of no considerable importance with a population of less than 1,000 with few industries and no modern improvements.

By 1905 Fairmont's population had exceeded 20,000 and Monongah had reached 6,000. The growth was driven by a coal industry and supporting industry. Coal production in the Fairmont field in 1890 was 240,000 tons and by 1901 it had reached 6 million tons.

Home to the Watson Hotel, which was often described as one of the finest in the state, and the Fairmont Brewing Company, one of the state's largest brewers, Fairmont also boasted ten hotels, thirteen meat markets, thirty doctors in residence, and an office for the aforementioned Italian Consulate, Joseph W. Mariani, at 112 Main Street.

At the corner of Main and Adams streets, were the Fairmont Coal Company offices and the Consolidation Coal Company offices. Consolidation Coal had merged with the Fairmont Coal Company in 1901, and several of Camden's, Watson's, and Fleming's other enterprises, including the National Bank of Fairmont, the Fairmont and Clarksburg Traction Company, and the Fairmont Gas and Light Company, were all clustered near the center of town. The city's first skyscraper, the Watson Building was completed in 1911. The nine-story skyscraper was one of the biggest buildings in the state, and easily the largest in Fairmont. The Watson skyscraper so pleased the owners that one of The Fairmont Coal Company's baseball teams, which included

Monongah mine employees, was called the Skyscrapers, and a copy of the building's design appeared as the logo on the team uniforms.

The skyscraper's designer, noted Philadelphia architect Horace Trumbauer, also designed the baronial estate buildings of High Gate for James E. Watson, eldest son of patriarch James O. Watson, founder of the Fairmont Coal Company. High Gate would be built eight blocks south of the Watson Building on Fairmont Avenue by James E. Watson. James E. Watson had taken over the coal trade from his father in the 1880s and retired in 1900 to turn his attention to investments and the building of the finest estate in West Virginia. The actual building of High Gate was begun in 1909, and when finished covered an entire city block. Its three stories contained twenty-five rooms, a dozen baths, eight gigantic fireplaces with mantles carved from Italian marble, and five hundred windows. High Gate boasted flower gardens alongside tennis courts big enough to host large-scale regional tournaments. Fairmont residents liked to observe that the architect, Trumbauer, had also designed buildings for Jay Gould and the Vanderbilts.

At the center of town the newly completed Marion County Courthouse, with its gold-leaf dome, was a tribute to the economic might that was making Marion County one of the leading centers of the state and the region. The courthouse opened in 1900, reflecting the county's economic prosperity. The Beaux Arts-styled building had fluted columns supporting the porticoes, and within the tympanum, or triangular caps, were four decorative figures: a set of scales, an eagle with outstretched wings, a mining car, and a shovel held by a male figure, representing justice, power, agriculture, and mining. The firm Yost & Packard of Columbus, Ohio, designed the building and capped the dome with a classical figure holding the Scales of Justice.[58]

Fanning out from the center of town toward the south, two boulevard-sized avenues ran in the direction of the mining camps. Locust Avenue and Fairmont Avenue ran parallel to one another for roughly two miles. Locust

Avenue was dotted with farms and dairies, while Fairmont Avenue was the more developed section of the city. The Fairmont Development Company, a Watson-Fleming enterprise, designed and developed a corridor twelve city blocks long and six blocks wide on either side of Fairmont Avenue. Grand mansions dominated the crest of the hill that Fairmont Avenue followed, with large homes on the closest side street, Virginia Avenue. One block down, duplex houses for managers sat on Gaston Avenue. At the bottom of the hill on Virginia Avenue, machine shops and manufacturing plants sat next to the river. At the far end of Fairmont Avenue, from Ninth Street to Twelfth Street and beyond, was the Fairmont Farms enclave. Here lived Clarence Wayland Watson, his wife, Minnie Lee Owings, and several other Watson family members. Their estate, the Grange, had originally belonged to Clarence's father, J. O. Watson, and contained the stables that housed Minnie Watson's world-famous show horses. High Gate was located in the next block; A. B. Fleming, the company lawyer, lived across from High Gate and the Farms.[59]

Fairmont was served by the street car system (described at the beginning of this chapter), which was connected to the interurban light-rail system. The street car line made a large loop from downtown, out to Fairmont Avenue past Twelfth Street, across Country Club Avenue, where it intersected with Traction Park, and then proceeded down Locust Avenue and back into town. This light-rail system provided a means for the miners and their families to come to town on Saturday. For the mine owners, supervisors, and bosses who typically lived in Fairmont, it provided travel to the mines during the week. At the heart of the system was a double-arched crossing at the center of town in front of the Court House on Main Street in Fairmont, where the Monongahela Valley Traction Company was headquartered.[60] It was said, and not without justification, that no town in America had a better transportation system than Fairmont. Fairmont viewed itself as the coal city and ideal manufacturing center of the entire region, and not without reason.

IMMIGRANTS WANTED

Two thousand (2000) Coal Miners and Helpers, either experienced
Miners, with their families, or green laborers to learn coal mining
Under competent instructor.
All drift mines in the Monongahela Valley.
Average wages of Helpers from $2.00 to $3.00 per day;
Average wages Machine Runners $3.50 to $6.00 per day.
No Shaft Mines; All drift, located at Fairmont and Clarksburg, West
Virginia on the Baltimore and Ohio Railroad.
Height of coal seam was eight feet. Practically free from explosive gasses.

The Consolidation Coal Co., Inc.

I have investigated the conditions outlined in the above letter and find them
true as claimed. I find there are no labor troubles or difficulties in the Fairmont
field and that the statement of average wages earned is correct. I think the
above offer of employment a splendid opportunity for men with families seeking employment. The dwelling houses are comfortable and rent charges I find
reasonable.

John Nugent, Immigration Commissioner, State of West Virginia

As THE new century dawned and the industrial expansion spread, every sector of the U.S. economy faced labor shortages. The increased demand in the railroad, mining, and manufacturing industries absorbed all available labor and drew workers from rural communities to the cities. As a result, many industries turned to immigrant labor; farmers in Maryland and South Carolina farmers even recruited immigrants for work.[1] Railroads, steel mills, manufacturing, and mines all sought employees from abroad.

However, nowhere was the shortage of labor more profound or the demand more critical than in mining. Throughout the country, coal mining relied on large numbers of strong men to perform the difficult manual labor, and nowhere was the need greater than in the booming West Virginia and western Pennsylvania coal fields. Between 1870 and 1880 the coal production of northern West Virginia and western Pennsylvania more than doubled, from 17 million tons to 42 million tons. The increase continued into the 1890s, resulting in what W. Jett Lauck called, on page 35 of *The Bituminous Coal Miner & Coke Worker of Western Pennsylvania*, "a remarkable increase in the operating forces." In 1870, bituminous mine workers had numbered only 16,000 men, but by 1909, the number was approaching 186,000, an increase of almost 1,100 percent in 39 years.[2]

Immigration patterns were shifting dramatically during this time. By 1890 the traditional immigrant groups—Irish, English, Welsh—had declined so significantly that recruitment efforts shifted focus to southern and eastern Europe. In Marion County, the shifting immigration pattern was especially pronounced. The burgeoning coal industry caused the population to increase from 12,107 in 1870 to 32,430 in 1900; during the last decade of the century, the population increased 56 percent. Much of this increase was due to the influx of Italian and Polish immigrants specifically brought in to work in the mines. By 1910, Italian miners were by far the largest immigrant group, registering more than 2,185 of the new residents, while 798 were registered from the Austro-Hungarian Empire.[3]

By 1906, Monongah was populated principally by immigrants from Italy, the Austro-Hungarian Empire, the Russian-controlled Kingdom of Poland, and a smattering of Turks, Greeks, and African-Americans in addition to the first- and second-generation Irish, Welsh, Scottish, English, and German who had settled in the area and come to work when the mines were first opened.[4] In order to deal with this multicultural workforce, instructions at Monongah mine portals were posted in seven languages, reflecting the diversity of the workforce, although the instructions were of limited help because many, if not most, of the immigrants were illiterate.

From the company's earliest days, Senator J. N. Camden and his associates had focused on immigrant labor as part of a strategy to provide cheap labor for the newly opened mines, as well as to help thwart unionization efforts. From 1897 through 1902, labor unions, particularly the Knights of Labor and then the United Mine Workers of America, undertook extensive unionization efforts at Monongah. Although unsuccessful, the push for unionization encouraged the mine owners to replace the homegrown part of the work force with immigrants. During Camden's early years of operation, when he was beleaguered by labor unrest, he first considered black workers as strikebreakers and replacement workers but rejected the idea in 1890 because of the potential for racial diversion and animosity. When a coal broker suggested the use of 'Negro' labor rather than 'foreign' labor which is "almost sure to give you trouble as soon as they are settled in," Camden wrote,

I note what you say in regard to colored labor, and I have no doubt it is more reliable labor if we could get plenty of it, but this is a contingency that I want to avoid if possible as the Monongah district is an old settled country, and would protest furiously against an introduction of colored labor there.[5]

Camden, and later, Watson and Fleming and the Fairmont Coal Company, became the leading importers of immigrant miners in the region. By the turn of the century, the merged Consolidation Coal Company and Fairmont Coal Company employed company labor agents who were sent to Europe where they recruited in the villages and small towns of Italy and the Polish section of the Austro-Hungarian Empire. In addition, in the name of economic development, the state of West Virginia set up an immigrant labor recruiting office directed by the commissioner of immigration. This office would send state labor-recruiting agents to Europe to recruit workers on behalf of state companies. The recruits were normally inexperienced single males. In return for a small payment or simply the promise of a job, they would sign a contract binding them to employment with, for example, the Fairmont Coal Company mines, which they were assured were safe and desirable. The labor agent would direct the men to a steamship office in Naples or elsewhere where they could have a one-way steerage passage booked.

From its earliest days, a special passage arrangement existed between the Fairmont Coal Company, the B&O Railroad, and at least one steamship line. As early as March 27, 1868, the B&O Railroad entered into a supply-sales agreement with the North German Lloyd Steamship Line; after the B&O's affiliation with the Fairmont Coal Company, the agreement was expanded to provide immigrants' passage across the Atlantic to Baltimore and rail transportation to their destination—in this case, Monongah. In return for passage, the Fairmont Coal Company and the B&O Railroad supplied coal to the Steamship Company "at less than current market rates."[6] This advantageous arrangement contributed in part to the fact that, by the last decades of the century, the port of Baltimore became the principle port of entry for immigrants destined to work in the coal mines of West Virginia and Pennsylvania and the second largest port of entry on the eastern seaboard. Because of its reach over the mountains and into West Virginia, the B&O Railroad became the principle transporter of immigrants from the eastern seaboard to the mines and mills of Pennsylvania, Ohio, and West Virginia.

Upon arrival in Baltimore, the immigrant men were loaded directly onto B&O trains, which headed west through Cumberland to Fairmont and Wheeling. The B&O Railroad had an economic interest in seeing to it that the immigrant miners arrived on time and safely, because the B&O was the controlling shareholder in the Consolidation Coal Company, parent of the Fairmont Coal Company, which operated the Monongah mines. From the moment these new immigrants arrived on U.S. soil, they were under the control of the mine employer. Even before experiencing the freedom of America, the immigrants were indentured servants, bound by the labor contract and indebted to the company for passage, money, and tools.

The immigrants generally spoke little English, if any. Many had grown up in rural farming communities and had no experience with industrial workplaces, much less mines; but if their backgrounds did not prepare them for the rigors of mining, it may have made them more willing to accept the living conditions in the coal camps. Early experts concluded that their background led to little dissatisfaction in the coal camps:

the standards of living of southern and eastern Europeans who have entered the bituminous mines have been so low that neither the conditions of employment nor the rates of pay have as a rule constituted grounds for dissatisfaction.[7]

The recent immigrant workers also faced hostility on the job:

The feeling has become strong among the natives and older immigrants that a certain social stigma attaches to working in the same occupation or alongside the recent immigrant. This has led to the segregation of the races at work, even when they live in the same towns and company rows.[8]

In 1900, mining towns were isolated from the ordinary flow of life in the United States. Coal camps and villages were frequently located in rural locations such as Monongah, where the immigrants and their families were cut off from the daily commerce of the economic centers. The Monongah interurban rail, which was part of the Camden, Watson, and Fleming interest, was the principal means in and out of town. In several ways this isolation worked to the disadvantage of the newly arrived immigrant:

That isolation facilitated control over the town by excluding outside troublemakers and alternative employment; it allowed management to impose discipline through eviction from the community as a penalty for breaking the rules—such as joining a union or trying to promote one.[9]

The presence of armed company guards who traveled on the train and patrolled the town, especially at the first sign of labor trouble, added to the sense of isolation. There were very few, if any, institutions or groups to which the immigrants could turn for help.

The Italian Miners

Among the miners waiting to go to work at mine No. 8 on the morning of December 6, 1907, were Angelo DePetris and his brother Orazio or Crazio DePetris. Dan Dominico and his son Leonardo joined the DePetris brothers at the entrance of No. 8 around 5:30 A.M. Orazio DePetris was with his son Felice who only recently had been hired as a motorman, operating a gathering motor that collected the filled mine cars, pulling them to the surface. The motorman job was considered a step up from his father's pick work position.

Orazio and Angelo had been among the first Italians to be recruited and hired to work in the new Monongah mines.[10] They had left their village of Pesco Costanzo, Italy, in March 1889, and traveled by train across the south of Italy to Naples Bay. There they boarded the ship, *Alsatia*, which stopped in Palermo, Sicily, and then set out across the ocean, arriving in New York City on April 18, 1889. They boarded the train to Baltimore and, from there, traveled on to Fairmont and Monongah.[11]

After several years, Orazio returned to Italy when his wife became ill and stayed in the old country for four years, returning to Monongah only a little over a year before, in 1906, where he resumed work in the mines. Although all of the older men had been in the country for several years, they spoke little English and relied on Felice for English translation.[12]

By 1905, the largest group of immigrants in Monongah were from Italy, many from the central and southern provinces. They were peasants from small villages in the provinces of Campobasso, Calabraia, Benevento, Aguila, Catanzaro, the Abruzzie Molise, Potenz, and Terra di Lovoro in the economically destitute section of the Italian boot. Recruited by labor agents, they signed a contract, and traveled by train or boat to Naples where they reported to the U.S. immigration office. There each immigrant was interviewed by U.S. immigration officials, who determined whether they were acceptable as immigrants to the United States. The immigration officer inquired as to their destination, background, health status, and most importantly, whether they had money for the passage and a job in America. Those who failed to meet the criteria were rejected and sent home. Those approved would travel aboard ships like the *Patria*, the *Elysia*, or the *Olympia*, steaming out into the Mediterranean then to the Atlantic for the trip, which was typically between three weeks and a month long and then on to New York or Baltimore. Upon arrival in New York, most boarded trains to Baltimore, and then proceeded on the B&O to Fairmont, afterwards taking the spur line to Monongah.[13]

In the first years of the Monongah mining operation, many immigrants arrived in Monongah. When they passed striking miners whose jobs or houses they were to take, the reception was often hostile. At the station in Monongah they were met by company agents who assigned them to houses in one of the sections of town, typically where other members of their ethnic group were living. The company agent, who was frequently a member of the company security force, also directed them to the company store where they would buy, on credit, miners' boots, caps, lights and food rations. At the store, they could also buy the mining tools they needed (e.g., pick and shovel); each man was required to purchase all the necessary mining equipment himself. For these and other reasons, the large majority of immigrants were in the company's debt from the day they arrived.

A typical Italian miner's story is told by Judy Prozzillo Byers, who currently heads up the West Virginia Folk Life Center at Fairmont State College and is a wonderful promoter of oral history. Her grandfather was recruited from the hills of Benevento, in southern Italy. He traveled by ship from the Bay of Naples to Ellis Island, then to Monongah where he worked double shifts and learned English. Soon he had saved enough to go back to Italy, marry, and return with his bride. He also brought along with him several men he had *sponsored* from Benevento, which means he loaned them the money for their passage; they worked in the Monongah mines to pay back their debt and lived as boarders with the Prozzillos—Mr. Prozzillo being the house boss and Mrs. Prozillo cooking and cleaning. They all lived on Camden Street in one of the Italian sections and raised vegetables to supplement their mining income. The house was directly behind Our Lady of Pompeii Church, and Father D'Andrea often visited and joined in the meals.[14]

The Polish Miners

Just after Orazio and Angelo entered the mouth of No. 8 on that 6th day of December, 1907, two other brothers entered, Stanislaus and Peter Urban (also identified as Peter Rosebeiq). Around 6:00 A.M., they went to the first right of the first heading to the eighth room. There were no mine cars available, so they began to dig and shoot the next load.

Stanislaus, the older of the two, had come to Monongah first in 1892. He was married to Mary, and they had four children. They had come from the Village of Czonolas near the town of Kolbreszowa in the province of Galitzia in what was then part of the Austro-Hungarian Empire, and is now southwest Poland. Stanislaus and Mary were in their mid-twenties with two girls and two boys, all between the ages of one and seven. Peter and his wife immigrated a short time later and Peter began to work in mine No. 8 just six months before.[15]

Polish immigrants constituted the second largest immigrant group among the miners at Monongah. The Kingdom of Poland also was known as Congress Poland because it had been partitioned in 1772 and again at the Congress of Vienna. In the late eighteenth century, the Kingdom of Poland had been conquered and was divided between the Russian Czar's Empire, the Austro-Hungarian Empire, and Prussia. In addition, the last decades of the 1800s were a period of great instability in this area of Eastern Europe and in the Russian and Austro-Hungarian empires in general. Insurrections, overpopulation, and periodic droughts led many young men to seek a new start in the New World.

Along with this instability, a recent technological advance emerged that made immigration both more affordable and more accessible: the development of ocean-going steamships. Steamships powered by coal allowed for quicker trips and lower fares than the sailing ships had, permitting larger numbers of immigrants to strike out for the New World.[16]

But if the promise of the New World was not enough, the threat of the war added urgency to many young men. Conscription posed a great risk for many of the young men of the Polish region. During this time, the Russo-Japanese War was raging in the Far East, and Czar Nicholas was conscripting young men throughout the Empire for service in the Russian army. Further south, in areas controlled by the Austrian-Hungarian Empire, conscription was common and supplied combatants for armies to fight in distant locations in order to support the aging empire.

In addition, many Polish immigrants came from poor agrarian districts and were landless farmhands or the owners of *dwarf farms*, family farms that had been subdivided over time into parcels so small that they could not sustain a family. Thus, recruiting agents from mine companies found willing takers among the young men of the area. Prospective immigrants traveled first by cart or rail to Bremen or Hamburg then to Keil where they boarded ships with names like *La Normandie*, the *Amalfi*, or the *Augusta Victoria* and steamed for the two- to three-week trip east out of the Baltic across the North Atlantic to Baltimore or New York, where many boarded B&O trains to Fairmont and Monongah.

Initially, these men came alone or with brothers, cousins, or neighbors. As savings from work accumulated, money was sent back or the men themselves traveled back, visiting families or bringing wives and families back with them to the new country. In Monongah, Polish immigrants, like their Italian counterparts, would typically live and socialize with their countrymen; inside the mines, crews tended to work with family and friends.[17]

The Irish Miners

On June 22, 1852, the B&O reached Fairmont and a short time later, Francis H. Pierpont and J. O. Watson opened up the first mine in Fairmont just up the hill from the B&O Train Station. The railroad continued building through the summer and fall, reaching Wheeling and the Ohio River by the end of the year.

The B&O, the nation's oldest rail line, had completed the most expensive and first rail expansion across the Appalachian Mountains largely by using

Irish immigrants. Work began in Cumberland, Maryland, on November 5, 1842, to extend the line west through Fairmont to Wheeling and the Ohio River. By the autumn of 1851, the track building project involved five thousand men, most of whom were Irish immigrants who, having fled the artificial famine or been forced off the land by the application of the English Poor Relief Laws, sought work constructing the rail line through the mountains. Thousands of men were employed, with wives and families living in railroad shacks nearby and moving west as the line progressed. One Irish immigrant's family history describes the railroad construction journey and how, during the year of 1852, many railroad construction workers recognized that they would soon be out of work. Many of those workers settled in the mountains of West Virginia, bought land to farm, and soon went to work in the booming mining industry.

In early 1847, English lawmakers passed the Poor Relief Bill. A two-part Act, it first advanced a ten-million-pound loan to Ireland, one half to be expended in public works and the other half to relieve the poor. Soup kitchens, called outdoor relief, were to be organized throughout the country.

By April, nearly three quarters of a million fathers were enrolled in the relief work. Assuming an equal number of wives and two or three children per family, Ireland's relief roles at the time represented almost four million people, nearly one-half of the countries population.

The second provision of the Poor Relief Act was called the Quarter-Acre Clause. It provided that any farmer wishing to obtain "outdoor relief," i.e. food, had to surrender "all rights to any land ownership he might have above one quarter of a statute acre."

As a result of this continuing famine and the English policies, escape became the only answer, and yet again, the Poor Relief Bill addressed the issue and provided assistance to such people wishing to get out of the country and settle elsewhere.[18]

On July 26, 1847, the John S. DeWolfe, a Braque, sailed from Killala, a small port in County Mayo, Ireland. Among the 362 passengers were Kathrine Flannery, a 55-year-old widow, her married daughter, Cecily Erwin, and son-in-law, 33-year-old Philip Erwin, as well as her unmarried daughter Kathrine. On August 9th, after a difficult passage during which many passengers died, the boat arrived at Saint John, New Brunswick. A short time later Grandma Flannery and family sailed to Boston where Philip Erwin found "contract work" grading for the railroads. Following available work, the family moved to Maryland where work was found for the B&O's westward rail line construction project from Cumberland, Maryland, to Fairmont and Wheeling, Virginia.

As the railroad construction reached Fairmont and the end of the railroad construction project neared, the family settled in Marion County, first in Barnsville, then in Section 37 and Downs until a few years later when they bought a home in Fairmont in the 1850s. Through the next forty years, the family flourished farming and working for the railroad. In 1873, Philip and Cecily Erwin's daughter, Mary Agnes, married Michael Kennedy, of a family that had also emigrated from County Mayo and worked railroad construction in much the same way as had the Erwins.[19] In 1900, the Kennedys bought a farm near Fairmont from the Fleming family and built a ten-room house. At about that time, Mary and Michael Kennedy's daughter, Ellen, married Daniel Thomas Purcell. Purcell had begun work in the mines at a young age and by the early years of the 1900s, had worked his way into mine management supervisory position.

A second group of Irish immigrants had become miners in other mines in Maryland including in the original Consolidation Coal Company mines in the Georges Creek Basin of Maryland. This minefield was located near the towns of Eckart Mines and Frostburg, above Cumberland. By the end of the century, those mines had been worked out and were closing when, in 1901, the Fairmont Coal Company and Consolidation Coal Company merged. Many of these men and their families moved to Monongah and Fairmont as the new mines opened and because of their experience, these miners were frequently entry level or midlevel management positions as foremen or superintendents.[20]

The Greek Miners

In the 1900s, the island of Tenedos in the Dardanelles Strait, eight miles off the Turkish coastline, was part of the Ottoman Empire. Although the population was predominately Greek, the islands were ruled from Istanbul, Turkey.

Anestis Stamboulis was born on the island of Tenedos, near Bozcarda, Turkey, on May 3, 1888. At the age of 16, he left home and went to live in the monastery near his home. Anestis was not a monk, but lived as a tenant and sought work in the area, which was a common practice at the time. In early 1907, Constantius Limnion, a Greek who had immigrated to the United States some years earlier and was acting as a recruiting agent for mining companies in West Virginia, solicited young men in Tenedos to come to work in the Monongah mines. Limnion lived in Wheeling, West Virginia, and was securing employees for the Fairmont Coal Company's mines at Monongah. Limnion made arrangements for Stamboulis and several other young men from his village to book passage on the M.V. Gentry sailing from Patras, Greece, on June 7, 1907, to New York.

In all, 13 young men from Tenedos were on board. Stamboulis was 20 years old at the time, 5-feet 5-inches tall, and single. He had a total of $10 in his pocket and traveled third class to America, seeking a new life. In late May, he and the others left Tenedos by ferry and sailed to Athens, where they then made their way to Patras. There they boarded the M.V. Gentry and sailed through the Mediterranean and out across the Atlantic. On June 24th, after a fourteen-day passage, they docked in New York City harbor and passed through Ellis Island. A train took them to Baltimore, where they boarded a B&O train bound for Wheeling. In Wheeling, Limnion gave his recruits instructions and then took them on the train back to Fairmont. At Monongah, Stamboulis was assigned to a boarding house with his traveling companions, one of whom was Michael Saltos, a fellow traveler from Tenedos. Saltos had not gone to Wheeling, but had stopped in Cumberland, where he met relatives and from there traveled directly to Monongah. Within days, all went to work in the Monongah mines.[21] The mines at Monongah employed such a large number of men that recruits were gathered from all corners of the globe.

The Others

A small number of Turkish miners added to the multicultural mix that constituted the Monongah work force. A substantial number of black miners worked alongside the immigrants, most having been brought into the Monongah mines as strike breakers during the strikes of the late 1890s and the early years of the 1900s. Recruited principally from southern West Virginia, these men had the worst lot of all in terms of housing, location, and work assignments. Black miners were denied access to any skilled or management position, and their children were not allowed in any of the schools. The African-American section of town, called Africa by most of the American-born European miners, was the furthest removed from the center of the coal camp.

Summary

In 1900, the U.S. population was 76 million. Within 10 years, immigration had raised that number by 8 million; by 1910 the population of the country had increased by 21 percent. Immigration peaked during the first decade of the new century, higher than ever before in the United States. Much of this influx resulted from the demand for workers to fuel the industrial expansion, and coal mining was integral to that expansion.[22]

This mass migration also sparked one of the strongest waves of anti-immigration sentiment in U.S. history, as previous immigrants, now natives, grew concerned about both economic and cultural impacts of the new arrivals. These new immigrants were not from the same countries or cultures that had come before. They were considered less desirable by the Anglo Saxons who had migrated earlier. On Friday, July 6, 1906, the *New York Times* ran a story on the Immigration Commission and its annual report about

the continuance of the disproportion of the less desirable races. Last year 850,000 landed here, the previous greatest number having been 788,289 in 1905. It was in that year that Hungarians displaced Italians as the greatest contributors to the dilution of the Anglo-Saxon race. In the earlier years our National stock was recruited chiefly by those of near lineage like the British of the several varieties and even the Germans were almost kin, being cousins not far removed.

The arrival of Austro-Hungarians at the head of the list is unwelcome for several reasons. Their illiteracy and disregard of law are high, and they are among the race which settled in the east, only one-fourth going west. They are not skilled workers, contributing hardly anything but crude muscle to the country of their adoption.[23]

But if the first decade of the new century saw the rise of anti-immigrant sentiment, it also witnessed the rise of the Progressive Era. The era came to its fullest with the ascendancy of Teddy Roosevelt to the presidency following the assassination of William McKinley. McKinley was shot by a disgruntled immigrant who had lost his government job. Roosevelt, a Republican from an aristocratic, wealthy New York family, was faced with the inequities that decades of unfettered capitalism had wrought upon American society, especially among immigrants in basic industries like mining. He applied some of the reform lessons he had learned as governor of New York to some of the worst injustices facing children, as well as immigrants, with regard to wages, hours, and working conditions. He adopted a number of the policies that the populists and labor unions had championed during the previous decades.

While not an ideological foe of big business, Roosevelt did not feel obligated or beholden, either. It was either Mark Hanna or Henry Frick, both mining industry barons, who said of Roosevelt, "We bought him, but he wouldn't stay bought."[24] Nor was Roosevelt a captive of the union movement. He was not afraid to adopt, albeit in modified forms, some of the reforms labor and others had championed. His concerns were the excesses of big businesses, and for that matter, big labor.

When Roosevelt saw big business running roughshod over the miners in Pennsylvania in 1902, he reacted. At that time, the anthracite miners of Pennsylvania were responding to the call of John Mitchell, president of the UMWA. On behalf of some 100,000 miners of different ethnic backgrounds laboring in the central Pennsylvania coal fields, Mitchell demanded reorganization of the union, a raise in pay, and an 8-hour day. When Mitchell called for a walk-out after the companies flatly rejected all of his demands, the miners surprised even the union leadership by walking off and staying off the job.

George F. Baer, the industry spokesman and one of the most prominent mine operators in the country of the day, infuriated Roosevelt when he wrote in an open letter to the press:

The rights and interests of the laboring man will be protected and cared for, not by the labor agitators, but by the Christian men to whom God in His infinite wisdom has given control of the property interests of the country, and upon the successful Management of which so much depends.[25]

Roosevelt responded to this arrogant stupidity by letting the operators know that if federal troops were to be used, it would be to protect the miners and not the mine operators. The strike succeeded and the miners obtained both a raise and reorganization of the union.

In northern West Virginia, however, Roosevelt's efforts were limited. For most miners—especially the immigrants—working conditions, wages, and safety and health concerns were ignored. Elsewhere, miners—particularly immigrants—were intimidated by the company supervisors and security guards and were unwilling to join unions. They were left to the whims of the mine operators, particularly in West Virginia, and especially in Monongah.

"HIRE BANDS OR ANYTHING THAT IS NECESSARY"

"There is never peace in West Virginia because there is never justice."

—Mary Harris "Mother" Jones

WHEN J. N. Camden's Monongah Coal & Coke Company opened the mines at Monongah, their business strategy was two-fold: to mine coal at a lower cost than their competitors and to operate in such a way that they would be able to supply coal during periods of labor unrest. Their chief competition worked out of the mines in Connellsville, a little more than 50 miles north, and they wanted to continue mining despite expected, periodic slowdowns and interruptions at other West Virginia and Pennsylvania mining districts. Both strategies were contingent upon Monongah Coal & Coke Company being able to operate their mines without their miners joining labor unions like the Knights of Labor or the United Mine Workers of America (UMWA).

In March of 1890, the Monongah Coal & Coke Company shipped its first load of coal to market, but as the washing and preparation plants were not wholly operational and the rail transportation system was not completely operative, most of the coal was sold locally. Shortly thereafter, the plant and rails were completed and shipments were begun to more distant markets.

From the very first, the Monongah mines had labor trouble. Almost immediately after the first coal was sold, disagreements arose over the amount of wages paid to the miners. This was a result of both the introduction of new technology and of the policy of paying mining laborers less than the prevailing rates at surrounding mines. Camden had introduced recently developed electric cutting machines into the mining cycle in the Monongah mines. Designed to save time and expense, this new equipment created new functions or jobs and resulted in machine operators being paid at a different rate than traditional contract miners. In fact, as entirely new positions, the rates were different from those of any other job in the mines. In addition, new equipment such as electric motors and electric rail locomotives operating the coal haulage systems also affected traditional job classifications and wages. The new equipment was more efficient, but it was also more complicated than, say, horse-drawn carts. The new technologies improved coal production, but they also increased the danger of explosions and the risks to miners' health by creating more coal dust.

When the first Monongah mine opened, Camden set out to undercut the prevailing wage scale as a matter of policy, the rationale being that the immigrant miners he was actively recruiting were less experienced and therefore less valuable than the native miners. As immigrants, the miners were also less likely to join a union or go on strike. The wage difference was only pennies per ton, but as wages were already low, every cent mattered. For example, the Gaston Mine in Fairmont was paying the miners 32 cents per ton for cutting, blowing down, breaking up, and loading; and the Montana Mine, in which Camden and J. O. Watson held an interest, was paying 35 cents per ton for these same jobs. In some locations in the Monongah mines, the cutting was being done by machine and a price had to be established for the cost of the coal loading. Camden had the rate fixed at 17 cents per ton, well below the daily wage that was generally paid for loading alone. Immediately, the miners asked for a minimum rate of 25 cents per ton for loading with the electric cutting machine, and the company refused. On April 15, 1890, just one month after the mine opened, miners at the Monongah mines went on strike and all were immediately fired. Within a week, although most miners had buckled to the company's position, labor union organizers arrived from the nearby Pennsylvania mine fields where they had only recently succeeded in establishing a new scale of wages adopted by miners and operators.

Organizing at Monongah was difficult. The initial crews who were recruited as miners were typically local farmers who considered the mine work supplemental to their livelihood as farmers and were not interested in unions. The immigrant miners had been recruited in the old country and were so fearful that they were reluctant to join a union. Furthermore, the company completely dominated every aspect of society in Monongah. Soon, the union agents were sent packing back to Pennsylvania and the miners accepted the reduced rate.

But in June, as a result of labor shortages, the Gaston and Montana companies gave their miners an increase of 5 cents per ton and also increased the daily wage for laborers. At Monongah the company continued at the low rate and many of its miners left and took other jobs. This, coupled with the shortage of railroad cars, caused production to decline sharply.

Partly as a result of these business reversals, on September 11, 1890, the first company president, S. W. Colton, Jr., resigned, and reorganization was undertaken by the Camden-controlled board of directors. In October, Camden was voted president and his son-in-law, Baldwin D. Spilman, was named general manager. As would become the practice at the Monongah mines over the next several years, the company management was frequently related by blood or marriage. In an effort to revive the flagging production, Spilman ordered that the mining machine operators be paid by the ton as opposed to by the day. As a result, production increased dramatically. Shortly after the reorganization, in November, 1890, the company showed its first gain.[1]

However, Spilman believed wages, although lower than at surrounding mines, were still too high. A number of jobs were not affected by the electric machines: undercutting the coal seam with handheld cutting machines, drilling with handheld augers, setting explosive charges, blowing down the wall or face of coal, and breaking up and loading the coal into mining cars all paid 25 cents per ton for *room work* (rooms driven off the header or main entrance where the coal is mined) and 30 cents for *header work* (a development opening).

Spilman recommended to Camden and the Board a five-cent reduction of each rate. Camden and the Board agreed, despite their expectations of a strike—which occurred immediately.

Union organizers were, once again, soon working with the striking miners. Although it was late November, Spilman moved to end the strike by evicting all strikers and their families from the company houses. By December 12, 1890, most of the men had returned to work, although some miners still held out.

On that day, a fight between a striker and a company agent occurred at the picket line, and one of the striking miners was shot. As a result, the Marion County Sheriff, who was also a Camden company employee, made several arrests among the strikers, and within a week, all who could returned to work. The strike had been completely broken.[2]

Spilman, in his six-month report to Camden on the state of the Monongah Coal Company, describes the period:

On November 1, 1890, the books of the company showed a loss of $13,728.75; in November, 1890, we had only a small amount of business on old contracts, but for the month showed a gain for the first time.

In December we had a strike on hand which lasted three weeks and which cost the company between four and five thousand dollars. The result of the strike, however, was a great gain to the company in that it reduced the cost of mining 5 cents per ton and brought order and discipline out of absolute chaos.[3]

Camden and Spilman had not only broken all opposition and undercut the prevailing wage scheme, they also had established the Monongah mines as a nonunion stronghold, possibly one of the goals of the low-wage strategy.

Pressures Build

Coal profits and production increased through 1891 and 1892, but labor unrest smoldered not far under the surface. In June of 1892, Spilman submitted his resignation as general manager, at the same time organizers for the Knights of Labor called a strike and the mines were closed for a week. Although Camden again beat back the strikers, a water shortage at Monongah—caused by a continuing shortage of railroad coal cars and an unseasonable drought in northern West Virginia—resulted in inadequate washing of the coal and customer complaints about the quality.

But events in Washington, DC had a more significant impact on the company's management. On January 11, 1893, West Virginia's senior United States Senator John E. Kenna died, and on January 24, 1893, the West Virginia legislature elected J. N. Camden to fill the unexpired term of two years. Camden had long been active in Democratic politics in West Virginia and was clearly the unanimous choice of the Democratic Caucus, which held the majority in both houses of the state legislature. Although he relinquished the presidency of the Monongah Coal & Coke Company by the end of 1893, he remained an active board member and continued serving on the executive committee. He also retained presidency of the Monongahela River Railroad, despite the fact that the United States Senate was actively engaged in the development of governmental policies that directly affected the coal and railroad industries generally and Camden's interests in particular. Such a conflict would be unusual by today's standards, but was accepted in the 1890s.[4]

Also in 1893, one of Camden's principal distribution agents collapsed financially, leaving the Monongah Coal & Coke Company without a distribution agency on the Great Lakes. In late 1893, prospects for Monongah Coal & Coke Company were bleak. The Monongah mines had produced only 40,000 tons in any one month, barely enough to break even and less than half their capacity. The 1893 monthly production average was less than 25,000 tons; forty thousand tons a month were needed to break even.[5]

A solution Camden pondered was to merge the Monongahela River Railroad Company, a highly profitable company thanks to the tariff agreement with the B&O, with the Monongah Coal & Coke Company. The idea was to then sell the combined company to the B&O. However, B&O management was not interested.[6]

Throughout 1894 and by the beginning of 1895, the economic outlook was dismal for Camden and the Monongah mines, despite paying the lowest prevailing wages and successfully thwarting union efforts. The general economic downturn that began nationwide in 1893 was growing more entrenched, and the coal transportation problem, getting the Monongah Mine coal to market, was as serious as ever. The B&O had neither sufficient coal rail cars nor the desire to provide them. By early 1896 the B&O itself faced financial difficulties and went into receivership. The reorganization efforts, influenced by Senator Camden, stood to benefit the Monongah mines by placing a greater emphasis on the shipment of coal and the acquisition of adequate numbers of coal cars. About that same time, Camden secured an order for 100,000 tons of coal from the Great Northern Railroad, resulting in the Monongah mines working at full capacity. By the mid 1890s, West Virginia's coal industry, particularly the Monongah mines, had captured an increasing share of the Great Lakes market. In 1895, 236,967 tons of West Virginia coal shipped to the lakes, ranking the state third behind western Pennsylvania and Ohio.

In the labor unrest of 1894, Camden had hired black workers from southern West Virginia as strike breakers. He repeated this tactic in the strikes of 1896 and 1897, but with little success. Indeed, in 1896 and 1897, while other mines had gone back to work, the Monongah mines continued to strike, a result—it was commonly believed—of the below-market wage structure.[7]

Throughout the early nineties, wages had been pushed down as a result of a national economic downturn, and in April 1896, reflecting the improved coal trade and in reply to miners' demands for increased wages, Fairmont operators unilaterally raised wages 8 percent to 22 cents—except in the Monongah mines. The raise was an attempt by the mine owners to control local labor unrest and stem the spread of strikes from the Pittsburgh and Connellsville coal fields. As during other strikes, Monongah management sought replacement workers, both native and immigrant, as a long-term solution.

In the Fairmont coals fields, the striking miners, through the UMWA, made a wage offer and offered to sit down at a wage conference with the operators. They were rebuffed. Unlike the Pittsburgh and Connellsville operations, no discussions with the Fairmont owners were held. The miners demanded a raise to 35 cents per ton and an agreement from management to negotiate, which would have meant recognizing the union. Chris Evans, of the UMWA, offered to meet any operator, but this offer was flatly rejected by all the Fairmont operators. Having succeeded in neighboring coal fields, the UMWA called for a strike of the Fairmont mines, including the Monongah complex.[8]

Initially, the strike succeeded to the point where fifteen African-Americans who had been brought in as strike breakers joined the strike. Unlike earlier efforts, the strike lasted several weeks and the Fairmont UMWA chapter was formed. By Friday, August 13, the strike had gained national attention, and the country's major national labor organizations were convened in Monongah.

Samuel Gompers, president of the American Federation of Labor; J. S. Sovereign, general master workman of the Knights of Labor; and Michael D. Ratchford, UMWA president, addressed the striking miners at a rally. Some other mines in the area had returned to work, but the Monongah mines had only a skeleton crew, despite the fact that the company was offering $2.00 a day to strike breakers. More African-American strike breakers from southern West Virginia were recruited, but soon they either joined the strikers or disappeared. Other nearby coalfields were experiencing unrest during the same period.

At the Monongah Convention, in addition to the strikers and their supporters, four U.S. Marshals attended. The local Fairmont papers reported that the speakers were orderly and were presented with flowers by the wives of miners following the meeting. The strike continued through the end of August, when immigrants from Italy and Poland recruited by Monongah mine labor agents began arriving at the ports of New York and Baltimore. There they boarded B&O trains that carried them to Monongah, past the striking miners to the houses from which those miners and their families had recently been evicted. The immigrants were put to work in place of the strikers. Bitterness toward the Monongah mines spread even to the local news organizations.

The *Fairmont Free Press* editorialized about Camden's mines on October 17, 1897:

The only place where there is still contention is at Monongah where it is a hard matter to get the old men back. The importation of Negroes to take the place of the strikers has been the one serious blow to the propriety of the company, and it is not likely to make headway under the present system of labor and miners.

There is a great deal yet to be said about the treatment of the miners at Monongah by the officials which is the real grounds of so much trouble and the cause of so much discontent, and which will not doubt be brought out before long. All that has been gained in grinding has been lost in the last strike and more.

It will pay Cole Fichinger (the mine superintendent) to investigate into the events that have heretofore existed there and to learn from the men themselves what is the real cause of the discontent. There is a reason for Monongah being idle where all other mines were at work.[9]

The strike at Monongah continued, although many strikers moved away as immigrants took their places at work. Then, on July 4, 1897, the front page of the *Fairmont Free Press* reported that Monongah Coal & Coke Company was again cutting wages:

On last Friday a big cut was made in the wages of the miners at Monongah to take effect immediately which brings the price of mining at that place down to a figure that seems really out of reason. The company has done away with the weighing of the coal, and the cars are loaded by car measurement. The miners are required to load each car with a ten inch square top, and the estimated quantity is from two and one-half to three tons on each car, for which the company allows sixty-five cents.

The machine man has been reduced to 18 cents, a corresponding cut in wages to pick miners.

This last reduction puts the miners' wages beyond the reach of a living, let the work be as heavy as it will.

The following Monday morning, July 5, some 800 Monongah miners stayed away from work. The *Fairmont Free Press* reported a rumor that many of the men recently hired had secretly been card-carrying union members. That same morning, Eugene V. Debs, president of the Railway Union, arrived and registered at the Arlington Hotel in the community of Palatine, on the east side of the river, just across from Fairmont. He immediately traveled to Monongah where he addressed the striking miners. UMWA organizers from Pennsylvania and Maryland, as well as Michael D. Ratchford, the president of the UMWA arrived and joined Debs and J. D. Malone, president of the Street Railway Union. The men spoke at rallies throughout the valley. The Monongah Company management brought a trainload of strike breakers who, after working one day, joined the strike and were immediately evicted from the company boarding houses.

But despite the union efforts, by December 16, 1897, five months after it had begun, the strike was broken. The striking miners had been forced out of town and new immigrant recruits took their places. By February 1898, the mines had resumed full production, and the union's organization efforts had collapsed.[10]

Mother Jones

By the turn of the century, the UMWA had successfully organized large parts of the coal districts of western Pennsylvania, particularly the Connellsville field, as well as large portions of the coal fields in Illinois, Indiana, and Ohio. The success of these efforts, however, was continually threatened by the non-union production of the northern West Virginia area, particularly the mines in and around Fairmont—and especially the Monongah mines.

The Fairmont Coal Company production competed directly with the Connellsville mine production, especially in the Chicago and the Great Lakes markets. Monongah mine coal competed with the Ohio, Indiana, and Illinois producers. The fact that the Fairmont companies, led by the Monongah mines, paid lower wages across the board meant that the three mines could sell their coal at a lower rate and thereby capture an increasing share of the markets, threatening the wages and unionization in the other states.

Recognizing this threat, in 1900 the UMWA renewed its extensive effort to organize the immigrant miners of Monongah and surrounding communities, but they were up against overwhelming odds. The organized police forces of Monongah and Marion County were either part of the coal companies' security force or were sympathetic with the mine operators' views. Union organizing in the coal fields was always difficult and often dangerous; armed company guards controlled access to the camps and either prevented union organizers from entering them or ejected them forcefully when discovered.

The mine workers' efforts were entrusted in part to a 60-year-old Irish immigrant, a former dress maker and mother of four, Mary Harris Jones or Mother Jones. Born in Ireland in 1830, Mary Harris moved to the United States, and while living in Chicago, she met and married George Jones, a member of the Iron Molders Union. Together, they settled in Memphis, Tennessee. In 1867, yellow fever swept through Memphis, causing the events she described:

Its victims were mainly among the poor and the workers. The rich and the well-to-do fled the city. Schools and churches were closed. The dead surrounded us. They were buried at night, quickly and without ceremony. All about my house I could hear weeping and cries of delirium. One by one my four little children sickened and died. I washed their little bodies and got them ready for burial. My husband caught the fever and died.[11]

After the deaths of her children and husband, Jones returned to Chicago where she established her home and set up a dressmaking shop. The shop burned down in the Great Fire of 1871. Overcome by the social inequities highlighted by the epidemic and fire, Mother Jones joined the Knights of Labor and, by 1891, had become an organizer for the UMWA.[12]

During her first years with the Knights of Labor, she was present at the B&O strike in 1877 where fighting broke out at the Haymarket Square; she was also present at the famous Pullman strike of 1894. By the end of 1901, she had been working in the coal fields of both southern and northern West Virginia under the direction of the then-new UMWA President, John Mitchell, who was just 30 years old, but effective and promising.

In 1900, Mitchell had initiated a strike of 100,000 anthracite miners. The operators, including J. P. Morgan and George Baer, had bowed to public pressure and granted a wage increase, although they denied the union reorganization. Similar strikes had met with failure in the Fairmont fields of northern West Virginia, although they had met with limited success in southern West Virginia. The Fairmont fields were proving to be among the most difficult mines in the nation to organize. Up to this point, the Fairmont Coal Company, under the combined leadership of Watson, Camden, and Fleming, had completely thwarted every effort to organize the miners.

In 1901, the Fairmont Coal Company and the Clarksburg Fuel Company, now part of the Consolidation Coal Company and under the control of Camden, Watson, and Fleming, operated all the major mines along the West Fork River. Indeed, the mines from the Pennsylvania state line above Morgantown to below Clarksburg, nearly 40 miles, were exclusively under the three men's control.[13]

Entrance to and egress from the Valley was also under the company's tight scrutiny. The principal means of transportation to Monongah from either Fairmont or Clarksburg was the interurban. Otherwise, one had to walk or ride a horse over dirt roads. The B&O lines, the Monongahela Railroad Company lines, and the Fairmont, Monongah, and Clarksburg interurban trolley lines were all owned and operated by the Watson, Camden, and

Fleming interests. The appearance of unwanted elements, such as union organizers, was duly noted.

The Fairmont Coal Company dominated the economy of Monongah as well as the nearby communities, including Fairmont. The post office and telegraph were located on company property, the houses and most stores where miners lived and shopped were company owned, and the water and electric power systems were either directly or indirectly controlled by Camden, Watson, and Fleming interests. The few doctors that were available were company employed, although their salaries were taken out of the miner's wages regardless of whether the miners needed the services. The town's elected officials, for the most part, were company officials who served in a dual capacity. The initial meetings of the town governments were held at the company office and then moved to an office donated by the Fairmont Coal Company.

Despite the earlier setbacks in 1901, the UMWA held a convention in Huntington, West Virginia, in an effort to revive their fortunes. Delegations from all the West Virginia coalfields met in October and set out a list of grievances, again requesting a meeting with the mine operators. Just as before, the Fairmont operators led the way in, rebuffing the offer. Frustrated, the miners unilaterally established a set of wages, which they demanded be met, and sent out a flyer announcing the rates in March of 1902.[14] After waiting for three months, the miners met and issued a strike call on May 24, 1902, to be effective June 7, 1902.

The Fairmont Coal Company mines and, more particularly, the mines at Monongah were to be targeted. In addition to attempting to persuade the miners at Monongah to strike, efforts were made to form groups of union miners who would march from locally organized mines to Monongah. A nearby mine at Flemington had been successfully organized a year earlier, and the plan was to march from Flemington to Monongah, a distance of some 30 miles, and gather support as the march progressed.

UMWA President John Mitchell had become familiar with the Fairmont Coal Company's antiunion attitude during the preceding four years. He had personally taken part in the earlier unsuccessful organizing drives, and wrote to Mother Jones, then working in Montgomery, West Virginia, in May of 1902:

I think the Fairmont [field] would be the place in which you could do the most good, as the coal companies up there have evidently scared our boys, and of course with good reason, as they have brutally beaten some of them. I dislike to ask you always to take the dangerous fields, but I know that you are willing.[15]

Mother Jones soon joined the strike commander, Thomas Haggerty, a veteran of the western Pennsylvania efforts, and another organizer, Joe Silver, to form the nucleus of the organizing committee. This group was joined by the local union president from Tunnelton, West Virginia, and Joe Poggiana, an Italian immigrant miner alleged to be an anarchist. Leaders also included Andrew Rashover and Tom Burke from Pennsylvania, as well as two midwesterners, William Beabilly, from Indiana, and Pete Wilson, from Illinois.

Early on the morning of June 7, 1902, Haggerty, Silver, and the other strike leaders, along with 140 supporters, began the march from Tunnelton towards Monongah. Mother Jones followed the miners in a horse-drawn buggy. Stopping along the way at many mines, they made their way in stages and arrived at Monongah on Monday morning, the first work day following the strike call. In Monongah, they had rented the Willow Tree School, a property on the west side of Monongah that had been closed in 1891 when the new, larger school had opened. Here, they camped out and periodically paraded on public roads and held rallies on the school grounds. The Willow Tree School property was a parcel of land not owned or controlled by the company and thus was available as a rally point. Mother Jones and others gave speeches while organizers spread out to speak to off-shift miners and families.

In anticipation of the union marchers' arrival in Monongah, Fairmont Coal Company's general counsel, A. B. Fleming, had prepared a Bill of Complaint against the union organizers, including Mother Jones. Upon their arrival, he promptly filed it with the Marion County Circuit Court in Fairmont. The judge, a colleague of ex-judge Fleming, supported the company's tactics and immediately issued an injunction. By Wednesday evening, Sheriff M. A. Jolleff, who had earlier in the week moved his office from Fairmont to the Monongah Hotel to be near the potential site of the civil unrest, received the injunction as well as a phone call from one of the Watsons, urging him to secure the union's organizers quickly before they had a chance to escape the county.[16]

The union organizers, leery of the Marion County authorities and having seen this legal strategy in 1897, had earlier the same day crossed over the Marion county line into Harrison County along Route 19, a distance of some six miles. Mother Jones began speaking to the 200 people gathered there. Despite the fact that he was outside of his jurisdiction, Sheriff Jolleff followed and approached the chief union organizer, Thomas Haggerty, and said he had injunction papers to serve and would certainly serve them as soon as Haggerty crossed into Marion County. Haggerty told Jolleff that the miners were in better shape to fight than in 1897.[17]

Jolleff started back toward Marion County but stopped and waited at the company store in Enterprise, a location still within Harrison County. As the marchers began to trickle past the store, he found Haggerty and the others and began to serve the writs, although the miners were still outside of the Marion County court's jurisdiction. The injunction prohibited Haggerty from returning to his quarters at the Willow Tree School. The Sheriff then returned to his temporary outpost at the Monongah Hotel. The following morning a warrant was issued for Haggerty's arrest and he was charged with violating the injunction. Jolleff and his men moved in, arrested him, took him to Fairmont, and locked him in the Marion County Jail.

Mother Jones took over the strike, which was showing some encouraging signs of success. Work at the Hutchinson mine near Fairmont had ceased as the miners joined the strike. John Mitchell was so encouraged that he wrote to Mother Jones:

I am overjoyed at the success of the strike movement in West Virginia, hire bands or anything that is necessary.[18]

However, at the Monongah mines, many—if not most—of the immigrant miners had remained at work and, among the immigrants, clearly the Italian miners—the largest contingent—had to be brought out if the strike was to succeed.

But now the union organizers were under threat of arrest if they left the school property or made any attempt at exhorting the miners to join the strike. Fairmont Coal Company guards surrounded the compound along with the Marion County Sheriff and local Monongah police officials.

On Friday, the surrounded miners exchanged taunts with the police and company guards. After a heated argument, a fight broke out between one of the guards and Daniel Grace, a member of the union group. Grace was immediately arrested and charged with intent to kill, a felony, making him ineligible for bail. He was taken to the Marion County jail under armed guard where he remained for two weeks until a grand jury, after a hearing, threw out the charges.

Later that same day, three union members and Mother Jones had set out from Monongah for Fairmont in an attempt to visit Grace, Haggerty, and the other jailed men. Jones traveled in a horse and buggy while three miners walked behind. On a narrow bridge along the public road, company guards set upon the three men and began to beat them. Mother Jones heard the shouts and raced back just as the interurban was approaching. She describes the next moments:

I ran onto the bridge, shouting, "Jo Jo! The boys are coming, they're coming! The whole bunch is coming. The car's almost here!"

Those bloodhounds for the coal company thought an army of miners was in the interurban car. They ran for cover, barricading themselves in the company's store. They left Jo on the bridge, his head broken and the blood pouring from him.

I tore my petticoat into strips, bandaged his head, helped the boys to get him onto the interurban and hurried the car into Fairmont City.

She later says, "We tried to get a warrant out for the arrest of the gunman, but we couldn't because the coal company controlled the Courts."[19]

But Fleming, unsatisfied with limits to the Marion County injunctions applying only as it did to Marion County and thus leaving the miners some maneuvering room, moved next into federal court in Parkersburg, Camden's home town. Here he sought a federal injunction from Federal District Court Judge John Jay Jackson, a contemporary of Stonewall Jackson. A federal injunction would be enforceable across county lines. In a novel legal pleading, Fleming contended that federal jurisdiction existed because a nonresident, one J. H. Wheelwright, a financial official with the parent company (Consolidation Coal Company, headquartered in Baltimore) held $60,000 in bonds of the Guaranty Trust Company of New York and these bonds were security for the debt of the Fairmont Coal Company. Wheelwright was also one of the single largest shareholders of Consolidation Coal Company, the parent and sole owner of the Fairmont Coal Company and would later become president of Consolidation. But Fleming argued in what must be described as contrived grounds that federal jurisdiction existed because of the multistate diversity.

The second aspect of the injunction was Fleming's request that a blanket ban be placed upon all demonstrations, even on the Willow Tree School property that had been leased by the strikers. Judge Jackson, a long-time friend of Fleming and Camden, was quite familiar with the Monongah mines, since each year he received from the company a free railroad car full of coal for heating his home from those very same Monongah mines. Jackson, who had become known as the Iron Judge as a result of his earlier harsh treatment of union organizers, issued what can only be characterized as a legally questionable injunction based on the grounds that Mother Jones, Haggerty, and the other strike leaders, including individuals both named and unnamed, had entered into a conspiracy that would irreparably damage the operations of the Fairmont Coal Company, thereby preventing it from paying its mortgage debt or bonds.[20]

On June 15, Federal Marshal C. D. Elliott served the injunction on Mother Jones at the Willow Tree School and stationed federal marshals around the property to ensure that the injunction was obeyed. The strikers were illegally driven out of Monongah and Marion County and were forced to move to Harrison County. Following this retreat, the company once more prevailed upon Judge Jackson; this time he banned all public meetings near company property. The miners had already scheduled a rally on a newly rented Harrison County property for June 20.

At the appointed time, the Union began the rally and Elliott and his deputies immediately arrested several of the organizers. Mother Jones was one of the featured speakers, and when the marshal sent one of those arrested to advise her that she had been arrested, Mother Jones proceeded with her speech:

I looked over at the United States Marshall and I said I will be right with you, wait till I run down. I went on speaking till I had finished. Then I said, Goodbye boys, I'm under arrest. I may have to go to jail. I may not see you for a long time. Keep up the fight! Don't surrender. Pay no attention to the injunction machine at Parkersburg. The federal judge is a scab anyhow.[21]

After she completed her speech, she was arrested, loaded with the others into a B&O train, and transported to the Wood County Jail in Parkersburg, eighty miles away. While the men were placed in jail cells, the jailer refused to put Mother Jones in a cell, offering her a hotel room. She refused, arguing she should be treated like the others. The jailer persisted, and Mother Jones was hosted by the jailer and his wife in their home.[22]

In an interview the next day, a *Parkersburg Sentinel* reporter quoted Mother Jones as saying "[W]e were arrested on our own ground which we had donated. We expect to fight this matter to the highest court." She also revealed that in all of her thirty years of organizing, including rail and other mine strikes, this was the first time the sixty-year-old matron had ever been arrested.

With the strike leaders in jails in Fairmont and Parkersburg, the federal marshals moved to completely destroy the strike movement. Every out-of-state organizer or participant was arrested and local leaders were also detained. The first arraignment was held shortly after the arrests in the federal court in Parkersburg, but arguments were not scheduled until after July 11. Following that hearing, Judge Jackson did not issue an order for two more weeks; all the while, the striking miners were losing pay, and their families—having been evicted—were going hungry. The court, by stalling its decision, was essentially siding with the company. Consolidation Coal Company and its attorney, Fleming, were completely controlling the strike; support among the strikers dwindled. Mother Jones and others had gotten out on bail but dared not to return to the strike scene. After being released, they boarded a railroad train bound for the UMWA national convention in Indianapolis, where they intended to plead for support for the Monongah strikers.

By 1902 the UMWA's organizing efforts had been divided into two major drives: in the West Virginia coal fields, and the anthracite coals mines of central Pennsylvania.[23]

John Mitchell, in the meantime, was faced with a dilemma. He was losing the northern West Virginia strike, but was holding his own and even beginning to succeed in the Pennsylvania anthracite strikes. As a result of being engaged in a two-front war, however, union resources were rapidly dwindling. At a special national convention in Indianapolis, the question of supporting both efforts was on everyone's mind. The union membership was split: some wanted to support both efforts, at Monongah and in the anthracite mines, while others wished to focus on what appeared to be more hopeful, the anthracite strike. Mitchell sided with those who wished to support the anthracite efforts, and in effect, give up on the Monongah strike. He attempted to convince the convention delegates to support only the Pennsylvania strike, thus dooming Monongah strikers.

As the issue was coming to a head, Mother Jones rose to speak. Taking the megaphone over Mitchell's objection, she described the hardships at Monongah and pleaded for support. But the delegates organized by the Mitchell forces voted with Mitchell and the anthracite-only strategy was adopted. Only the West Virginia delegation voted to continue their support.

The Consolidation Coal Company and the Fairmont Coal Company had cemented its approach to labor relations. For the next few decades, the companies led antiunion efforts at every turn. It would become part of the company's culture that unions were to be opposed with all means, both legal and extra legal if necessary.

As Judge Jackson wrote at the time,

I think that the time has come when this country should look to the coming events face to face, and what must soon transpire in this country—the conflict between two elements of society. Merely to gratify a professional set of agitators, organizers and walking delegates, who roam all over the country as agents for some combination, who are vampires that live and fatten on the honest labor of coal miners of the country, and who are busybodies creating dissatisfaction amongst a class of people who are quite well-disposed, and who do not want to be disturbed by the unceasing agitation of this class of people.

Indeed, Judge Jackson took special exception to the comments of Mother Jones:

The utterances of Mother Jones should not emanate from a citizen of this country who believes in its institutions. Such talk comes from communists and anarchists, and they cannot shield themselves behind appeals to the Declaration of Independence and the First Amendment. Freedom of speech cannot apply to reason or the destruction of the country's institutions. The abuse of free speech inspired the anarchists and assassins to take the life of our late beloved president. Your lawmakers, both federal and state, to consider the question whether freedom of speech should not be so restricted by statutes as to suppress seditious statements.

According to Judge Jackson, the miners' meeting in Harrison County at Pinnickinnick on June 20 had clearly violated the order of the court, as well as the limits of freedom of speech. Mother Jones was the principal transgressor, but the other defendants were present, applauding and cheering her while she was making her speech, and endorsing the sentiments that she uttered upon that occasion.

I cannot forbear [added the judge] to express my great surprise that a woman of the apparent intelligence of Mrs. Jones should permit herself to be used as an instrument by designing and reckless agitators, who seem to have no regard for the rights of others, in accomplishing an object which is entirely unworthy of a good woman. It seems to me that it would have been better for her to follow the lines and paths which the Allwise Being intended her sex should pursue. There are many charities in life which are open to her, in which she could contribute largely to mankind in distress, as well as avocations and pursuits that she could engage in of a lawful character that would be more in keeping with what we have been taught and what experience has shown to be the true sphere of womanhood.[24]

Six of the strike leaders were then sentenced to sixty days in the Wood County jail. Haggerty received an additional thirty days for a total of three months. Mother Jones's sentencing was postponed until the afternoon.

Fleming, on behalf of Watson, Camden, and others, had struck a great blow against the unionization efforts. Especially telling was the fact that the union's defeat had come just at the time the strike in the anthracite coal fields of central Pennsylvania resulted in a stunning UMWA victory that included the intervention of President Theodore Roosevelt on behalf of the miners.

However, the Pennsylvania victory also reflected the fact that while the powers of the coal interests and their political connections were quite strong in Pennsylvania, they had nowhere near the power of the coal operators in West Virginia. With Camden's assistance, Fleming had recently won the governor's spot in West Virginia. Camden had been a U.S. Senator, and Clarence Watson would soon serve as the junior U.S. Senator from West Virginia.

The political connections of the Monongah Coal & Coke Company (which was a Camden interest), the Fairmont Coal Company (run by Watson, Fleming, and others), the Consolidation Coal Company (with which Watson, Wheelwright, and Fleming were involved), and the B&O were stunning. They wove throughout West Virginia and reached every level of government in all three branches. The connections also stretched to the halls of government in Washington. The coal companies' power in West Virginia was such that they did not even have to exercise it with force; it was simply understood that the power of the coal companies would be shared with those who were helpful to them.[25]

The union efforts were completely trampled in northern West Virginia, especially at Monongah. In March 1903, the UMWA West Virginia branches met in Huntington and voted not to strike.

The powerful elite of West Virginia on both the Democrat and Republican sides of the aisle united in their opposition to union organization efforts, and after seeing the success of the Fairmont Consolidation Company, the southern West Virginia mine operations that wished to build on the success met in secret to decide on some general plan of resistance to union encroachments based on the successful strategy employed at Monongah.

Not until 1933 would the majority of the mine workers of northern West Virginia be unionized; the Fairmont Coal Company and the Monongah mines also remained unorganized until 1933.

The ramification for the miners of Monongah Nos. 6 and 8 would be felt much sooner; with the union firmly and convincingly beaten, the miners and their advocates had little, if any, means to raise safety and health concerns. The Italian and Polish immigrants and their coworkers were left entirely to their own devices and the company demands.

AND THE EXPLOSION CAME

One bright morning, the miner just about to leave,
Heard his dear child screaming in all fright.
He went to her bed, then she looked up and said:
"I have had such a dream, turn on the light."

> *"Daddy please don't go down in that hole today,*
> *For my dreams do come true some time, you know.*
> *Oh don't leave me daddy, please don't go away,*
> *Something bad sure will happen, do not go."*

"Oh I dreamed that the mines were burning out with fire,
Every man was fighting for his life.
And some had companions and they prayed out loud,
'Oh God, please protect my darling wife.'"

> *"Daddy please don't go down in that hole today,*
> *For my dreams do come true some time, you know.*

Oh don't leave me daddy, please don't go away,
Something bad sure will happen, do not go."

Then her daddy bent down and kissed her dear sweet face,
Turned again to travel on his way,
But she threw her small arms around her daddy's neck,
She kissed him again, and he heard her say:

> *"Daddy please don't go down in that hole today,*
> *For my dreams do come true some time, you know.*
> *Oh don't leave me daddy, please don't go away,*
> *Something bad sure will happen, do not go."*

Then the miner was touched, and said he would not go:
"Hush my child, I'm with you, do not cry."
There came an explosion and two-hundred men
Were shut in the mines and left to die.

> *"Daddy please don't go down in that hole today,*
> *For my dreams do come true some time, you know.*
> *Oh don't leave me daddy, please don't go away,*
> *Something bad sure will happen, do not go."*

—*"Explosion in the Fairmount Mines," Blind Alfred Reed, 1927*[1]

ABOUT midmorning on December 6, 1907, a load of nineteen mine cars was being pulled by a wire rope up the incline from the mouth of No. 6 mine just short of the *knuckle* or top of the trestle. As they were pulled slowly toward the highest point, an iron coupling pin snapped and the nineteen cars, each carrying more than two tons of coal, plunged 1,300 feet back into the mine portal.

J. H. Leonard, the miner in charge of the derailing switch located outside the mine portal, had just stepped onto the threshold of the building where the ventilation fan was housed. Upon hearing the noise, he turned back in time to see the string of cars break loose; he could see the switch twenty-five feet away but knew that he was too far away to be able to reach it in time.[2]

The cars raced back into the mine and crashed at the mine portal bottom. Along the way, the cars tore out electrical wiring and knocked down timber props, partitions, and curtains. When they hit bottom, a blast of air shot back into the mine entryways. The wreck disrupted the mine ventilation system deep within the mine, caused coal dust in the mine to swirl into the air, and forced methane gas from the voids and high spots.

At that instant, from deep within the mine an explosion rumbled, a terrible explosive report rocketing out of both mines, rippling shocks through the earth in every direction. The report was so loud it could be heard eight miles away in Fairmont. A second explosion followed immediately, and at the No. 8 mine entrances explosive forces rocketed out of the mine mouth like blasts from a cannon, the forces shredding everything in their path.

The No. 6 mine fan, which was equipped with a pressure gauge and clock to constantly record the pressure, showed the time of the disruption as exactly 10:30 A.M.[3]

What at first seemed like distant thunder in a few seconds was transformed into a road like a thousand Niagaras. Like the eruption of a volcano the blazing gas reached the surface and vomited tongues of red flame and clouds of dust through the two slopes. [4]

At the entrance to No. 8 the forces blasting out of the mine entirely obliterated the large brick power house, tearing the ten-ton, thirty-foot tall fan from its concrete moorings and, according to the *Fairmont Times*, hurling it across the West Fork River to embed in the hillside a half-mile away.[5] The wooden check boards containing the miners' identifying tags at each mine portal were completely destroyed, the brass tags scattered more than a mile into and across the river. The fire boss boards from both portals were gone. Huge eight-by-eight timbers and literally tons of mine equipment were hurled from deep within the mine, up and out of the mine entrance. At both portals the air was filled with smoke and dust. The fire and smoke shot up into the sky more than sixty feet. Debris continued falling for more than a quarter of an hour. Tragically, bodies of miners, who seconds before had been working, were carried with the force and debris and were obliterated. At No. 6, tons of earth were heaved high into the air and the many adjacent buildings were damaged.[6] At No. 8, one hundred feet of the mountainside was blown out by the force of the explosion, leaving a giant crater where the mine entrance had been. The remaining slope of earth was forever altered.[7]

J. H. Leonard, who had attempted in vain to reach the derailing switch in time, was blown down and covered with rubble. Months earlier, he had complained to his boss, Charlie Dean, that it might be impossible to keep the fans properly oiled *and* attend to the derailing switch at the same time, but Dean, the outside foreman and the man who had assigned Leonard both tasks, said the assignment would stand. Leonard had also raised his concerns to David Victor, the company's mine safety inspector: "I have the engine to look after and I have to oil the fan every few hours—slow the fan down and oil it—and there is right smart trouble with the belt slipping."[8] But Victor had taken no action to see that responsibility for the switch was given to someone else either.[9]

On that December 6 morning, the cars had stuck on the knuckle, which frequently happened, just as Leonard had gone to the ventilation fan house to check the fan. He looked back and saw the trip break loose and race back into the mine. As he saw the last two cars go by, he braced for the inevitable wreck at the bottom of the mine entrance. As he later recalled, "I stood there looking down the slope a little bit and the explosion came." He was knocked to the ground with such force that his arm and ankle were smashed. As the smoke rose out of the mine, he crawled under a section of the trestle to avoid the raining debris, which continued to blow out of the mine.

Carl Meredith, the foreman for the No. 8 tipple, was located across the river from the mine opening. At 10:30, he was on the loading track just opposite the mouth of No. 8: "I was out on the loaded track and was looking toward the mouth of No. 8 and the first thing I knew I saw timbers and everything flying in the air. . . followed by black smoke." He glanced around to see if any of the timbers were about to hit him.

Meredith noticed flame and smoke only after he saw the timbers, but he continued: "It seemed to me like the smoke was afire. It seemed to me it was a short distance up in the air, maybe fifty or sixty feet."[10]

Charles Honaker, 15 years old, a trapper, was caught at the entrance of No. 8; his body was blown 200 yards into the river and lost. Poor little Honaker, with clothing ablaze—literally a human torch—was enveloped in the fiery torrent. Several men who were in the mine near the entrances likewise were carried in the claws of death and strewn at the pit mouth like things disdained, while the greater work of havoc was wrought.[11]

The terrible force of the two explosions is beyond description. The large black power house, with its vast machinery, and the boiler room were virtually obliterated. Tons of brick and timbers were hurled through the air. At the entrance of the mine was a big iron grating with bars three inches apart. It, too, was carried across the river. The fan and grating were blown 600 feet.

Hyre Stalnaker was a carpenter working in the No. 8 shop on Friday morning. At 10:30 he felt and heard the report. As he started to come out of the carpenter shop, directly across from the mouth of the pit, the force of the explosion knocked him out and blew him back across the shop entrance and the length of the shop. When he came to, he was shocked to see that the force had caused the iron and shop machinery to give in; the entire contents of the shop were collapsed on the floor and every window was broken. When he recovered, he rushed across the bridge, where he saw Joe Newton about one hundred feet from the mouth of the mine "a colored fellow . . . he had some wounds on his head and the eye was knocked out." At the streetcar line, he found William Bice, a 40-year-old engineer, lying next to the wall, imprisoned by pieces of the wall and timbers. Stalnaker worked to free Bice, who had been in the powerhouse in front of No. 8 mine when the explosive force destroyed the entire structure. With the help of others, Stalnaker freed Bice and carried him to the streetcar, which miraculously was still operating toward Fairmont. The street conductor rushed him, bleeding nonstop, directly to the newly opened Miners Hospital in Fairmont, but shortly after his arrival he died from his wounds.[12]

Joe Newton, who was Bice's assistant, ended up suffering a compound fracture and lost his right eye. Pat McDonald, who had been standing near the No. 6 opening, had his face lacerated. Both were rushed to the hospital in Fairmont.[13]

At the moment of the explosion, Christiana Cerdelli, a 17-year-old woman, was standing in the doorway of her home on Hill No. 3 across the river from the mines. Roughly an equal distance from the No. 6 and the No. 8 entrances, she could see both portals. She first heard the explosion, and as she looked up at No. 6, she saw smoke billowing out of the mine. Turning to No. 8, she saw flame and smoke pouring out. Directly across from where she was standing, smoke flowed out of the toad holes surrounding the Saint Stanislaus

Polish Catholic Church. Toad holes were openings in the hillside near the mine portals; the ones near Saint Stanislaus made it look like the smoke was coming out of the church itself. The mine was a slope mine driven into the west side of the Monongahela River, which meant some of the interior mine rooms were quite near the surface. As miners removed the coal from the seam, the dirt overlying the seam would collapse creating a small opening or *toad hole*, as they were known in Monongah. For five or more minutes, Cerdelli watched in horror as flames and smoke filled the sky.[14]

Lester Trader, in bed but still awake, recalled that when the first explosion "hit, the whole house lifted, then the sound of a terrible roar and I felt the earth shaking with such intensity causing objects to fall from the shelves of the rooms."

Later he noticed that the top bricks of the chimney had loosened. "Then I walked to the door and the second hit occurred." He felt air from mine No. 8.[15] Dressing quickly he rushed to the mine No. 6 portal and saw the confusion and chaos. Smoke and flames were billowing out of the portal. He saw Superintendent Gaskill and Foreman Charlie Dean outside of the company office staring at the billowing smoke. At first, Trader, Dean, and Gaskill all thought that one of the fans had exploded, but it soon became apparent that the magnitude of the explosion could only mean that the mine itself had exploded. Now with both portals billowing smoke, and after hearing and feeling two explosions, the men knew that whatever the cause, explosions had traveled throughout both mines.

Sarah Ann Martin and her son Charlie lived on Hill No. 3 across the river from the portals, just above the stables. Charlie had been ill earlier in the week, but that morning he had gotten out of bed, preparing to go to the mine. His mother believed it would be bad luck to start back to work on a Friday and refused to pack his lunch, imploring him to stay home, so he did.[16] Now they watched in horror as the smoke and debris blew out of the mine, which continued for several minutes.[17]

Lee Curry, the stationary engineer for mine No. 8, operated the hoisting engine; he was in the engine house when the blast occurred: "I saw the glass in the house next to the mine portal shatter and I felt like I was in a jar." He ran out of the building and had gotten just twenty-five feet when he saw the smoke coming out of No. 8 and No. 6. As he looked across between the mines he could see the Polish Catholic Church. From a toad hole in back of the church he also saw smoke billowing above the church.[18]

E. R. Knight was the tipple foreman at mine No. 6. At the moment of the explosion, he was on the phone to John Talbot. A company shipping clerk who was at his desk in his office, Talbot was located between the company store and the superintendent's office. Knight's office was under the tipple of mine No. 6 and he had just counted 19 cars, which had been pulled up the grade from the mine to the knuckle. He saw the trip of cars break loose and run back into the mine:

We were talking about the railroad cars. We had placed our last car under the tipple . . . as I was about to tell him that, the trip broke . . . I felt the jar and saw the rope jerk and looked out of the window and then ran out of the shanty.

Before Knight could say anything about the cars dropping into the mouth of No. 6, Talbot told him he heard an explosion at No. 8 and dropped the phone. Talbot's office had two round bay windows, one facing No. 6 and one facing No. 8 mine.

Knight stepped out of the office: "It looked like dark brown smoke . . . lasting, I would say, from five to eight minutes."[19] As he looked toward the place under the tipple where the trip had broken, he saw that the pin that held the cars to the wire winch had broken. He picked up the part of the broken pin and put it in his pocket. Knight had looked for Leonard when he saw the trip of cars break loose to see if he would throw the derailing switch, but now Leonard was lying under debris in the fan house.

George E. Peddicord was an outside foreman at No. 8 and earlier had gone to the supply house to pick up chain buckets. As he was walking back up to No. 8 on the west side of the river, he felt the earth shaking, then a rumbling noise came up the river from No. 8: "I observed the timbers and debris coming out of No. 8."

He could not see the opening of No. 8, but the timbers were high enough so that he could see them. Immediately, he looked at No. 6 and saw the smoke coming out of the airshaft. "I noticed the difference in the color of the smoke. . . . The smoke that came out of No. 8 was black and that which came out of No. 6 was reddish brown."[20]

George Bice was a track layer in No. 8. On Friday morning he was not scheduled to work but was leaving his home near No. 8 mine and preparing to travel to Fairmont on the interurban. He had walked down to the station just above the No. 6 mine portal, out of sight of the No. 8. At the moment of the explosion Bice was just 330 feet or "33 lengths of 10 feet of steel rails" from No. 8 and a quarter of a mile from the opening of No. 6. He explained:

The street car had gone up—the one that passed the other one in Middleton. I thought I was late getting to the track and turned around to see if I could see the car coming and when I turned around, I saw the explosion. The first thing I saw was the brick, steel, timbers and smoke all together. It looked like the steel and timbers was just a little bit ahead—but very little—and there was a terrible smoke coming out of the mine.[21]

Immediately he heard a second report, coming from "down the river in the direction of No. 6." William Finley, the town sergeant, was standing outside of the company office when he heard a "heavy blast" and saw smoke coming out of the No. 6 mine.[22]

Will Jenkins was a blacksmith at the No. 6 mine. On the morning of December 6 a foreman from underground, Frank Moon, had called him to shoe a horse in the mine. The horse was missing calks, the spiked plate attached to the bottom of the horse's shoe to prevent slipping. At about 10:15, after he completed the repair, he came out of the mine and began to shoe a horse in the blacksmith's shed on the surface when he felt the explosion.[23]

A. J. Ruckman was in the mine office with Charlie Dean when they first heard a loud report and felt a concussion so severe that it shook the whole building. Together they rushed out to the porch. Dean first suggested that it was a boiler at No. 8 that had exploded, but just then a loud noise attracted their attention to No. 6. Looking down, they saw smoke coming out of the No. 6 airshaft—"pretty strong under high pressure." Ruckman recalls thinking, "from the appearance it looks like No. 6 fan house is damaged." He said to Dean, "Get men and material there as soon as possible and I will go to No. 8, and if that fan is not damaged, we will reverse it." But as soon as Ruckman approached No. 8 it became clear that it had suffered more damage than its sister mine.[24]

Andrew Daran had come to America in 1900 and worked at Monongah for five and a half years. On the morning of December 6, he had gone in No. 6 at about 6:30 and had begun loading cars. He soon began to feel ill and came out of the mine just before ten o'clock. He walked back to his house and lay down; at 10:30 he was awakened by the report.

After the explosion, Charlie Dean called J. H. Leonard at the No. 6 fan house. Dean ordered him to shut the fan down because "it was not doing any good." Leonard then began examining the damage to the belts and the fan itself as others at Dean's direction came to help. Dean then went to the No. 6 portal where Trader, Leonard, and Gaskill, who had come back from No. 8 with some others, formed the first ad hoc rescue party.[25]

Anestis Stamboulis and a few of his fellow Greek immigrants had become violently ill from eating the wild mushrooms that they had collected on Thursday, and they missed work that Friday. Others who made the crossing with Stamboulis, including Nick Saltos, had gone to work and perished.[26]

Instantly, news of the disaster was flashed around the world. In Austria, the Austrian Peoples' Newspaper carried a story that read, in part: "On Thursday, in the western part of Virginia of the North American Union, a coal-dust explosion occurred in the mines of the Fairmont Coal Company."[27]

ESCAPE AND RESCUE

This mustering of the Minutemen of the coal pits is one of the finest things in industrial life in America today.

> —Paul U. Kellogg, "Charities and the Commons," Vol. 19

$\mathbf{A}$T ABOUT half past five the morning of December 6, Angelo and Orazio DePetris, brothers, and Dan and Leonardo Dominico, father and son, entered the No. 8 portal and walked down the main entry. They began work in the second right south face off the first south. Here, they undercut the coal seam using short-handled picks, set off a round of explosives, and loaded one car full of coal.

After the first car had been loaded and taken out, just before 10:30, Angelo and Orazio had put off a shot in the coal face at the third left south section where the men had been working. Just as they bent over to pick up the loose coal that had tumbled down from face of the room, a powerful concussive force knocked them violently to the ground, pushing them hard against the mine floor and rib. They struggled to their feet before a second, equally powerful explosion and concussion knocked them to the ground again. The violent explosion smashed Dan Dominico to the ground with such force that his ear was badly cut and one arm injured so seriously he could not raise it.

But he had not seen any explosion or fire: "I didn't see anything; the jar came and threw me down and I didn't see anything."[1] Immediately, the mine began to fill with smoke, loud noises, and continuous blasts. Orazio testified that the blasts lasted for ten minutes or more. Leonardo Dominico testified,

I never seen anything at all . . . just knocked me down. I just seen smoke; I heard lots of noise. In fact the noise was accompanied by a concussion which knocked all the miners down, and the noise lasted for about ten minutes.[2]

The blasts, in addition to knocking the miners down, had extinguished their carbide lamps and knocked their canvas caps off their heads. Both Orazio DePetris and Leonardo Dominico had matches in their jacket pockets that day but the jackets, lunch pails, tools, and all the belongings of the four had been lost or destroyed by the blast.

Now, despite the darkness and smoke, they struggled to get back to the main heading by feeling the ground, trying to find the rails on their hands and knees, attempting to head out of the mine the way they came, by following the tracks. As they went, the smoke grew dense and they were forced to turn back.

Yet even as they turned, the smoke increased from deep in the mine. They crawled back past their working place, moving south toward an entry to a dead end where the hillside slopes down toward the river, lessening the distance to the surface. Here the younger Dominico, Leonardo, remembered seeing an opening or crack in the mine roof two or three days before, only fifty yards from the place where they had been working.

"We started to go this way on the track," Donato Dominico, Leonardo's brother, testified, "and came back around toward the hole to get out." His father, Dan Dominico, unable to move quickly because of his injuries, had to be helped by his son and the DePetris brothers. Slowly, they moved toward the opening, Leonardo estimated that it took about fifteen minutes to make there. Finding the toad hole, they struggled to grab hold of the side of the hole. Reaching up, they pulled themselves higher, helping and boosting each other up and out. One of the brothers hoisted himself up first, and a fellow miner, Jim Rogers, who was above the hole on the surface, saw the survivor and called to other observers who then helped the others out including the injured Dominico. As they were drawn out of the enlarged hole, smoke enveloped them and was so dense that those on the surface could barely make out the hole.[3]

When they arrived on the surface, they were facing the river just above the streetcar line looking towards Pentrose. Gasping for breath in the fresh air, they remained stunned for several minutes until finally they stumbled over to the crater of what had been No. 8 portal. By this time a large crowd—alerted to the rescue—gathered, and as word of the four miners' escape spread, the waiting crowds' hopes were buoyed. The hope that more miners would be found alive spread through the town.

No organized mine rescue teams existed at No. 6 or No. 8, or for that matter, in West Virginia or the entire country. In Europe, mine rescue teams and systems had existed for decades. Despite repeated disasters and emergencies, no system had been adopted in the United States. Each rescue effort was an ad hoc affair. A few companies had made efforts to organize teams, but it was primarily up to the mine superintendent. Neither Fairmont Coal/Consolidation Coal nor the state of West Virginia had established emergency procedures for disasters.

A. J. Ruckman, No. 8 mine superintendent, who had been in his office with No. 8 outside foreman Charlie Dean, recalled the first moments of the explosion:

We both went out on the porch and looked toward No. 8 as that is where the report sounded, but there was nothing visible—didn't see any smoke or anything. Then we were attracted to No. 6 by a loud noise and looked down and the smoke was coming out of the air-shaft pretty strong, under high pressure.[4]

Ruckman and Dean went immediately to the No. 8 portal, and their first thought was how they might re-establish ventilation underground. The blackboard, which would list the fire boss's report, had been blown away, along with any other danger signal indicators.[5]

Almost immediately after the explosions, a frantic call was made to the Fairmont Coal Company headquarters in downtown Fairmont. Lee L. Malone, the general manager, the man in charge of all of the company's mines, was told of the explosion. Malone had begun his career as a miner and had risen through the ranks to become the general manager of the Fairmont Coal Company. He had worked at Monongah Nos. 6 and 8 for most of his professional life and, according to his contemporaries, was a self-made man whos success was based upon raw talent. A fellow operator and president of the West Virginia Coal Mining Institute, J. B. Hanford, described Malone in 1909: "This man was surely a typical example of a self-made man, beginning in humble circumstances, he rose step by step."[6]

Malone gathered what staff he could find and raced to the interurban car station not a block from his office. Although the interurban line had been destroyed for a mile in the area of No. 8 and the electric trolley wire had been brought down between Monongah and Clarksburg, from Monongah north to Fairmont (to the No. 6 mine site) the trolley, telegraph, and telephone were fully functional. Malone commandeered the first available car and raced at top speed the eight miles to the mine skipping all intermediate stops, arriving within minutes of the explosions.[7] The scene was utter chaos. Almost from the instant of the explosions the families, neighbors, and fellow workers began streaming toward the mine openings. By the time of Malone's arrival, virtually the entire population of Monongah had gathered around the craters that had been the portals to No. 8 and No. 6.

The entire eastern section of the town of Monongah was built on top of the mines themselves, allowing the crowds to rush toward the entrances even as the purple smoke spewed out from the openings. There were few supervisors to take command of the scene, as most of the principal staff were below ground and, unbeknownst to those on the surface at the time, all dead.

Malone, recognizing the urgency of time in mine rescue situations, immediately began organizing rescue and rebuilding efforts. Ventilation had to be re-established. The explosions had completely destroyed the mine No. 8 fan, the principle fan at the mine, but had only damaged the fan at No. 6, which had been stopped. No ventilation at all was available in the underground workings. Malone was in touch with Ruckman, Dean, and some others by this time; he gathered what men they could find and the first efforts were made at restarting the No. 6 fan. The No. 8 fan, which was by far the larger and more critical of the two fans, blew across the river and was completely flattened; its wooden frame structure would have to be entirely rebuilt. Carpenters would be needed to build a structure to house a substitute fan. Malone had a crew gathered to begin the carpentry and ordered that timber be brought from the supply yard.[8]

J. O. Watson, II, a company officer, was in downtown Fairmont. He raced by horse and buggy to the maintenance shop on Fairmont Avenue and 12th Street. He had earlier called the interurban trolley barn on nearby Beverly Road and asked all who were available to help. Perry Vernon, who worked as a foreman at the mine, lived near the maintenance shop and was at the trolley barn by the time Watson arrived. Watson, Vernon, and others commandeered a trolley car and rode the seven miles to Monongah, arriving by 10:45 or 10:50.[9]

All the while, the shrieks and screams of the women and children grew in volume and intensity and the crowd's anxiety increased with each passing moment. They began to surge toward the now cavernous opening where the No. 8 portal had been. Some women ran back and forth along the track between the two portals crying out; some sank to the ground, sobbing uncontrollably. One beautiful blonde woman pulled her hair out in handfuls. Others took up a vigil on the upper crest at the hollowed-out opening above the No. 8 portal, creating an eerie backdrop to the frantic work below.[10]

Simultaneously with the two explosions there was a mad rush across the river on the part of friends and relatives of the hundreds of employees. The wives, children, and other relatives of the doomed men simply could not be controlled. The frenzied ones crowded to the many blackened holes from which the deadly afterdamp was oozing slowly. '. . . The terror-stricken women were tearing their hair from their heads by the handfuls and sinking their fingernails deep into their faces. They demanded to know the fate of their loved ones, but it was impossible to tell them anything.'[11]

The initial chaos continued for some time, as no one seemed to be in charge. Malone gathered some supervisors and mine security guards and formed them into an ad hoc security force, first trying to keep the crowd back away from the openings and then trying to make way for the mine rescue efforts.

By now, news of the explosion had flashed across the telegraph wires to the whole country. In Fairmont, carloads of volunteers boarded the trolley cars and headed to the mines. At the same time, an enterprising photographer had been gathering his equipment and was traveling to the scene. Over the course of the afternoon, the crowds grew to uncontrollable proportions. Volunteers were needed to go underground; experienced miners with some rudimentary knowledge of explosions, especially of afterdamp, were chosen.

But time passed before an improvised fan could be constructed at mine No. 8. Finally, Malone and the others began to bring some order to the scene.[12]

Rescue Efforts

Less than twenty-five minutes after the explosions, the first volunteers entered the No. 6 portal under the direction of General Superintendent J. C. Gaskill, Foreman Pete McGraw, and Fire Boss Lester Trader, along with a few carpenters. They began exploring with great anticipation. Everyone thought and hoped survivors would be found. Clearing the debris as they went, some of the crew spent time rebuilding the entryway. When they got to the slope bottom about 300 feet down, they found the remains of the wrecked train and the mine timbers and debris in a tangled heap.[13]

Crawling over the mounded material, they arrived at the bottom. Inside the coupler's shanty, the team found three miners. Two were lying on the ground, the third sitting on a bench, all dead. One of the victims, Fred Cooper, was lying on his back with his head to the door and his mouth wide open. John Herman was sitting on the bench on the other side of the shanty with his dinner bucket between his legs, his head and arms down. Lester Trader pushed his head back and coffee ran off his lower lip. Trader concluded that he had been drinking coffee when the cars hit bottom.[14]

In confined spaces such as mines, explosions often produce unusual patterns of injuries. They inflict multiple-system, life-threatening injuries on many persons simultaneously. When the explosion is of a high order of magnitude, it can produce a defining supersonic, overpressurization shock wave. In humans, there are four basic mechanisms of blast injury: primary, secondary, tertiary, and quaternary.

Primary injuries are caused by the force of the initial *blast wave*. The *primary impact* is the intense overpressurization, causing the concussion or *first impact* of a blast. Blast injuries can be anatomical or physiological changes resulting from the blast force colliding with the body's surface. Injuries can include *blast lung* (tearing, abrasion, hemorrage, or other lung injury caused by the force of a high-explosive detonation that may or may not include obvious external injury to the chest), middle ear or eye rupture, abdominal hemorrhage or perforation, or concussion with or without physical signs of head injury.[15] In the secondary category are injuries that result from flying debris, which penetrate the body surface. Tertiary injuries result from individuals being thrown bodily by the blast force, which can result in fractures and traumatic amputation and brain injuries. Finally, quaternary injuries are burns, crushing injuries, brain injuries, and breathing problems from smoke, dust, or toxic fume inhalation.

Gaskill and crew continued to climb over the wreckage of cars and material, exploring around the bottom and a short distance down the main entrance. All the stoppings and supports had been completely destroyed. As they moved farther into the mine, the rescuers began to feel that they would encounter toxic atmospheres such as *blackdamp* or *afterdamp*, and they reluctantly turned back and came out of the mine.

In addition to instantaneous death from concussions or the blast itself, miners and rescuers are frequently killed in the aftermath of an explosion when the mine atmosphere becomes poisonous as a consequence of the explosion or fire. Mine explosions and fires frequently produce *after gasses*, or lethal mine gasses that come in different, but related forms: *chokedamp*, *afterdamp*, *blackdamp*, and *whitedamp*. The word *damp* is derived from the German word *dampf*, meaning a fog or vapor. Each of these gasses is deficient in oxygen but rich in various lethal chemicals. Any one of these gasses can cause death.

Chokedamp is an atmosphere that causes choking or suffocation due to oxygen deficiency, the oxygen having been consumed by the fire. *Afterdamp* is a mixture of gasses that remain in a mine after air explosion or fire, principally made up of carbonic acid gas and nitrogen. *Blackdamp*, commonly thought to be carbon dioxide, is actually a mixture of 85% nitrogen and 15% carbon dioxide. Formed after explosions, it is depleted of oxygen and thus heavier than air, forming layers along the floor of the mine. It will extinguish any lights and suffocate victims who attempt to escape by crawling. *White damp* is nearly pure carbon monoxide and is extremely poisonous. Colorless, odorless, and tasteless, it is difficult to detect and is absorbed by the blood to the exclusion of oxygen: one tenth of one percent can be fatal in ten minutes.[16]

In his December 6th letter to his father, Lester trader had discussed the unpredictable interactions of gasses and coal dust:

The gasses in a mine or rather the elements that go to make up the gasses are the same after an explosion as they were before only in different combinations as the following illustration will show:

Composition of fire damp before explosion:

C	O	H	H
O	H	H	O
N	N	N	O
N	N	N	N

Composition of the after damp of an explosion of fire damp the elements of which the gas was composed in the first place being present only combined differently:

C	O	H	H
O	H	H	O
N	N	N	O
N	N	N	N

C —Carbon, O —Oxygen, N —Nitrogen, H —Hydrogen
Marsh Gas- C+H, Atmosphere- O+N, Carbonic Acid Gas- C+O, Steam- H+O

Nitrogen has no effect on an explosion but exists in a free state before and after the let go.

After the two major explosions, there were localized explosions or ignitions and burning fires that consumed the oxygen in the mine. Since the No. 8 fan was destroyed and there was no air movement in much of the mine, those who survived the initial explosions, primarily because they were not in the direct line of the explosive force, began to die of the lethal mine gasses and oxygen deficiency. Some attempted to survive by placing jackets over their heads, but they fell, one by one, suffocated.[17]

Neither the miners nor the rescuers had protective equipment or fresh air apparatuses. This lack of equipment would limit rescue efforts both in the early minutes and throughout the entire rescue effort. In fact, no fresh air headgear existed in the United States. Without such equipment, rescue efforts at Monongah and elsewhere were hampered, and progress was slow and labored. A crew leader would inch forward, his flame safety lamps held aloft to provide the only lighting and warn against the presence of methane gas. Occasionally, rescuers carried a small cage with a canary trapped inside to test the atmosphere. At Monongah, the crew sniffed and checked the air for odors, but the most deadly mixture in the atmosphere was the odorless, colorless white damp. Unfortunately, the most effective method of detecting gasses in the air was when a team member either collapsed or began to feel faint. In mines No. 6 and 8, all canaries underground at the time of the explosions were dead.[18]

It was after noon, an hour and a half after the initial explosion, when the first rescue crew came out of the No. 6 mine. Additional efforts would have to wait while ventilation repairs were completed. By early afternoon, the No. 6 fan repair was nearing completion, but the temporary frame for a fan at No. 8 was just getting started. Malone had ordered supplies from surrounding mines and lumber and steel braces from the supply yard at Monongah.

A second rescue effort was organized when, shortly before 4:00 P.M., moaning was heard near a toad hole above the No. 8 mine portal. A group of miners who had been working nearby to remove wreckage got a rope and started in. Skinny McGraw, a railroad man of slender build, was lowered on the rope through the hole. After a few minutes, he and the men who had followed him underground saw a miner, still alive, sitting on the body of another man. As they came close, the man attempted to drive them off, but after a struggle, they were able to subdue him.[19]

Peter and Stanislaus Urban (Rosebeiq) had entered the mine at about six o'clock that morning. They had gone to the first right of the first heading seventh room. There were no rail cars available for loading coal, so he and his brother started to dig the next round of coal, and by about 10:20 they stopped to have lunch. While they were sitting down having lunch, Peter heard a report or noise, and he asked Stanislaus if he had heard it too. Stanislaus said, "Oh what happened, I don't think anything happened."[20] But instantaneously, they both heard the second explosion and after momentary confusion they both started to run. At the grand jury hearing, Peter later testified in Polish "then I don't remember nothing."

When the rescuers arrived, Peter Urban was sitting on the body of his injured brother, Stanislaus, trying to protect him. Peter and Stanislaus had run to escape the explosion but Stanislaus fell and Peter stopped to try and help him up. He was unable to move Stanislaus, and they remained there for five and a half hours. Underground, the rescuers attempted to remove Stanislaus, but just then, he expired. Stanislaus, a father of four, would be brought out days later.

After the initial struggle with Peter, McGraw and the others were able to subdue him and bring him to the surface through the toad hole. There he broke away and, rushing through the spectators, ran toward the river only to be caught again at a fence and taken to his home. As word spread of Peter Urban's rescue, hope once again revived with the belief that the rescue team then preparing to go underground would find other survivors.[21]

The rescue work was slowed by the lack of mine ventilation structures on the surface but also by the collapse of the entire ventilation infrastructure system within the mine. All the brick or block partitions used to direct the air throughout the mine were destroyed, and temporary stoppings made of brattice had been completely obliterated. Before deeper penetration of the mine could be attempted, temporary partitions had to be constructed, an effort that slowed the rescue efforts to a tedious pace.

As more and more time passed, the realization grew—particularly among more experienced miners—that chances were diminishing that others would be found alive. Time was the critical consideration after the multiple explosions and subsequent fires. Despite the fact that bodies had been found, there was hope that miners located further back into the mine could have survived. However, as Malone and other mine professionals knew, time was the enemy. The work continued into the night, and by the early hours of Saturday morning, the work progressed more rapidly. With each passing hour, crowds outside the entrances grew, and by Saturday morning virtually the entire population of the town was at the site. Volunteers from other mines and the curious walked or rode the interurban from Fairmont and the surrounding camps.[22]

Among the volunteers were Fairmont physicians, Dr. F. Hill and Dr. J. R. Cook. Nurses also came, hoping to treat the wounded. Malone ordered teams of experienced supervisors and craftsmen from all of the company's surrounding mines to come to the site to help speed the rescue.[23]

Restaurants in Fairmont and Clarksburg made soups and sandwiches for the rescue teams and the victims' families. Make-shift kitchens were set up near the mine portals to support the workers.[24]

By Friday evening, a third rescue party was formed. At 9:00 P.M., as the ventilating air pushed into the mine by repaired fans through cleared main entries, rescuers began to investigate the side entries and rooms that had been further away from the explosions.

As each team moved forward, they stumbled over the dead bodies of miners and horses. By midnight they had reached 700 feet from the entrance when the poisoned air drove them back. Fresh recruits replaced them. As the rescuers came out, the crowd begged for information, calling out the names of loved ones. The rescuers shook their heads. Nearly all the bodies were unrecognizable, and no signs of life had been seen. Imagine a handful of reckless, bedraggled men going into the cavern with lanterns with sulfurous fumes in their faces and dragging out the charred bodies of men, some with their faces burned off. That is what Monongah looked like.[25]

The rescuers found only one additional man alive. John Tomko, who was referred to by a company official as "a big Slav," was found far back in No. 8 by a rescue party on Saturday. Tomko and his wife Barbara lived in Monongah with their three children. Originally from Alsobaskocz, Hungary, John had come to Monongah with his brother George, who also worked in No. 8. When John was found, he was a raving maniac and rushed with great fury upon the men who approached him. When he was calmed, the rescuers started for the opening with him, but the poor fellow died before reaching the open air.

George Tomko's body was found nearby.[26]

The scene underground was one of unspeakable agony and despair. As more and more teams entered and returned, finding only bodies, the horror of the catastrophe settled in. During the night the effort began to shift from one of searching the length of the mine for survivors to one of recovering the bodies.

Late Friday evening, Clarence Watson, company president, arrived from Parkersburg. Jere H. Wheelwright, company vice president, and others from the Consolidation Baltimore office also arrived on a separate train. B&O Railroad President William Murray, who owned a substantial interest in the mines and also transported all of the coal produced by both mines was in

New Martinsville, West Virginia, and ordered a special train—he also arrived late Friday.[27]

During Friday afternoon, agents for the company had begun to prepare for the worst. Transport wagons and crews were hired. W. S. Thomas Transfer Co., a Fairmont firm, sent all available wagons and teams to the mines. A temporary morgue was set up at the First National Bank of Monongah, a newly established enterprise owned by Watson and others, and pressed into service. As Saturday dawned, rescuers began to bring bodies out of the entries. In No. 6, 34 bodies were assembled near the base of the slope. Hope of finding any survivors had faded. At 9:10 Saturday morning, Watson telegraphed J. N. Camden: "Rescuing work progressing faster and if not interfered with, most of the mine workers will be reached to-day. Have lost all hope of finding any men alive."[28]

Afterdamp, Explosions, and Roof Falls

Every undertaker in Fairmont was contracted and the supply of coffins available in the surrounding towns was immediately exhausted. By early Saturday afternoon, a Fairmont undertaker placed an order for 100 coffins with the Muskingum Coffin Company of Zanesville, Ohio.[29] It was to be the first of several orders. The Muskingum Coffin Company went into emergency production, working around the clock in order to meet the demand.[30]

At the bottom of mine No. 6, 300 feet down the incline from the mine mouth, work was progressing on cleaning up the wreckage of the strings of cars and the electric motors. The rescuers climbed over the pile-up and found bodies beyond it, but made no attempt to remove these to the surface. They moved on, partly because it would have been impossible to carry the bodies over the debris, but more particularly because they did not want to lose any time in reaching other sections of the mine where still-living men might have been imprisoned.[31]

By Sunday afternoon in No. 8, flames that had been smoldering in the mine broke out as fresh air reached the interior. The rescuers were required to evacuate, and it was expected that many bodies would be completely destroyed.[32] Three fires were found and extinguished with water. Within the mine workings of both No. 6 and No. 8, virtually all props and timbers were blown down and large falls of roof were found in every section but one in both mines.

The rescuers were faced with horrible scenes. A headless body sat in the seat of a cutting machine, its hands still gripping the handles of the machine. The rescue effort had become a recovery effort and was now better organized. Mappers accompanied every crew. The location of each body was noted on a special map, and that information was used to help identify the victims. A body found near a railroad track would be assumed to have been a tracklayer. If a miner was found in a room, it was assumed he had been assigned to that room.

Those miners who were in the direct line of the explosion force were the most mangled. Some were completely destroyed, others were split open as a result of being thrown violently against the mine. "Legs and arms of others were blown or mashed off by the debris as it fell on the victim," reported the *Baltimore Sun* on page 12 of its December 12 edition, which also pointed out that bodies were so thoroughly destroyed that only small parts survived and would never be recovered or accounted for.

For some, death was not instantaneous. Some miners were found suffocated; one held a pencil and paper in his hands. Several miners were found holding their glass safety lamps, attempting to relight them as the afterdamp extinguished both the lamp flame and the miner. One man was found clutching his handkerchief in his right hand, trying to cover his mouth in a futile attempt to block the gas. One miner was found with a spoon in his hand, eating his last meal.

By the end of Wednesday, 320 bodies had been found. Watson ordered a temporary halt to recovery operations, as fires had broken out anew in sections of No. 6 and No. 8 and the rescue crews had been working around the clock for six straight days. By that time, every section of the mine had been entered and finding survivors was impossible. As a result of the explosions, extensive roof falls had occurred throughout the mines, and bodies were buried under tons of roof strata. The rescue teams made no effort to remove these roof falls, and therefore those bodies were still entombed. A new clean-up crew of nearly 100 men began that Friday, a week after the accident, to remove the roof falls so additional bodies could be found.

Watson now revised his estimate of the number of victims and admitted that the amount was simply unknown.

It is not yet definitely known how many miners were in Mines No. 6 and 8 at the time of the explosion. In fact, the efforts at recovery were shifted to recording the location and counting the number of bodies. They would no longer attempt to determine the number lost, but would rely instead on a census being conducted by the company auditor, Robert Cunningham.[33]

Monongah W. Va
Dec 6. 1907

Mr Ernest M. Trader
    McKeesport - Pa.

    Dear Papa. — This bring the second letter [I]
have written in answer to your several most welcome
ones in the last two weeks, I will try and get
it a little farther on the way to McKeesport [than]
where the first one stopped (in my inside coat
[pocket])

    We [are all] young very [good] health [at]
present owing [I think] to the [dry] settled [state]
of the weather we have been having. It has
been quite cold here for over a week, snow
almost [every] day, but melting almost as fast
as it falls.

    The [railway] did not [pass] in Clearing
[House] checks [as] we had expected but all the
[boxes] were [gone] checks on [the] company
[bank] in Fairmont, I deposited [mine] in our [own]
bank here. [It is] hard to tell what the result
would have [been] if the foreigners had been
paid in the certificates as they are so [hard]
to make [understand] even [more simple]

Composition of [the] ... damp before explosion

marsh gas

H	H	H	H
C	O	O	O
O	M	M	M
	air		
M	M	M	M

Composition of the after damp of an explosion of fire damp

C	O	H	H
O	H	H	O
M	M	M	O
M	M	M	M

the elements of which the gas was composed in the first place being present only combined differ[ently]

C. Carbon   O Oxygen   M. Nitrogen   H Hydrogen.

Marsh Gas.	C & H
Choke damp	O & M
Carbonic Acid gas.	C + O
Steam.	H + O

Nitrogen has no effect on an explosion but exists in a free state before and after the let go

I guess that's enough of mine talk for Eugenia. who likes mine talk so well so I will sidetrack to some topic as far away from it as the earth is from the sun.

Grace Dearlove is to be married on the 19 of Dec and Mayne is going to attend so I expect she will most likely stay at home for Xmas. I would have liked to come too but cannot see my way clear either financialy or from a business view so will spend Xmas — at Daves

Trader's illustration, from his December 6, 1907 letter, of the elemental composition of firedamp before and after an explosion. (A&M 3574, Davitt McAteer Collection, West Virginia & Regional History Collection, WVU Libraries)

Above: Graveyard from the Monongah mine disaster showing separate Polish and Italian burial areas. (Photograph by Allen; West Virginia & Regional History Collection, WVU Libraries) **Below:** Another view of the graveyard from the disaster. In this photograph, Polish graves are on the left and Italian on the right. (Photograph by Boland, Dec. 12, 1907; West Virginia & Regional History Collection, WVU Libraries)

Community members await news at the portal to mine No. 8. (Photographer unknown; possibly Guerin Johnson, an Alabama photographer thought to be in Monongah at the time of the disaster)

Above: Investigation and recovery teams were constantly working inside the No. 6 mine during the week following the disaster. (Photographer unknown; WV History OnView #002546, West Virginia & Regional History Collection, WVU Libraries)
Below: Miners had to undercut the coal wall in preparation for blasting. (Photographer unknown; Mine Safety and Health Administration, Bureau of Mines file)

Above: Undercutting the coal wall to prepare for blasting was rough, exhausting work. (Mine Safety and Health Administration, Bureau of Mines file) **Below Left:** A Wolf Safety Lamp (Royce J. and Caroline B. Watts Museum, West Virginia University) **Below Right:** Body after body was removed from the mines following the explosion. (Photographer unknown, possibly Guerin Johnson; author's personal collection)

Above: Following the explosion, access to the rescue area was limited to a few rescuers at a time. Here, men await their shifts. (Photograph by Boland, taken Dec. 8, 1907; West Virginia & Regional History Collection, WVU Libraries) **Below:** The immense fan housing from the No. 8 mine was demolished. (Photograph by Boland, taken Dec. 7, 1907; West Virginia & Regional History Collection, WVU Libraries)

Above: The explosion at the No. 8 mine created a 60-foot scar in the earth. (Photograph by Boland, taken Dec. 7, 1907; West Virginia & Regional History Collection, WVU Libraries) **Below:** On the day after the explosion, a large crowd gathered to observe as bodies were carried from both mines. (Photographer unknown, possibly Guerin Johnson; author's personal collection)

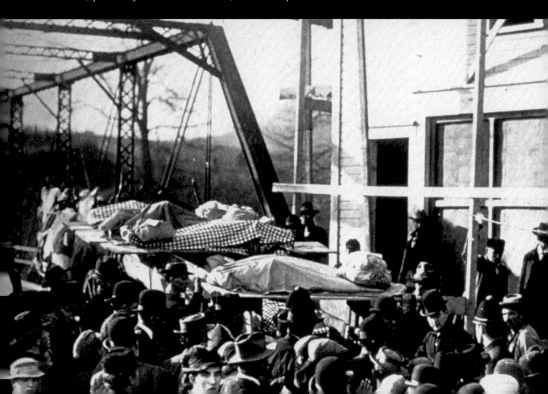

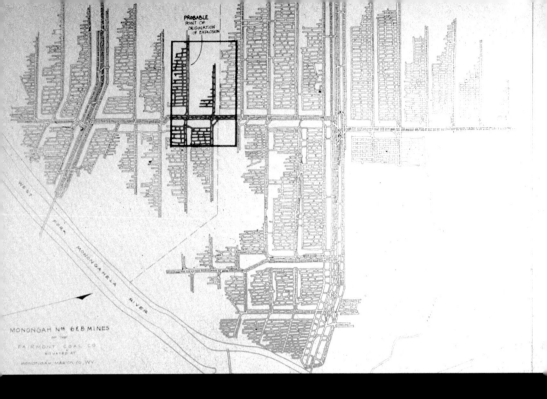

Above: A map shows the probable origin of the explosion and the connection points between mines No. 6 and No. 8 (Jim Stevens, graphic artist; author's personal collection) **Below:** Joseph A. Holmes, First Director of the U.S. Bureau of Mines (Photographer unknown; author's personal collection)

Above: The view from the trestle where the railway cars broke loose, looking back at the mouth of the No. 6 mine. (Photograph by Boland, taken Dec. 6, 1907; West Virginia & Regional History Collection, WVU Libraries) **Below:** A printed letter of thanks to the Carnegie Hero Commission, signed by members of the Monongah Mine Relief Committee.

Fairmont, W. Va. January 2nd 1908.

To The Carnegie Hero Fund Commission :

Whereas, on Friday morning December 6th, 1907, there occurred at Monongah, W. Va. in Mines Nos. 6 and 8 of the Fairmont Coal Company, an awful disaster, resulting in the death of 361 Employees; and

Whereas, as a result of this large death list, approximately 250 women were made widows, and 1,000 children, some of them yet unborn, were left fatherless, and deprived of their only means of support; and

Whereas, The Carnegie Hero Fund Commission very generously contributed the large sum of $35,000.00 toward the contemplated fund of $200,000.00 for the relief of these widows and orphans ;

Therefore, be it resolved, that we, The Monongah Mines Relief Committee in behalf of the beneficiaries of this fund, thank most heartily the members of the Carnegie Hero Fund Commission for their liberal gift of $35,000.00 to our Relief Fund, and for their kindly thought of the women and children who lost their bread winners in the Monongah Disaster.

We believe that you as a Commission, by helping the helpless and stimulating the strong ; by rewarding heroism, and relieving suffering, are establishing a new type of philanthropy that appeals to the best instincts of humanity.

Furthermore, we feel greatly indebted to you for sending to our aid Messrs. Frank M. Wilmot and Geo. A. Campsey, who by their intelligent advice and keen business suggestions, enabled us

A photograph of Monongah taken some years after the disaster. (Photographer unknown; author's personal collection)

Above: Inspectors from West Virginia and other states standing in front of the craters at the mouth of the No. 8 mine. This photo was taken during the investigation after the explosion. (Photographer unknown; WV History OnView #002546, West Virginia & Regional History Collection, WVU Libraries) **Below:** Coffins for victims laid out on the main street of Monongah. (Photographer unknown; author's collection)

Above: The houses in Monongah were intertwined with the workings of the two mines in 1907. (Photographer unknown; author's personal collection) **Below:** Four generations of Trader men. (Merle Dowd Family Files)

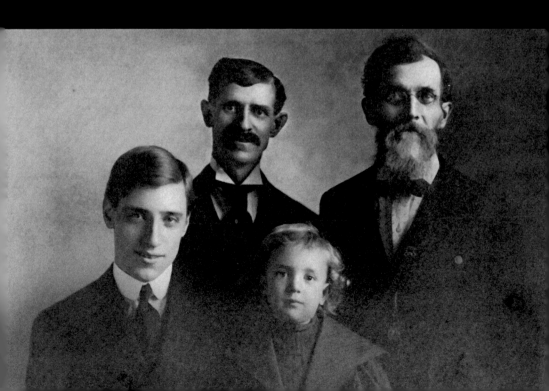

Lester and Mayne Trader, approximately 1906. (Merle Dowd Family Files)

Above: Lester Trader's home in Monongah. (Merle Dowd Family Files) Below: Men and women of Monongah wait for news of their relatives on the interurban track between Fairmont and Monongah. (Photographer unknown; A&M 3574, Davitt McAteer Collection, West Virginia and Regional History Collection, WVU Libraries)

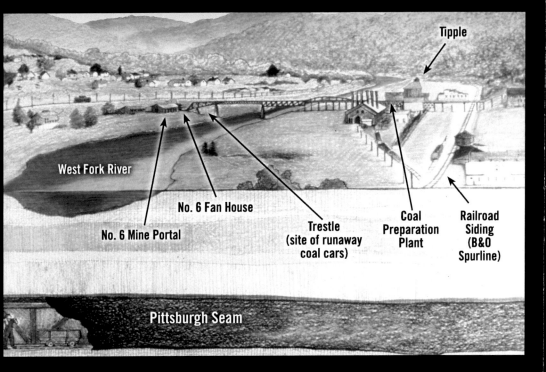

Above: A drawing reveals the arrangement of the coal trestle and preparation plant for the No. 6 mine and illustrates the operations' relation to the Pittsburgh seam. (Jim Stevens, graphic artist; author's personal collection) **Below:** Map used by Assistant Chief Engineer John Graham Smyth to indicate the location of bodies in the No. 6 and No. 8 mines. (Scanned with the assistance of the West Virginia GIS Technical Center, West Virginia University; author's personal collection)

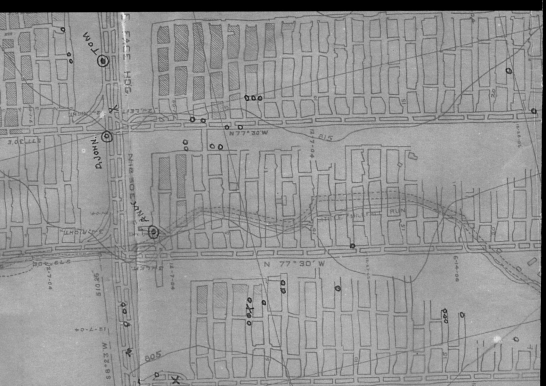

"THEY ARE ALL GONE"

At the man-way of No. 8 mine Monongah, was a check board with numbers pressed into the tin tags that swung on its pegs. The black fury that swept up the entry December 6, scattered the checks like confetti—what else, when it laid hold of a great steel plate of the fan, and rammed it into a clay bank across the Monongahela River.

The lost checks stood for lost men—foolish, tinkling little name plates they had been for the hulking coffin of the hills. . . .

— *Paul U. Kellogg, "Charities and the Commons," Vol. 19*

FRIDAY night, December 6, and early Saturday morning, December 7, the first bodies were brought from the mine. As they were brought out, they were examined by Dr. F. W. Hill and others who had volunteered and had come out of Fairmont.[1] The miners' bodies were placed on wagons and carried across the river to the main street on the west side of town. There they were placed in the First National Bank, which had been converted to a temporary morgue.[2] There the Marion County coroner, E. S. Amos, and the company payroll clerk, George Gibbons, collected items found on the bodies, attempted to identify each man, and recorded the name or lack thereof into twin sets of books that the coroner and the company were keeping. The ordinary and most reliable means of identification was the brass or tin numbered checks that each employee was supposed to carry.

Two checks were placed on a master board outside of each mine entrance; as each man went to work, he would place one check in his pocket and one on a board set close to the entrance to indicate he was inside. The numbers were preassigned for each shift. But because the boards had been destroyed in the explosion, this identification system was useless. In addition, as State Mine Inspector R. S. LaRue testified, the Monongah mines did not use brass tags.[3] In many instances there were no checks found on the bodies, an indication that many men and boys had been working 'off the books'—in effect, as subcontractors—which meant they were working for a miner and being paid by that miner and therefore not on the company records. The practice was common in the industry and at these mines.[4]

Early on Saturday, the first group of bodies was taken to the bank, the temporary morgue. After examination, each body was laid out in a black suit supplied by the company and the effort of identification began. As part of that effort, families of the dead began to stream through the rooms. Autopsies had been performed on the first corpses in an attempt to identify the precise cause of death; suffocation, burns, and concussion were the prominent causes, but the bodies were in varying conditions. By early Sunday, eighteen bodies had been identified, removed from the morgue and taken to the miner's homes. Those bodies that could be, were embalmed, dressed, and laid out.

But by the end of the weekend, many bodies were not identifiable. When that was not possible, these bodies were taken directly from the mine entrance to the graveyard and buried immediately. Widows and family members were permitted to view the bodies and attempted to identify them. The effects of the explosions varied. In some instances the bodies were perfectly preserved and recognition was immediate; in other cases, the bodies were so badly disfigured or mutilated, identification was impossible.[5]

In the first hours of the recovery, bodies were brought out of the mine and loaded onto the horse-drawn carts; crowds of families and onlookers would surge forward, frightening the horses and causing difficulty in moving the bodies. On Saturday afternoon, while pulling a load of coffins, the horses became frightened by the crowd and bolted, overturning the cart and tossing the bodies to the ground. The horses raced through the throng and ran headlong into the river along with their driver and his assistant. As the cart hit the water the driver was violently thrown out and seriously injured.[6]

That evening, the company officials ordered the rescuers to store the bodies at the bottom of the shaft and arranged that they be moved through town or to the graveyard only after dark when the crowds had diminished. Throughout the week, bodies collected in the mine, assembled at the shaft bottom, and were transferred to the morgue or the graveyard.

By Sunday, December 8, all Consolidation Coal Company officers and employees from mines throughout the area had been brought into service. All of the sixty-four Consolidation Coal Company mines were closed and some of the 20,000 company miners and their supervisors were ordered to Monongah.[7]

The day before, Governor William M. O. Dawson had called out the National Guard: Company H of the First Infantry, under the direction of Colonel M. M. Neely, who later became West Virginia's U.S. Senator. The Governor was concerned about potential disturbances among the immigrant families as well as the throngs of sightseers. Neely and his men erected white tents next to the cemetery to be used by his men, to be used by the rescuers and as a second morgue, and to be used by the grave diggers. Order was beginning to take shape, but on both Saturday and Sunday the crowds again threatened to overwhelm the special police force that had been hastily organized. During the weekend, enormous crowds of the curious rode the inter-urban from Fairmont or walked to view the dreadful site. By one estimate the crowd exceeded 25,000 people, so large that one enterprising photographer had begun selling postcards with pictures of the rescue or recovery efforts.[8]

On Saturday, by order of the Marion County Sheriff, all saloons and bars were closed and no liquor sales were permitted in the county. Slowly the bodies were brought out. By Sunday, the company had hired three Fairmont undertakers to be in charge of the bodies and burials: Musgrove & Sons, R. I. Cunningham, and Jones & Company. Because of the huge number of bodies, the three principal undertakers hired twenty other undertakers from Fairmont and surrounding towns.

Late Friday, the day of the disaster, as the magnitude of the disaster was be-ginning to unfold, it became clear that burial sites would be needed for hun-dreds of bodies. The existing potter's field would be insufficient. The Italian and Polish Catholic churches, only recently opened, did not yet have grave-yards established and were not equipped for such a calamity. The Fairmont Coal Company hastily donated two one-acre parcels for St. Stanislaus and Our Lady of Pompeii. These parcels sat adjacent to one another on the west side of the river a mile or so south of the exploded mine.

Since there was concern that each body should be buried within the cor-rect ethnic graveyard, a double barbed-wire fence was stretched down the hill to separate the graveyards: Polish graves on the left and Italian graves on the on the right. The gravediggers consisted of Consolidation Coal Company and Fairmont Coal Company employees, and included surviving miners from mines No. 6 and No. 8. The National Guard troops had also been stationed at the gravesites because there had been instances or rumors of per-sons changing the names on graves. The presence of the troops also helped to quell emotional reactions by the victims' families near the graves.[9]

The National Guard tents were set up on the north side of the Italian graveyard, lined up in typical army formation, with the graves in front, so numerous as to resemble military trenches. Separating each grave was one foot of earth. Seven rows roughly seventy yards long stretched from the top of the hill down to the bottom. Each grave was seven feet eight inches long. Separating each row of graves was a row of six feet of earth.[10]

Further south of the Polish graveyard, the bodies of other ethnic groups, Greeks and Turks, were interred. Those victims' graves were segregated and buried a short distance down the hill and across the lane in unmarked graves. Black victims and other nationalities were buried further away from town.

By Sunday, December 8, the first funeral masses were begun in the churches of Fairmont and Monongah. In Fairmont, priests at St. Peter's Roman Catholic Church conducted funeral masses, while some Protestant churches both in Monongah and Fairmont held services for the victims who were their members.

On Sunday, Bishop P. J. Donahue arrived by train from the diocesan seat in Wheeling. He was joined by Father Arsenius Boutlou,[11] Pastor of St. Peter's Fairmont, who had come to Monongah Monday morning to meet with company officials and to assist the Reverend Joseph Lekston, pastor of the St. Stanislaus Polish Church and Father Joseph D'Andrea, pastor of the Italian parish Our Lady of Pompeii.

The Italian parish had lost the most parishioners in the explosion, and Father D'Andrea had also lost his brother, Victor, who was the father of three and whose wife, Maria, was six months pregnant. Both priests had been working without rest since Friday morning and were close to exhaustion. Bishop Donahue speculated that over 80 percent of the dead were members of those two parishes. He also met with relief committee officials and suggested that the two pastors be added to the then-forming relief committee. Bishop Donahue then assisted at the obsequies or funeral rites of twenty-six dead at St. Stanislaus Church and met later that day with family members.[12]

But by late Sunday, it had become clear that the number of bodies, both identified and unidentified, was outpacing the capacity of the families to identify them and of the morgues to embalm them. In one case, a beautiful Polish girl remained for a while beside the casket that contained the body of an unknown victim. She sobbed as if her heart were breaking and, in her few words of English, declared that her father was in the mine.[13]

Identification in some instances was easy, as the dead had no mark or sign of injury. In other instances, the bodies had been brutally manipulated and disfigured, beheaded, burned beyond recognition, limbs torn away. As Monday dawned, more and more bodies were brought to the surface, and the trauma repeated itself countless times. The bank-turned-morgue was overwhelmed, and the coffins and bodies were in the street in front of the bank itself.

By Monday morning, December 9, trains from New York, Baltimore, and Washington brought representatives of several governments to look after their citizens' interests. The Austrian government sent a representative to look after the Austro-Hungarian miners' interests. The Italian Consular G. D. Caldara, who already resided in Fairmont, had rushed to Monongah on Friday afternoon, shortly after the explosion.

And beginning on Monday, the weather worsened and rain poured down steadily all morning, as five priests prepared to hold funeral masses at St. Stanislaus Church. The coffins of the first twenty miners were arranged on the first floor of the church. Paul Kellogg, a writer and staff member of Charity and the Commons, a New York City charitable organization, observed,

Many of his people had come early to the church, a-foot, with bowed heads, sorrowing in low voices, sometimes a woman half led up by her companions, to that basement where the coffin lids closed in on blistered, swollen faces and parts of men. Four or five women wept convulsively. An older woman read from a religious book held to the flickering light of a candle at the head of a closed coffin. A peasant, ugly with her pitted face, but beautiful in her great sorrow, bent often and kissed the lips of her husband. All of a sudden there was a cry more piercing than the others. It was from an old mother who had lost seven—her husband, a son, two sons-in-law, and three nephews. She had come upon one of them and the people with her could scarcely hold her. She threw her head on the casket, and spoke to the boy fondly, trying to caress the crumpled face with poor, wrinkled hands. She had moaned all the way that morning from her lonely house to the church door, giving infinite sorrow to those who heard, and here her grief had at last found vent. Outside, rain continued depressing the almost impossible situation further.

At the end of the street were store buildings, and the Italian woman who kept one had let them leave a coffin box on her steps until the right household should be found. She told me of a country-woman, the mother of four little children who had lost her husband, one son of nineteen and a trapper boy of thirteen: "Women cry all time," she said:—of another with three boys killed:—of the man and seven boarders killed at No. 151—"All married, old country. No see t'all, no see. He can find. All burn." Standing at the head of the street, she pointed out with stretched finger the houses in a row on the bluff where the shawled women sat and waited. "First hous', he no come out. Nixa hous', two men nine clock he go out"—and she raised and lowered her arm in a counting of the houses, one after another.

Later on, Kellogg encountered a woman and her daughter who he described as "West Virginians." In response to his question of who lived on the street or rows, the mother explained:

At 109 Mrs. Larkin's left with three, her oldest twelve and the others're five years and two. They're Slavish in the houses next for a spell and I don't know so much about them. But Mrs. McLaren at 113 has eleven children, some grown and married, thank God, and the Slavish woman at 118 has two little ones. There's a young husband killed at 119—they weren't married for long and she's all broke up. She's one child but Mrs. Wright at 120, she's got five under fourteen year and her man gone. That's the way it goes on the lower row. The upper row's worse—every house but one. And that big house down the road a piece—that one and the one next to it they're the same family—married children—there're fourteen dead there. . . . the children of the McFarleys, all little ones and not a bite to eat.

Kellogg further describes other women in mourning (quotes presumably indicating direct statements by eyewitnesses):

. . . the Italian mother "where I got the peppers," with no money and no English and "two little bits of children." The Slavish wife who "tore blood out of her face," the two crazed women on the hill who, rumor had it, had to be tied down to their beds. . .[14]

In some cases, the women had no food or money as they were living on each day's pay. When there was no pay they were without. In some cases even where there was food the mothers were so distraught as not to be able to prepare anything. Then the guide pointed to the house just over mine No. 8 where the widow of the English machine man lived, "who tore out her beautiful yellow hair in grabs."

Maria deGaetana Abbnte lost three; her husband Francesco and two sons, Carlo and Joseph. She was now alone with four living children and pondered returning to her home town of Castrovillari, Italy.[15]

Kellogg next described talking with five sisters and a mother whose husband and brother George had both been killed and how the father had been singing "Nearer my God, to Thee" as he went to work the morning of the explosion. As tragic as the deaths were, the girls commented, "Oh, we know he's dead, but if we could only get his body out of the pit. . ." The list went on. One man and his son left five other children, the youngest but a year old. His family was one of the fortunate ones; he had paid up an insurance policy on Thanksgiving Day. Others were not so fortunate. One woman was left with forty-five cents when they brought her husband home.[16]

When the coffins of the identified parishioners were brought from the temporary morgues, they went to the house or the church basement. Then the coffin lids were closed for the last time. In this makeshift funeral parlor, many of the families gathered. The scene was one of despair: women weeping, a widow held up from collapse by her companion, the woman at the front of the coffin read prayers from a religious book brought from the old country, lighted only by candles.

Father D'Andrea worked nonstop. For three days he neither slept nor bathed, but continually ministered to his flock, guiding the drivers of the casket carts to the correct homes. D'Andrea had held funeral masses for the first bodies recovered on Sunday or Monday. All day Monday, a drizzling rain and overcast sky caused a mist to hang over the valley. The weekend crowds were gone, much of the excitement was over, groups of men stood nearby the mine entrance. Women wandered aimlessly.

Everything was sober and uncertain. The relief workers, explorers and brothers and men waiting their times to go in, closed like shadows beside the black of the mine mouth or stood out, restless silhouettes against the background of steam and smoke and mist. Seemingly, from every pore of the earth there rose a white cloud.

Here for sixty hours, the men had worked feverishly, unafraid to bring blackened bodies out of the ground that they might be counted, and put back, and here at this same pitiful commission, they were to work for a week to come.

In town, the weight of events wore down. Near the bluff above the mine portals . . . and at its edge sat in a heavier silence, a group of shawled women, waiting. . . . Two

Slav women, with big-boned, grief-wrenched faces, were walking up and down the street, going nowhere. They wore great shawls and diagonally across their breasts were the papoose-like bodies of their babies, wrapped in with a knack, which is handed down by the mothers of the old Country.[17]

But as soon as the exploration of the mines had begun, there was the recognition that many bodies were entirely destroyed by the force of the explosion and the number of dead would never be fully known.

As more and more bodies were brought out, the identification process became more routine. By Tuesday night, 149 bodies had been recovered, and by 6:00 P.M. on Wednesday, 221 had been brought out. By Thursday at noon, 297 bodies had been recovered, and by Friday, 338 bodies had been removed, according to the first page of the December 19, 1907, edition of the *Fairmont Free Press*. In addition to the men, some 40 to 50 horses and mules were removed. As time passed and removal became more difficult, the rescuers turned to lye to destroy the decomposing animals—and no doubt, also men's bodies.

Underground the efforts were horrific. John Graham Smyth, assistant chief engineer for the company, was placed in charge of the recovery underground. Smyth reported to E. Scott outside, who reported to Ruckman and Malone. Smyth sent notes to the surface, asking for more rubber boots because the leather boots were not lasting in the flooded mine. He also requested more lye for sprinkling on dead stock. It was taking more than five pounds per head. Deodorizing squads went ahead of the rescuers, trying to minimize the dreadful condition. Smyth argued with the surface that the cotton gloves being supplied were inadequate and that rescuers needed rubber gloves as well as a solution to wash with after handling each body. Scott declined Smyth's request for rubber gloves citing the cost of such gloves.[18]

Mindful of other concerns, C. W. Watson, Consolidation and Fairmont Company president, invited the visiting mine safety experts to dinner at his home, LaGrange. On Thursday, December 12, Frank Haas, the assistant general manager, wrote to Smyth underground:

Arrange to get your party on the 4:30 car for Fairmont without fail. Dr. Holmes, Mr. Hall, Dr. Smelly, Pres. Bush and the two French gentlemen and Mr. J. W. Paul are invited to a dinner at C. W. Watson residence at 6:15 p.m. Inform the gentlemen of this and that it is not a formal affair. You will have to make the 4:30 car in order to give them time to get cleaned up.

P.S. Send reply that all concerned understand by bearer Jim McGraw to G.E. Peddicord.

According to the *Fairmont Times*, a magnificent dinner was held at The Fairmont Farms, hosted by C. W. Watson, complementary to President B. F. Bush, of the Western Maryland Railroad.

Joseph A. Holmes and Hall were with the U.S. Dept. of Commerce, Technologic Branch office, which had been charged to look into whether there was a role for the federal government in the safety affairs of the United States mines. The two French gentlemen, Mr. Jacques Caffauel and M. Dumaine, were from the French mine safety government authority and happened to be in the country when the explosion occurred and had traveled to Monongah to be part of the investigation.[19]

At the temporary morgue, if Gibbons or anyone else could identify a miner's body, he would look up the man's address. After being embalmed and dressed in a black suit, the body would be placed in one of the waiting coffins, loaded on the cart, and sent home. A silver watch was found in the pocket of Joseph Alexander, stopped at 10:42. A gold watch belonging to

Charles B. Hofaker was still running. Many of the drivers were unfamiliar with Monongah, including the W. S. Thomas Company drivers who were from Fairmont, and much confusion occurred. Both the parish priests were frequently called upon to direct the body to the proper house. On Saturday, Father D'Andrea had also begun to survey the victims among his parishioners, out of which he counted some 174 dead. Father Lekston had estimated 110 dead from his parish.

Through Saturday, if no identification was made within several hours, the dressed body would be placed in a coffin and buried as an unknown. But as the bank morgue filled beyond capacity, bodies were taken directly from the mouth of the mine to the tents serving as the temporary morgue at the cemetery. Others were taken to the basement of St. Stanislaus and Our Lady of Pompeii. Overwhelmed by the numbers, the process was disorderly.

As of Saturday evening, embalming became difficult even among the bodies identified because of the number of bodies, yet less than one-fourth of the death toll had been accounted for.[20] A more expedient burial system had to be adopted. This had led to C. W. Watson's request for immediate burial. Besides the sheer number of bodies, however, was the concern that the widows' situation could spin out of control. The wives and families of some of the victims were greeting the bodies with emotional outbursts and the funeral masses were wrenching affairs, full of sadness and forlorn reactions. The conditions in the homes themselves grew more desperate:

Women and children have been found absolutely destitute of food and without clothing sufficient to protect them from the wintry blasts. These women, many of them the extremely ignorant foreign type, are just beginning to realize the enormous scope of the calamity. Instead of now sitting mutely on the porches of their humble cottages and watching the great mob of sightseers they are haunting the mines in search of husbands and relatives. In many instances they still refuse to believe these have been lost."[21]

The company officials who were acting as census takers discovered one house in which nine miners had been killed. The father, Michael Sari, three cousins, and five male boarders had all died in the explosions. Sari was survived by his wife, Maria Szalaga Sari, and pretty six-year old daughter, Mary. The cousins, John, George, and Stephen Sari all left widows in Czeke, Hungary.

On Monday, funerals were continual in both the Polish and Italian churches, beginning at 9:00 A.M. and continuing until late in the afternoon, which amounted to some forty services. At the cemeteries, burials were also continual, and following the custom from the old country, each family member would throw a handful of earth into the grave and say a final prayer.

Also on Monday, Company President Clarence Watson contacted the Marion County Board of Health and sought their help in expediting the burial procedure, citing the danger to health in Monongah because of the decomposition of bodies. There was also concern that the grieving and hysteria could begin to spark anger, and Watson believed the situation threatened to spin out of control. The Board of Health and the Board Supervisor, citing public health concerns, issued an order on Tuesday, December 10, initiating new accelerated identification and burial procedures, directing that burials were to occur immediately, which would mean without funeral Mass. Viewing and identification times were reduced to a maximum of four hours. The Catholic parishes would have to hold whatever services they could at the graveyard if any service at all was to be held.

Many of the widows were distraught at having lost their husbands, their sole source of support, while they had small children to feed. Some expressed a desire to return to their home countries, "feeling that the few short years of the country of liberty has brought them nothing but grief and suffering."[22]

On Tuesday and Wednesday, large numbers of bodies were brought out of the mines. Some funerals were conducted, but more frequently the bodies went from the mouth of the mine to the graveyard and were buried immediately. If identification had been made, a simple prayer service might be held; if not, the bodies were simply buried.

Out of thirty houses on one block on Camden Avenue, twenty-seven didn't have a man left in them. Nineteen men lived in Andy Sticke's home, all related, and all were killed in the explosion. The widow could be found in the church basement, paying a last tribute to her youngest son, San Angelo.

By Wednesday morning, newspapers were reporting that 142 bodies had been recovered. Rain and snow continued to fall, casting the entire valley in a desperate gloom. A number of bodies from the far reaches of the mine interior were completely intact and were embalmed immediately and buried within three hours. Effort at identification was restricted to less than one hour.

Families who were not members of the Catholic churches had to make separate arrangements for burial. Several widows had no money to pay for burials, and their loved ones had to be interred in the potter's field.

At midweek, bodies were still being brought out of the mines in large numbers as widows in small knots stood guard by the morgue, hoping to catch a glimpse of their loved one. Rumors of an epidemic surfaced as many of the bodies being recovered were maimed and black from decomposition. The Marion County Board of Health issued a second order:

There is imminent danger of an epidemic of disease breaking out in Monongah. Scores of men working in recovering the dead are prostrated. Their illness is undoubtedly due to their exposure to the feral air and terrible stench created in the mines by the decaying bodies and the cadavers of animals. So urgent is the necessity for observing the strictest of sanitary measures that all of the streets in Monongah were heavily sprinkled with lime this afternoon. The odors emanating from the morgue and its vicinity are unbearable.[23]

By Tuesday or Wednesday it became clear that the company had no accurate account of the number or the names of the victims. Watson ordered a survey of the area. R. T. Cunningham, the Fairmont Coal Company auditor, was placed in charge of the survey of Monongah and the surrounding area in an effort to determine the amount and the names of the miners killed. Company employees, traveling in teams of two, canvassed the neighborhoods with translators, attempting to find out the number of miners missing. The Cunningham List, as it came to be called, would be referred to as the authoritative reference supporting the contention that the number killed was limited and below the estimates that the company officials had originally stated. But it was hopelessly inaccurate, failing to count entire houses of dead immigrants because no one survived. The Cunningham List was also limited to Monongah and the nearby coal camps.

By Wednesday, all hope of finding miners alive had vanished. The recovery was becoming more horrific and tedious with the passage of time. Once located, bodies now had to be carried a distance of a mile or more underground just to get to the mine mouth, and the system of identification and counting led to considerable confusion results in the number recovered.

To complicate matters, water from rain and the creeks had gotten into the mines through the enlarged portals resulting from the explosion, making recovery that much more difficult.

Bishop P. J. Donahue, having assisted on Saturday and Sunday, returned to Wheeling Wednesday after assisting the priest and visiting the homes of some of the victims. Upon his return he began plans for how to assist in placing children in homes and orphanages when necessary.

On Wednesday, December 11, more than fifty funerals were held, according to the front page of Thursday's *Fairmont Times*, and "on each casket there was a bunch of American Beauty roses or white carnations." It turned out that Miss Elizabeth Watson, daughter of the Company treasurer S. L. Watson, had ordered the flowers.

The company doctor, Dr. Reidy, a former staff member of the Baltimore City Hospital, was assigned to deal with shock among the widows. In one instance, the widow of miner Martin Bosner Zulu, was only 24 years old and the mother of two young sons, aged three and five. Her husband had worked seven years in the mines, and the young woman trudged back and forth to St. Stanislaus to await any news of her missing husband. She had no family in West Virginia, and her elderly mother and brother were poverty-stricken in New York City. When she rejected offers of assistance, a neighbor asked her what would become of her if she didn't let her mother and brother know of her situation. The widow answered, "Oh, I will die."[24]

Anna Jagos lost her husband Paul, and her brother and two grandsons, Paul and Marton Hanyik. All that remained of her family were four small children, for whom she was the sole support. Her home in Verbocz, Hungary, was thousands of miles away but she was thinking about what to do and shortly determined to return home.[25]

On Thursday, the body of Charles D. Wise, the chief engineer of the Monongah Coal Company was found. Wise was a surveyor for Camden's Monongah Company, not that of Consolidation Coal Co. or Fairmont Coal Co., and probably the most prominent man to die in the explosion. The body was found in a sitting position a half-mile from where his overcoat was located. He had wrapped his waistcoat around his head. Wise had survived the explosion and attempted to find his way out of the mine but had lost his way in the blackness and was overcome by afterdamp. Wise had served as a surveyor, taking surveys of the interior of the mine to ensure that the coal owner Camden and others were properly paid by the mining company Consolidation Coal.[26] Wise left a widow and two boys, one two years old and one two months old.

The following Sunday, December 15, the three principal churches in Monongah reassembled their flocks. The pastors, Fr. D'Andrea, Fr. Lekston, and the Rev. W. O. David of the Monongah Presbyterian Church, held their morning services simultaneously. A public service was also held in the cemeteries in "memory of many victims who were interred before being identified. The last resting places are in many instances designated only by stakes driven into the ground at the head of graves in which is inscribed the number of funeral."[27]

"WE KNOW SO LITTLE ABOUT HOW THESE EXPLOSIONS OCCUR"

President C. W. Watson of the Fairmont Coal Company said yesterday that he was now thoroughly convinced that the disaster in the two mines was caused by an explosion of coal dust, but said he could not account for the ignition of the dust unless it had been through the careless use of an open lamp.

—New York Times, December 8, 1907

WATSON'S statement, coming as it did on Saturday while the mines were still on fire, the first day after the explosion and before the mine interior had been explored, is suspect. According to Lester Trader, the theory was made up by David Victor, the Chief Safety Inspector for the company on the day of the explosion and was then used by Watson.[1] It appears to have been an effort to place the blame for the ignition at the feet of the immigrant miners.

On the day of the explosion, Clarence Hall, the nation's leading mine explosive expert, was at the Naomi mine near Fayette City, Pennsylvania. He had been investigating the causes of the mine explosion that claimed the lives of 34 miners on Tuesday, December 2, four days before the Monongah disaster.[2]

Hall was one of the few federal government experts working within the Commerce Department attempting to come to grips with the terrible toll coal mining was claiming in lives in the United States. At the time there was no federal government agency with responsibility or jurisdiction over mining. Earlier in the year President Theodore Roosevelt had called for the creation of a bureau of mines, to address the question of wasted resources resulting from improper mining practices; as almost an afterthought, the bureau might also be charged with gathering information concerning explosions and methods of prevention. On Friday afternoon as news of the Monongah disaster spread, Hall boarded a train in Fayette City and rushed to Monongah.

Upon arriving at Monongah, Hall was interviewed and countered Watson's statement. He put the debate about accident causes into its starkest form when he issued the statement:

These fearful catastrophes seem to be recurring every short while. Today we hear of one accident in Pennsylvania and one in West Virginia. The next day it is Illinois and the following day Montana. They not only are increasing in number, but also growing more terrible in the numbers of persons injured and killed. There is more danger in the deeper mine and when an explosion does occur it kills more men because of the increased number exposed to this danger.

When I enter a mine these days it is with fear and trembling. We seem to know so little of these gas and dust explosions. Sometimes I feel that the poor miner has not a ghost of a show for his life when he enters a mine.

It cannot be claimed that all these explosions are due to the carelessness of the miners. In this country we do not yet know who much of any given explosive can be used safely in the presence of coal gas or coal dust. The fact that nobody knows where or when these larger reservoirs of deadly gases are to be met within the mines makes the situation doubly serious.

What we need is more intelligent legislation, more rigid regulations and better practice connected with all mining operation. To treat trouble just now in bringing about safer conditions is the fact that we know so little about how these explosions occur.[3]

As the magnitude of the explosion became known, other investigations were added. West Virginia Governor William M. O. Dawson directed Colonel Joseph H. McDermott, then speaker of the West Virginia Legislature and political ally with A. B. Fleming, to act as his personal representative. James W. Paul, director of West Virginia's Department of Mines and the state's chief inspector, had already come to the site shortly after the explosion. Paul was familiar with these mines as he worked for the Fairmont Coal Company before his state employment began and indeed would seek employment from Watson in the coming years.

Investigative teams also came from the Ohio Department of Mines and the Pennsylvania Department of Mines. By coincidence, French and Belgian mining experts, M. Jacques Caffarul (Inq. Au Corps des mines and Director de la sation de Essails de Lieuim) and M. Dumaine (Iq. aux mines d'Angin) were in Fairmont preparing to examine the Monongah mines. Dr. Joseph A. Holmes, also from the Commerce Department and a geologist and colleague of Clarence Hall, would arrive later in the week from Washington.[4]

The Fairmont Coal Co.'s investigation team was led by Frank Haas, the company's chief chemist and assistant general manager, and included W. H. Bailey, formerly the assistant general superintendent for the company; H. V. Hesse, general superintendent of Consolidation Coal Company in Frostburg; and Dr. Henry M. Payne, professor of mining engineering from the West Virginia University School of Mines.

On January 10, Haas testified that the team found that the explosion likely originated in the heading designated second right entry off of the first south main No. 8 mine. They were unable to determine the actual origination point, but concluded that it was a powder explosion, as they had found two empty powder cans that had the tops and bottoms blown out and a deposit inside of them. This is also the place where they found the evidence of the highest temperatures and a lunch pail with tracings of soda that they concluded were caused by the exploding powder.[5] After first spending considerable amounts of time attempting to discount the contribution run away coal cars had on the explosion, Dr. Payne testified that the origin was, "In the second crosscut between rooms 21 and 22 in the second right entry of the first south in mine No. 8," because it was here that they had found the greatest evidence of heat and flame. Their theory was that the cans of powder were exploded by a boy who had brought the supplies to the cutting machine operator and then taken some of the powder to set it off as a prank to frighten the mine machine operator:

All boys that work in the mines where powder is used will testify to the fact that they are always inclined to steal a little powder. They have various ways of playing with it; and others want it to play a trick on the machine man by making what we called a spit-devil—that is dampening it and squeezing it up in a ball, lighting it and then running away from it: It would be my opinion that this powder was ignited by that boy.[6]

Payne was asked whether he was saying that the explosion was caused by a joke: "I didn't say that," he answered. "I say if the boy was the cause of it, the possibility is that he was trying to play a joke on the machine man. The powder didn't ignite itself."

The Consolidation/Fairmont company teams finding was in conflict with the finding of every other investigative team not only as to the location of the explosion's origin, but to the sheer speculative nature of laying the blame on the shoulders of a boy.

Notwithstanding Dr. Payne's speculation, two principle theories emerged as to the proximate cause of the explosions. The first was that the string of nineteen or so runaway coal mine cars carrying nearly thirty tons of coal at the top of the tipple broke away and rocketed back down the inclined track into the mouth of No. 6, wrecking violently. At the bottom of the portal, the cars tore down the electric power lines and caused sparks that ignited methane gas or coal dust, causing the resulting explosions. Several experts would adopt this theory and several would argue against it. During his testimony, company Superintendent Gaskill was asked by Chief Inspector Paul if he noticed any signs of short-circuiting or electrical malfunction caused by the runaway train when he lead the first rescue team to the bottom of No. 6 portal. He said he noticed none.

The second theory was that one or more blown out or overloaded shots improperly loaded and set off by immigrant miners exploded causing the ignition of gas or coal dust in a room of the No. 8 mine, setting off explosions throughout the two mines. Each of these theories had implications for the mine company, the West Virginia Department of Mines, and the miners themselves. The potential liability of the Consolidation Coal and Fairmont Coal companies was significantly higher if the trip of cars caused the explosions rather than the miners, both legally and from a public relations standpoint.

Also, the West Virginia Department of Mines and the mines' inspector with on-ground responsibility, R. S. LaRue, were far more culpable if the cause was other than a blown-out shot. If accumulated dust caused the explosion, the company and state would be implicated, especially in light of the fact that the recent inspections by LaRue gave the mine a clean bill of health. No inspector could be blamed if an unforeseen event such as a foreign miner disregarded known safety rules and improperly loaded and discharged a shot.

The teams from Ohio, Pennsylvania, and West Virginia conducted investigations and developed reports. The federal effort under the direction of the Technological Branch of the United States Geological Survey included both Hall and Holmes. Investigations were also conducted for the governments of Germany, France, and Belgium. Finally, the company itself conducted an investigation.

The most insightful investigation was conducted by the Ohio inspectors. The Ohio investigation team was headed by George Harrison, a British born and trained mining engineer who had started working in the mines of England at the age of eight. Their team arrived Wednesday, December 11, and had made a thorough examination of both mines. Their report was critical of the mining practices and engineering procedures followed by the company.

Harrison's testimony at the January 1908 inquest in Marion County conceded that both mines were equipped with the most modern fans and machinery, but was sharply critical of the application of mining practices:

In a number of instances we noted that working places—both rooms and headings—especially in No. 8 mine, were driven a long distance beyond what is known as the 80-foot limit between the breakthrough.

According to Harrison, the driving of the rooms and heading beyond the 80-foot limit increased the danger of explosions and falls because of inadequate ventilation and increased gas liberation and the amount of unsupported roof exposed.

It is reasonable to assume that in the quiet of the mines—especially if the barometer was low and weather conditions favorable—gas would generate and ascend to the highest and most favorable points and would remain there until disturbed by the action of moving bodes and diluted by a mixture of common air.

The Ohio team discounted the possibility that the explosion was caused by the runaway train, arguing that there was no evidence of explosive forces at the No. 6 slope and that the bodies of three miners at the bottom fall-shanty close to the wreck site bore no marks of violence. They did not, however, dismiss the importance the train wreck had on the explosion in general:

If the runaway trip occurred just previous to the explosion, which seems to be the general statement of those present, then we have no hesitation in saying that it may have played an important part in making the explosion possible.

It can be well imagined how fifteen loaded cars weighing four or five tons each, running uncontrolled 1,200 feet down an eight percent grade into a mine opening which was the inlet of air, would cause such an extremely abnormal force as to raise the dust in the air and dislodge the latent gasses in the most remote parts of the old workings in all sections of the mine, and drive these elements of danger on the open lamps of the miners in their working places.

Then the report suggested that the gradual rise of the mines as they followed the coal seam from No. 6 to No. 8, some 50 feet, would also cause gases to migrate in the direction of No. 8. They concluded that the explosions occurred in No. 8.

But more damning was their finding evidence of "great want of skill or practical experience in the locating and drilling of holes, as well as the want of judgment in the use, and in many instances the very excessive use, of blasting powder."[7] In two places they found evidence that an explosion had occurred that could have been the originating explosion.

On the No. 1 right air course to main west heading, they found that a seven-foot cut was made in the coal and one blast had been fired, the hole, having been drilled very high and pointed upward. The blast blew off only a portion of the coal, leaving two feet of the hole and failing to break down the coal that it was intended to remove. The coal that had been freed was thrown back 25 to 30 feet; the coal was charred and there was much dust around the face of the heading, as if an explosion had taken place.

There were no signs of any miners being in place after the explosion. The miners' tools were lying in the breakthrough leading to the parallel heading about twenty-five feet back—just as if they had been placed there by persons for safety while firing the blast. The heavy iron tracks just outside the room entrance "were twisted and torn and thrown outward for twelve or fourteen feet and the body of a miner, who had evidently been in the breakthrough waiting for the blast, was scattered around the breakthrough" to the parallel entry and outside of the breakthrough in a dozen or more pieces. The miner's body was so dispersed that it had been overlooked by the exploring party one week earlier.

A second possible explosion origin point occurred in the No. 31 of second right off first south heading.

The hole was drilled towards and bearing on the left rib of the room. The front of the coal was blown off, but three feet, nine inches of the hole remained.[8]

Again the coal liberated by the blast was charred and showed signs of an explosion; nearby, a five-ton gathering motor and several cans were thrown across the track or piled up by the explosive force. But equally damning was their finding that blown-out shots were a common occurrence and "that life and property are always in danger under such conditions and circumstances."[9]

Harrison's report then gave the timeless comment about virtually all mine explosions:

There will no doubt be many theories as to the cause of the explosion—all more or less sustained by facts—but no one is left to tell the tale or give any reliable fact information as to the condition of the mines or defects of the ventilation in the inner working places, or the dangers that existed on the morning of the explosion resulting from roof falls, or other causes during the previous day when all work in the mine was suspended. It is more than doubtful if ever the real or original cause will be known.

Then he continued:

It is our opinion that the explosion may have occurred in either mine, and could have been caused by a miner's lamp coming in contact with gas, or by a blown out shot, raising and igniting the gas, but the effect of the greater force is most visible at the heading of the leading heading on the No. 8 side.

Then, he turned to the issue of connecting mines:

At a point near the connection of the two mines there has been a whirlwind of force and destruction, and a division of the force is evident—going both towards No. 6 and No. 8 territory—increasing in volume by a series of new explosions. . . .

In one of his most telling comments, Harrison, considered one of the nation's leading safety experts, spoke to the overall shortcomings at Monongah:

What ever may be the conclusions of theorists and experts, suffice it to say that from a practical standpoint, at the time of the explosion, both in West Virginia and in other states or wherever they occur, they cannot occur except where there is an accumulation of those destructive elements sufficient to cause such appalling results and a favorable opportunity for setting them in motion.

The report continues that in older times it was thought that such casualties were the result of vengeance from a supreme power and that they were unavoidable. But the Ohio team concluded that, in general, some mine companies throughout the country lacked the necessary concerns for the miner's safety.

It is impossible for such things to occur if a proper knowledge of the accumulating dangers is possessed by those in authority looking after the inside of the mines and they exercise the necessary diligence to steer clear of that point of danger, if the necessary facilities are provided for doing so. We feel that the sacrifice of over six hundred lives by mine explosions in Pennsylvania, West Virginia and Alabama during the present month ought to stir the loyal sensibilities and teach a never-to-be forgotten lesson to those connected with mines, prompting every possible precaution against such calamities.

Taking aim at the Monongah mine:

We are not disposed to criticisms, and particularly not in a friendly way, but we are not clear as to the advantage to be derived from the system of driving seven parallel main headings. It is clear, however, from what we have all seen that in the Monongah case they acted as storage chambers for mine dust which we consider one of the greatest sources of danger at those mines.

And referring to the fact that No. 6 and No. 8 were connected, they concluded,

The great evil of connecting mining properties is also forcibly presented in this case by doubling the number of the dead. In the annual report issued by the department in 1904, we wrote a rather strong comment against the dangers and evils incident to the connecting of mining properties. . . .

The practice of connecting mines had been prohibited in a number of states including Ohio and Pennsylvania, but the mining industry, including the Consolidation and Fairmont Coal Companies, held such sway in West Virginia legislation that the practice was common in West Virginia mines. The Harrison report continued:

We fear that if there is not some checks in this direction and more care exercised about the connection of mining properties, that the time is not far distant when the subject will be presented to the people in such a serious aspect that a prohibitory law will be enacted.

Finally, the Ohio inspectors expressed what was becoming a commonly accepted response to the overwhelming nature of the problems faced by various states:

Close observation and striking recent events justify the further prediction that if the general conditions of the operating mines in the various states is not soon covered by adequate Federal laws that the sacrifice of human life in the mines has merely just begun.[10]

Finally, Andrew Roy, an Ohio geologist and mine safety authority wrote a damning indictment of West Virginia mines:

More men are killed by explosions in the State of West Virginia then in any state in the Union, or in any country in the world. . . . where the men have no organization, the mine-owners pay little or no attention to the law, generally speaking.[11]

On December 22, 1907, M. Jacques Caffanel, Ingininer au Corps des mines Directuer de la statin d'Essals de Lievin heading the French investigation delegation, arrived in Fairmont and registered at the Manley Hotel. The next day, escorted by company officials Haas and Smyth, the team visited the No. 6 and No. 8 mines.

In a statement to the press, Caffanel referred to the recent explosion in France. Earlier in 1906, on March 10, in the northern coalfields of France, the Couriers mine exploded, killing 1,100 miners, making it the largest coal mine disaster in world history up to that point in time.

The Couriers horror as you know was somewhat similar to that of Monongah. I made a thorough investigation of the French mine and my knowledge gained there will be a help to me here.

The phase that impressed me the most was the terrific heat caused by the explosion. Why? We found conditions today which convince me without a doubt that the temperature was many times greater than that which resulted in the Couriers horror, in my country. . . . In one place in particular, in mine No. 8 today, we encountered evidence of higher temperatures than I even believed could be caused by an explosion.[12]

Caffanel stated that it was his opinion that coal dust was the cause of the Monongah disaster. In reaching contrary conclusions regarding the proximate cause, the German and Belgium inquiry reports concluded that the runaway cars were the initial cause of the explosions.

The West Virginia Department of Mines report was the most exhaustive of any of the analyses. It included separate sections written by each of the state inspectors and a lengthy discussion by the director in which he was joined by the majority of the inspectors. The majority concluded that the explosion originated at the face of the third left entry off of second north in No. 8 mine.

They also attributed the explosion to large quantities of dust, which was being created by use of electric cutting machines, and "this being conveyed to all conceivable parts of the mine by a high velocity of air and under these conditions we do think this explosion was caused from coal dust."[13] Inspector R. S. LaRue's findings were contrary to the majority finding. LaRue had inspected the mines before the explosions and held that the explosions were the result of the runaway trip and the tearing down of the electrical wiring in the No. 6 portal. Inspection teams from other states and countries discounted LaRue's theory because of the appearance of coked coal and the intensity of the fire in the No. 8 mine and the absence of evidence of fire in the No. 6 portal and entry. One West Virginia inspector, Frank E. Parsons, was among the West Virginia inspectors siding with the company and suggesting that it began on the third left butt entry off of the second north in No. 8 in cross cuts separating room numbers 13 and 14.[14]

In 1909, Frank Haas, chief chemist and assistant general manager, produced the official company report for the disaster,[15] which inexplicably became the only report in the official United States Bureau of Mines files in Washington, DC, and the only report in the official file of the West Virginia Department of Mines in Charleston, West Virginia. That report no longer blames a boy for the accident, but instead cites a blown-out shot as the cause of the disaster.[16]

MONONGAH MINE RELIEF
FUND IN AID OF SUFFERERS FROM THE
MONONGAH MINE EXPLOSION

There seems to be as much danger that the public will overdo in relief work as that it will not do enough and I verily believe that quite as much harm is done through the former as through the latter.

—John D. Rockefeller, Jr.

to Mabel T. Boardman, American Red Cross President

February 7, 1908

IN THE company blacksmith shop, large pots of soup were simmering, along with gigantic pots of coffee. The initial rescue support efforts were spontaneous: Those with something to contribute did so. Neighbors brought food and clothing. Ethnic suspicions and distrust evaporated, each person helping however they could. The parish priests consoled the grieving and hysterical widows, and helped with locating children and making certain that the widows and orphans had someone to look after them. Father D'Andrea's survey was in part an attempt to see that each family was looked after.

On the day of the accident, as news of the explosion and its impact spread, neighbors of the victims' families began to offer assistance. Three separate committees were hastily organized within the first days of the explosion in Monongah. Mayor W. H. Moore, along with members of the town council, organized a committee of Monongah citizens, called the Monongah Relief Committee.

In Fairmont, committees sprang up at various churches, then these groups organized themselves into two relief groups: the Central Relief Committee of Fairmont, headed by Fairmont Mayor W. E. Arnett, and the Union Relief Committee, made up of women from the churches of Fairmont and Monongah. The Central Committee "was comprised of prominent citizens of both towns, Monongah and Fairmont, and has shown both zeal and sound common sense in dealing with the situation it had to face."[1] Each committee worked to deliver food and clothing to the wives and families of the miners.

On Sunday, December 8, 1907, the Central Committee of the American National Red Cross meeting in Washington sent out an appeal on behalf of the Monongah victims to every branch in the United States. It was an unprecedented appeal following an industrial disaster. The American Red Cross authorized each of its branches to receive and forward contributions for the families of the dead miners of Monongah.[2]

On Wednesday, December 11, Frank M. Wilmot, Manager of the Carnegie Hero Fund Committee of Pittsburgh, arrived in Fairmont.[3] Three years earlier on January 25, 1904, Andrew Carnegie had watched as a coalmine disaster in the Allegheny Coal Company mine in Harwick, Pennsylvania, just south of Pittsburgh, claimed 181 lives. That day, a massive explosion destroyed the Harwick Mine. According to news accounts, the mine's management was either in the mine at the time of the explosion or too stunned to react. Selwyn M. Taylor, 42, a mining engineer from Pittsburgh who happened to be nearby, organized rescue efforts that same afternoon. Selwyn and others found 17-year-old Adolph Gynia severely burned at the shaft bottom and brought him to safety. Selwyn advanced further into the mine only to be overcome by afterdamp; he was brought out, but died the next day.

A second man, Daniel A. Lyle, a coal miner working in a nearby mine, responded to an appeal for rescue workers. Lyle, having worked at his own mine that afternoon and most of the night before, went into the mine in search of others. He was also overcome with afterdamp, leaving a widow and five children. Carnegie, having built a steel empire in Pittsburgh and himself a mine owner and operator, sent a donation of $40,000 to match the public's contributions for the widows and families of the 181 victims. But Carnegie was also moved by the acts of heroism of Taylor and Lyle who had "sacrificed their lives in an endeavor to save their fellow man."[4]

Shortly thereafter, Carnegie established the Carnegie Hero Fund Commission and donated $5 million dollars to recognize "civilization heroes" and to provide assistance for "those disabled and the dependents of those killed helping others."

What had so moved Carnegie was not the explosion and miner's deaths, but the deaths of Selwyn M. Taylor and Daniel A. Lyle. The wives and families of Taylor and Lyle were left entirely destitute; no corporate liability would attach because these would-be rescuers were Good Samaritans with no employment relationship. In addition, these rescuers could not be covered by Pennsylvania Workman's Compensation statute both because no such statute existed and because it wouldn't have covered volunteer rescuers in any case. To direct the fund, Carnegie appointed a board of industrialists and social activists who were responsible for weighing application for the awards, which consisted of a gold coin and a monetary grant.

But the Harwick experience had taught Carnegie and the Commission staff the inadequacy of local efforts in the face of such overwhelming demands following a major accident. After Monongah, Wilmot immediately recognized the overwhelming long-term need facing the Monongah survivors and the temporary nature of the local relief committees' efforts. He organized a meeting of the Central Relief Committee in Fairmont and the Monongah Relief Committee for the purpose of merging the two groups, expanding their membership and mission. Wilmot outlined an organizational structure that recognized the extent of problems facing the widows and families. It also was apparent the local committees reflected the conventional wisdom that responsible citizens would have to look after the poor downtrodden immigrants and the now-fatherless families.

No representatives of the Italian and Polish-Slavic communities, nor any representatives from the Catholic churches in Monongah and Fairmont, had been appointed to these initial committees. Bishop P. J. Donahue, who had arrived Sunday, had first raised the issue with some of his fellow clergymen of expanding the committee's membership. His suggestion, along with Wilmot's urgings, led to enlarging the committee structure, a change that corrected the lack of immigrant representation of the relief committees. The merged committee was to be called the Monongah Mine Relief Committee and its expanded membership included Governor W. M. O. Dawson, Bishop P. J. Donahue, Rev. Joseph Lekstrom, and Rev. Joseph D'Andrea, among others. From this expanded membership of twenty-four officers, an executive committee and a subscription committee were chosen. Wilmot, on behalf of The Carnegie Hero Fund, donated $35,000 to the newly organized committee. Wilmot also met with Watson and Fleming and other company officials to discuss their role in the relief efforts.

In a separate but related effort, Dr. Edward T. Devine of New York City had traveled by train to Monongah in the week following the disaster to assess the situation first hand. He was the editor of *Charities and the Commons* and General Secretary of the Charity Organization Society of the City of New York. Dr. Devine was a man with wide experience in the handling of relief efforts. Upon his arrival, he conferred with the local committees and stressed the necessity, and suggested a method, of collecting a correct list of the women and children and "their true condition."[5] Dr. Devine had also called his friend and associate, Miss Mabel T. Boardman, head of the national office of the American Red Cross, which led to the nationwide appeal.

Boardman suggested that Margaret F. Byington, a trained social worker, might be dispatched to assist with the relief efforts. Byington was an employee of the Red Cross, but at that time she was working on a study of industrial deaths and accidents in the mines and steel mills of Pittsburgh and Allegheny County in Pennsylvania.[6] The study was financed by the Russell Sage Foundation, in cooperation with the Charity and the Commons and would later produce the Allegheny County Calendar of Industrial Death, a timely seminal publication that helped push the issue of mining and industrial workplace deaths to the front pages of the country. Through Devine's and Boardman's efforts, Byington was loaned temporarily to the relief committee.

The Red Cross's involvement in this disaster constituted a dramatic change of policy for that organization. It marked the first time that the Red Cross had provided assistance in a man-made disaster. Previously, the Red Cross participated only in the event of natural disasters, and the change constituted a break in the policy established by Clara Barton to avoid man-made industrial situations.

Margaret F. Byington was a graduate of Wellesley and Columbia University, where she received a masters degree in social work. Upon arrival in Monongah, Byington immediately embarked upon an intensive survey of the survivors, as per Dr. Devine's suggestions, and developed an extensive survey form, which the four local priests were asked to have each widow and family complete, despite every participants' exhaustion. The difficulty of undertaking an onerous survey, given the circumstances, was compounded by language barriers and by the illiteracy of most of the widows. However, according to Devine's and Byington's plan, these forms, once completed, would help determine the various needs of each family and what would be best for them.

The forms included questions about the victim's nationality, family, property, ownership, savings, plans of the widow, insurance, and condition of clothing. In addition, the interviewer was to note appearance, intelligence, cleanliness, indications of thrift and health, as well as the command of English. Progress was slow as significant numbers of widows spoke no English, and the committees interviewers were not conversant in the multitude of languages spoken. Priests were then called upon to commit long hours to helping fill out forms.

The Committee was ostensibly independent of the Fairmont Coal Company and its parent, Consolidation Coal Company. In fact, initially, the company was hesitant about supporting the committee's efforts, fearing a public relationship backlash. However, following meetings with Wilmot and others, they soon became supportive and assigned "various employees in the offices of the Fairmont Coal Company and others to work nights, Sundays and other extra time helping the Subscription Committee to address envelopes and in sending out its appeals."[7] Watson and Fleming had been cautious about endorsing the notion of a public appeal for funds and were concerned about what effect such an appeal would have politically, and particularly what effect the company's endorsement of such an appeal would have on the general public. In his meeting with them, Wilmot apparently convinced them that such response would be well received.[8] In fact, later the relationship between the company and the committee became quite close when officials of the mine served as members of the committee itself.

Robert T. Cunningham, the Fairmont Coal Company Auditor who had conducted the survey of homes, was assigned to serve on the Relief Committee, and in this capacity, was the liaison from the company to the committee. He provided information between the company officials and committee members and staff; his role was instrumental in seeing to it that the interest of the company and its principals were looked after. This was particularly significant with respect to the issue of the number of victims, an issue in which Cunningham was intimately involved. Margaret Byington, in early 1908, wrote to Cunningham, "I have been comparing the two lists and find that they agree except in the following instances. . ." Then after describing where the families of two of the victims were living she continued,

I have cards started for Paul Goff, John Goff and Frank Kroger (three other victims which were on the Relief Committee list, but not on the official company list), none of whom are given in your lists. Are these mistakes and shall I destroy them? I trust this will bring our troubles with these names to an end.[9]

The Goff brothers and Kreger had only started working in the mine on December 4, two days before the blast. They were kept on the list, but Byington's reliance on Cunningham and her offer to destroy the files indicates the willingness of the committee and its staff to support the company's interests.

Company officials—notably President Watson—would later exercise influence over some of the committee decisions. Ultimately, they would use the committee for their own purposes and against the victims' own interests. Watson and Fleming both came to view the Relief Committee as supportive staff to be used for their own ends.

Though Cunningham kept a close watch on the Relief Committee activities, Watson received a list of all contributions and contributors on a weekly basis. Other company officials also were active in the background. F. W. Wiltshire, the head of the Fairmont Coal Company's New York City office, requested a refund for the "Kollock subscription" because he had contributed twice, sending $15 on two occasions. But the company's involvement was to be kept secret. Wiltshire directed Cunningham to have Sands, the committee treasurer, write a letter to Kollock with a refund. Cunningham replied, ". . . will have to make a refund in Kollock's name as do not want Coal Company's name to appear in the matter."[10]

The task of assisting 252 widows and 1,000 fatherless children left without any means of support was monumental. The Committee initially estimated that $250,000.00 would be needed to provide any basic permanent form of relief.[11] Immediately, an appeal letter was prepared, setting forth the scope of the disaster and the extent of relief needed. On December 14, just seven days after the disaster occurred, the appeal was telegraphed throughout the entire country and released to the assembled media. The Relief Committee members were enlisted to send letters to newspapers throughout the country. Bishop P. J. Donahue wrote the following appeal:

My dear Sir:

I need not rehearse to your readers the details of the appalling calamity at Monongah. They have been set forth in all their sad features in your esteemed journal. Most of the unfortunate dead have now been transferred from the cavernous mines to quiet graves. But what of the three hundred widows and the more than one thousand fatherless children? Their immediate wants are generously provided for, but what of the next pay day and all the future pay days, when the grimy bread winner shall no longer return with his hard earnings in his pocket to fill with love and sunshine his humble home?

It is to help these helpless ones far away from their native land and not even knowing how to use our language in appeal, that I make this plea. They can only stretch forth empty hands and with streaming eyes crave shelter and bread.

As a member of the Relief Committee I respectfully request that you invite the contributions of the charitably disposed. If some local committee would kindly take this matter up, I feel confident that many would give a little to those suddenly bereft of love and bread and even hope save in the generosity of others. In some way homes and shelter must be found for the women and the little ones, even if compelled to build another institution.

Very respectfully,

(Signature Affixed)

Bishop of Wheeling

#14 13th Street

Wheeling, W.Va.

December 14, 1907[12]

Coming as it did just days before Christmas, the appeal was widely publicized. Then on December 27, 1907, a second appeal was published simultaneously in 2,000 newspapers throughout the nation, frequently accompanied by editorials encouraging support of the victims.

Additional appeal letters were mailed to specialized groups and individuals, to lists of churches lodges and breweries, to secret societies and wealthy industrialists. In all, some 80,000 letters were sent out at a cost of $2,810.89. Consolidation Coal and Fairmont Coal Company officials were deeply involved behind the scenes in these solicitations. Company officials sent telegrams and letters to friends and business acquaintances across the country and the largest twenty-five cities nationwide. Requests were made for copies of telephone books in order that they could be used to develop mailing lists for the Relief Committee. Telephone books were chosen rather than city index books because the latter books would contain too many names of people that might be able to give or might protest. Lee Malone also intervened with company suppliers and encouraged contributions. Malone wired A. T. Watson, the company purchasing agent in Baltimore and a relative of Clarence Watson, directing him to ask the Remington Typewriting Company whether they would donate the use of three typewriters for ninety days and suggesting that the coal company would guarantee their safety. Watson made the arrangements.

The volume of response and the amount of contributions was unparalleled. Locally, Bishop P. J. Donahue, on behalf of the Wheeling Diocese, gave $5,337.40, and Father A. Bouthlou, pastor of St. Peters Church in Fairmont, gave $192.00. The Hungarian government, which later became disenchanted with the committee and filed a formal complaint against it with the State Department concerning the funds distribution, gave $1,610.00.

The United Mine Workers of America, which had been so thoroughly defeated in its organizing efforts at these very mines a few years earlier, gave $1,000.00. The president and vice president of the United States, Theodore Roosevelt and William Howard Taft, and the secretary of interior, Gifford Pinchot, each donated $100, $50, and $25, respectively.

The responses from within West Virginia amounted to $43,160.19. Miners in nearby mines contributed most of that sum. Across the country, benefit concerts were held. In Baltimore $50.00 was raised at the Academy of Music benefit; at the Medinah Temple in Chicago, a concert raised $204.60; and in Fairmont, a benefit was held at the Grand Opera House and $76.88 raised.

Donations came in all amounts: Adolph Coors of Denver sent $25.00; E. E. Deems and M. M. Deems from Baltimore each sent $.10; and from Independence, Missouri, the Amalgamated Association of Iron and Steel Workers of Kansas City Bolt and Nut Company sent $41.50. Campaigns were started in Chicago and New York City to raise $5,000.00 for the families. As news of the accident and especially its magnitude spread, national organizations sent representatives to assist the local efforts on the ground. School children collected donations in Winchester, Virginia: one group sold a railroad car of apples and donated $302.50. In Hampton, Virginia, the First Baptist Church Colored donated $400; and in Newport, Vermont, the

Baptist Church and a Congregational Union meeting donated $9.50. Matt Ulrich from the Deepwater Saloon in Galveston, Texas, sent $1.00. All told, Galveston citizens who had recently suffered in the terrible storm earlier in the year gave $127.00. Local unions were prominent among the donors. The Bricklayers International Local of Uniontown, Pennsylvania, gave $250.00. Also in Uniontown, the Lyric Theater held a benefit performance and donated the $42.80 in proceeds. The German Baptist Church of America General Missionary Society collected $18.81. Miss Susie Uban and the Sunday school class of Andover, Ohio sent in $7.00, and the Sears and Roebuck Company in Chicago gave $250.00

In Pittsburgh, the Post Dispatch newspaper had started a separate relief fund on the day after the disaster that raised $1,135.27. Each donation was meticulously recorded, including $.25 from Florence Hopkins of Salem, Ohio. A Charity Day held by the women of Sandusky, Ohio, raised $556.52.

From Paris, Frances Pol and Taffanel Dunaime sent $50.00. The American Colony in Dresden, Germany, raised $104.70. The Grand Lodge of Elks and the Grand Order of Eagles each contributed $1,000.00. In Fairmont, $29,859.98 was raised; in Minneapolis, St. Paul, over $2,000 was collected. Contributions from New York City totaled $2,799.00, which included $100 from the Borden's Condensed Milk Company, $5.00 from Victor Herbert, $2.50 from Margaret Turnbill, and $100.00 from Alfred G. Vanderbilt. The community of Pittsburgh raised $13,272.00, and nearly $1,000 was received from individuals in Chicago. Mount St. Joseph College in Maryland gave $2.00. The Fairmont Coal Company gave $17,000.00, and the Monongah Company gave $2,500.

The disaster did not have a significant negative impact on the Consolidation Coal Company and Fairmont Coal Company's corporate profits. On January 31, 1908, the Consolidation Coal Company Board of Directors met in Baltimore and declared the Regular Quarterly Dividend of one and one-half percent, and an extra dividend of two percent, payable January 31, 1908, to the stockholders of record, January 23, 1908.[13]

In addition to money donations, goods and provisions poured into Fairmont and Monongah by train. H. B. Weisharpel Co. of Baltimore sent ten cases of macaroni. The Dewey Brothers Company of Blanchester, Ohio, sent one barrel of Dewey's best flour. Capitol City Dairy Company of Columbus, Ohio, sent twenty-seven cases of butterine. Individuals and companies from across the country sent cases and barrels of children's and infant's clothing, shoes, and toys.

Surviving miners from the Monongah mines gave $250.15, and the tools of the miners who had died in the disaster were sold and the $79.60 donated to the relief fund.

The Muskingum Coffin Company of Zanesville, Ohio, that was working overtime to supply some of the coffins, donated $50.00. From Louisville, Kentucky, children of various Sunday schools in the Crescent Hills area of the city collected and sent $18.02.

Churches, fraternal orders, newspapers, brewery associations, and banks were also prominent among the givers. Most were individuals who gave small donations. By the middle of February, over $140,000 had been received.[14]

Now the task became how to develop a fair system of distribution. Byington, the professional social worker using the survey forms of the victims, made an effort to develop an equitable distribution system. As she would write, "The task proved a lengthy but interesting one."[15]

Relying heavily on the experience of the Carnegie Fund at the Harwick disaster, the committee struggled with issues such as whether widows who remarried before the distribution should be treated the same as those who remained single. Father Arsenius Boutlou, the Pastor of St. Peter's Church in Fairmont and a Relief Committee member, successfully argued that those who remarried should receive equal payment. One significant issue was whether payment should be made to parents and families in the old country and on what basis. The committee's conclusion was that these parents and brothers and sisters would be included if dependency on the miner at the time of the disaster was proven—in short, if the miner had sent or been sending support money prior to the explosion.

Almost from the start, Byington's efforts created tension and animosity among the victims, families, and friends. Conflict had begun shortly after her arrival, and it centered on the stress between the need for immediate relief, which was a matter of urgency for most families and their priests, and the need for order that a more structured response would maintain. Byington wrote to Mabel T. Boardman of the American Red Cross National Headquarters in Washington:

Father D'Andrea . . . accompanied me to all the Italian families and friendly, though because of his poor English, our discussion of the situation was rather limited. Father Lekstrom, the Slavic priest, disappeared for nearly a week, without giving the committee an accurate list of the names of his people which resulted in some difficulties about giving out the money. I saw Father Lekstrom soon after my arrival and he seemed cordial and friendly. I presume that the difficulty has arisen because this priest felt that the entire responsibility for their people should be left with them, and that the money should pass through their hands. It may be that this would have been wiser for the present. Also, bureaucratic failures add to the ill feelings.[16]

On January 18, 1908, Miss Boardman, as Red Cross president, wrote to Bishop Donahue. As the letter in the American Red Cross Archives shows, she was explaining that because many of the victims were members of the Catholic church, "it only seems right to let you know" of the Red Cross's efforts and the involvement of Byington. Bishop Donahue, who along with the local clergy had been in Monongah burying the dead and ministering to the families and had actively served on the committee since shortly after the disaster, appears to have been a bit taken aback.

Bishop Patrick J. Donahue was born in Little Malvern, England, of Irish parents, and had studied at St. Gregory's College and the University of London. Following his immigration to the United States, he graduated from George Washington University Law School in Washington and practiced law for seven years before entering the priesthood. In 1893, he was appointed Bishop of Wheeling, and with his polished manners and distinctive style, had a commanding presence.[17] In a letter, Bishop Donahue replied to Miss Boardman:

I beg to acknowledge receipt of your favor of January 18th advising me that Miss Byington was at Monongah aiding in the relief work there as a representative of the Red Cross Society. This I knew from several attendances at the meetings of the General Relief Committee . . . but at the same time I thank you for the courtesy of your communication. It affords me gratification to write you that I shall be happy to do all I can myself and to direct the local pastors . . . I am using every effort to collect cash subscriptions also."[18]

As noted earlier, Bishop Donahue had made a substantial contribution to the Relief Committee on behalf of the Wheeling Diocese, giving $5,337.00, while the American Red Cross contributions amounted to only $3,462.11 when it withdrew from the campaign.

After much deliberation, the committee settled on what it hoped was a fair distribution system. Distribution was on a pro rated basis without regard to financial status, place of residence, or nationality of the family. Again relying on the experiences of the Hardwick disaster, lump sum payments were made in most instances to the widows on behalf of them and the children. However, if the widows were not capable of handling the money in a lump sum in the opinion of the committee staff members, it would be parceled out over time. The 222 widows received $200.00 each, totaling $44,400. Widowed mothers received $200.00, for a total of $4,600.00, and each of the 483 children received $174.00 each. Dependent families of 62 unmarried men got $200.00 each, or $12,400. There were 339 total dependents in Europe, 233 in Italy, 73 in Austro-Hungary, and 29 in Russia.

As many of the widows and families lived in remote sections of Italy, Russia, Poland, Turkey, and Austro-Hungary, considerable efforts would be necessary to locate the relatives. A subcommittee dealing exclusively with the relatives was established and set upon its task of dealing with questions of foreign survivors of the miners who worked.

This subcommittee devoted its energies almost entirely to gathering the information and obtaining the necessary proofs of the dependents living in foreign countries. This proved difficult because so many of the victims were unknown by the survivors in Monongah, and in a great many cases, the men were using names that were given to them by company clerks who could not or did not take the time to determine the correct spelling and pronunciation or their original home address. Since payment for work in the mines at the time was in cash or scrip, there was little in the way of a paper trail.

The committee, at the urging of the priests, began distributing partial payments just after the end of the year:

By the first of January, the food sent in was exhausted, and families had since been receiving a weekly cash allowance of $2.00 for each widow and $.50 for each child under 16 years. This amount was to be deducted from their share of the final distribution.[19]

In addition to the efforts of the Monongah Mine Relief Committee, an independent group called the Ladies Association continued to work with women who were sick and pregnant. Some seventy of the widows were pregnant at the moment of the disaster. But Byington also determined that her professional services would be helpful with some of the families:

In the process of gathering information, it became evident to your representatives (Mr. B) that there were a number of families needing advice as to their plans or encouragement in securing work, and occasionally one where it would seem wise to break up the family owing to intemperance or other moral defects.[20]

Such defects were addressed by Ms. Byington in conjunction with "some of the ladies who had been most active in the relief work." Byington, with the blindness that self righteous zeal brings to some, next observed that the need here would be lengthy and that "there is no organization in existence to meet such needs as would be . . . in a large community." For this New York City professional, the rural mountains of West Virginia offered greater challenges than the San Francisco earthquake. Charitable efforts of the Catholic churches, with whom the victims were so clearly tied, were not worth her mentioning. She did, however, see fit to recognize that the local committee members, including the governor, priest, bishop, mayor, and others could learn.

Throughout, the local committee showed itself most willing to accept the assistance and suggestions of outsiders to secure the best possible solution. The locals, it appeared, could learn at the hands of a professional like Miss Byington, and Byington in fact acknowledged the controversy surrounding her role. "Doubts arose as to the wisdom of this. . ."[21]

Byington and the other 'professionals' had serious concerns about the objectivity and neutrality of the Catholic Church representatives. The essential conflict was that while Ms. Byington and the Red Cross searched for an equitable formula to be used to distribute the money, the victims had immediate needs, and the Catholic priests were being called on to meet these immediate needs. Paul U. Kellogg, a colleague of Dr. Devine, was in Monongah preparing the long article for his organization, Charity and the Commons. Kellogg was also the director of the Russell Sage Foundation's Pittsburgh Survey, the organization from which Byington had been detailed, making him in effect Byington's boss. He was concerned that the immigrants' priests were overstepping their bounds when acting as representatives and attorneys for the survivors.

This role, Kellogg wrote Donahue, would disqualify the priests "to judge whether or not a possible recipient actually falls within the scope of the relief fund." Donahue disagreed with Kellogg and with the entire process of surveying the victims in order to find out what their needs were.

I confess that I am at a loss to understand where all the difficulty lies in processing a correct list of the relatives and dependents of the mine disaster. If they were given to understand that no notice would be taken of them unless they came forward and proved their claims upon the fund, all concerned would soon display the necessary audacity.[22]

The company involvement with the Relief Committee increased over time. The Masonic Lodge, which had donated the use of an office for the committee, was at that time under the presidency of Lee Malone, and Clarence Watson, company president, was soon directly involved in committee affairs. Indeed, the company accountant, R. T. Cunningham, joined the Monongah Mine Relief Committee while continuing to be connected with the Fairmont Coal Company and J. E. Sands, one of the initial investors in the Camden undertaking was treasurer. On his private telegram line, Watson wired Cunningham concerning an appeal letter of March 1908:

Have heard of some letters sent out by Relief Committee think it is too late to send out appeals at this time and they are creating very unfavorable impressions. Unless Committee has good reason, please see if they will not withhold these circulars. . . .[23]

Howard Fleming, postmaster and a committee member, as well as a brother of A. B. Fleming replied to Watson, "about 100 letters to which . . . mailed to multimillionaires . . . so that now it is too late to recall them. There will be no further appeals or subscriptions."[24] That ended the sending out of appeal letters.

The committee was also used to dispel rumors and to cover up for earlier promises of help made by company officials and corporate family members. On the Sunday after the disaster, Bishop Donahue had suggested that an orphanage be established for some of the fatherless children. Mrs. C. W. Watson, Clarence Watsons' wife and well-known socialite in New York City, was quoted in the New York papers a few days later as saying that an orphanage would be opened and might be financed by the company. The committee, as delicately as possible, as Mrs. Watson was quite active in working with the committee, directed Mrs. Watson away from this idea and her "public references to it." The committee also wrote letters dispelling the rumors that the company was taking full financial responsibility for the victims' families.[25] Records indicate only one instance in which a child was sent to the Home of the Good Shepherd in Wheeling, an orphanage operated by the Wheeling Diocese. Isabel Siletta, daughter of Antonio Siletta, was registered in the house on April 8, 1908, and the funds for her were put into a trust to be paid to the Home.

But if the outpouring of generosity was evident from persons of all economic levels, it became an issue with those who were wealthy, some of whom gave and some of whom chose not to give.

John D. Rockefeller, Jr., received an appeal letter from the Red Cross and he chose to respond, not once but three times. On December 27, 1907, Rockefeller wrote a reply to Boardman's letter, mentioning that he had received an appeal letter from the Monongah Mine Relief Committee and stating,

Since the Committee in charge of this work is local, and since, so far as I am able to ascertain, no committee has been organized in New York to co-operate with the local committee, nor has any public effort been made in New York to secure funds for the committee, we are at a loss to know what is needed in premises and how far the people of this country at large should be called to contribute to this fund.[26]

Of course what he failed to mention was that he personally and his company, Standard Oil, had been financially interested in the Monongah mines since they opened. As one of the nine founding principles, along with Senator Camden, he was one of the original Monongah Coal & Coke Co. shareholders. Moreover, Standard Oil, through the subscriptions in 1880, was the third largest stock subscriber. In addition, A. B. Fleming, the company lawyer, was on retainer for the Standard Oil Company in West Virginia. Monongah Coal & Coke Co. was leased to Consolidation Coal Co. and the Fairmont Coal Company. Thus, Rockefeller through Camden had an interest in the now merged Consolidation Coal Company and Fairmont Coal Company at the time of the explosion. In fact, several years after the explosion, in 1922, Rockefeller bought controlling interest in the Consolidation Coal Company. On January 29, 1908, Rockefeller wrote a second time, again declining to contribute and expressing opposition to the committee interest to help miners' families back in the native countries:

It is evident that more harm than good would be done by further contributions at the present to the sufferers from these two mining disasters [referring to Monongah and the Darr explosion of December 19, 1907]. It is fair to question as to how far the charitably inclined people in this country are under obligations to provide for the relatives in foreign countries of the miners who lost their lives. The obligation seems to me very remote.[27]

Miss Boardman wrote back to Mr. Rockefeller expressing her agreement.

Finally, on February 7, 1908, Rockefeller wrote a third time, this time arguing that the committee was overdoing the relief work:

There seems to be quite as much danger that the public will overdo in relief work as that it will not do enough, and I verily believe that quite as much harm is done through the former as through the latter.[28]

These immigrants, it seems, risked being pampered by the Relief Committee, and rumors had it that the committee had already reached its goal. The final records of the committee show no contribution from Rockefeller and none from the Standard Oil Company. Nor are any contributions shown from J. N. Camden personally, although his company, The Monongah Company, was receiving royalties from the No. 6 and No. 8 mines, and donated $2,500.00. Camden's donation was, in fact, made by the Fairmont Coal Company on his behalf for the Monongah Company. Senator Camden later made a $100 contribution to a fund raised in Parkersburg, then deducted the $100 from the amount he reimbursed the Fairmont Coal Company for the Monongah Company payment. In a letter on his behalf, the Monongah Mine Relief Committee was asked to refund to the Fairmont Coal Company the $100, so that the FCC would not see $100.00.[29]

The Red Cross also received correspondence from a fellow coal operator who thought that the Fairmont Coal Company ought to take care of their own responsibility:

According to the published ... of the Company, they are making a great deal of money over and above their fixed charges, and it does not seem to me that it is quite in order for the Red Cross to be called in to contribute when that Company should take care of its own people.[30]

In addition to the monies paid to the families by the Relief Committee, the Fairmont Coal Company as a final settlement paid each widow $150.00 and each child under age 16, $75.00. As no Workmen's Compensation law existed in West Virginia, and owing to the fact that the Marion County Grand Jury had exonerated it of all responsibility, the company was under no legal obligation to pay the survivors or their families anything. And indeed, it drew the line rather sharply at widows and children, parents, siblings, or other family members. Thus unmarried miner's families without children received nothing, and any voluntary payment was not a common practice in this era.

Some contributions were made with what appeared to be ulterior motives. The Rockdale Powder Co. of York, Pennsylvania, sent $25.00, but asked that a list of companies who were extensive users of explosive powder be provided. The committee, after consulting with the Consolidation Coal Company officials, supplied a list.[31] In the end, contributions and interest totaled $155,263.92, less than the goal of $250,000. It was believed that the lesser amount was collected because, after the Pennsylvania State Red Cross Society sent out its appeal letter, the current newspapers carried a statement that the Monongah Mine Relief Committee had reached its goal of $250,000. In any event, the Red Cross withdrew from the campaign after having raised only $3,462.11 for the Monongah disaster.[32]

Some miners had taken out insurance against just such a calamity, and indeed, on the morning of the explosion a life insurance salesman, following the common practice of the day, had entered the Monongah mines to sell insurance to the miners. He was killed in the explosion.

According to the Committee records, one hundred fifty victims had insurance. Some of the insured were identified as 'Americans' while the majority were 'foreigners'. The payments to the American miners was a modest $25.00 average because these policies contained a provision limiting the insurance company's liability considering that the miners "occupation is an especially hazardous one and . . . in the event of a general accident or catastrophe, the liability would be greatly limited."[33]

However, some of the newly minted immigrant miners had insurance purchased from numerous fraternal orders or benevolent organizations frequently related to the various ethnic groups. These organizations developed insurance schemes especially directed to insuring the head of the household. The Slavish Society, the German Beneficial Union, and the Ancient Order of United Workman had policies covering men who were killed at Monongah. These policies did not have the limiting clauses of the 'American' miners' policies and thus the liabilities were considerably higher. All told, these foreign policies carried a total of $60,000 liability.

In virtually all cases, these insurance companies would have had no liability if the deaths had been proven to be the result of the wrongful actions of the Fairmont Coal Company. The Marion County Grand Jury's complete exoneration of the Company meant that all such mitigation was lost, and those insurance carriers were fully liable.

Officials from foreign governments were recruited by the committee to assist in locating the victim's families in remote sections of their countries. Initially, these officials helped to locate and identify families of victims, as well as to provide translations for correspondents working with company officials. But as the full impact of the Marion County Grand Jury decisions became felt, these foreign governments were compelled to deal with the Monongah Mine Relief Committee.[34]

By virtue of the Jury's decision, the Consolidation Coal Company, the Fairmont Coal Company and the principles Watson, Fleming, and Camden, were effectively removed from the responsibilities for the widows and families since the employee was dead and therefore, they had no responsibility. All dealings with the victims and their families were taken over by the Monongah Mine Relief Committee, and the company encouraged this transfer of responsibility. The Fairmont Coal Company forwarded correspondence between European governments and the widows and children through to the committee, which caused the foreign counsels to become increasingly involved with the committee; the interaction was not always amiable.

The Relief Committee had engaged the New York law firm of Kneuth, Nached, and Kuhne (KNK), a firm with experience in banking matters, to track down the victims' families and relations in their home countries. KNK contracted with the committee, and charged a fee of one half percent of each check amount plus 75 cents per payment. For that amount, the firm would send the Monongah Mine Relief Committee check to the bank nearest the residence of the beneficiary, who was then required to establish his or her identity with the local bank. The local bank would then disburse the check—less fees and handling expenses. The law firm's fee became a concern to a point that the law firm wrote to the committee justifying their compensation:

Considering the clerical work which is connected with the execution of such payments, these conditions are very moderate. While our charge is minimal we have to pay our European friends quite a high commission.

What exasperated the foreign counsuls' officials was that much of the work of locating and contacting relatives was being done by themselves while the law firm was being paid for the service. More irritating was the fact that each recipient of a check was also required to sign a document supplied by the committee. That disclaimer read: "This amount, please understand, is a gratuity to which you have no legal right or claim, and you are indebted solely to the general public of the United States of America for the same. . ." The form went on to advise the recipient in what could only be viewed as moralistic arrogance.

The Committee is making this payment direct to you with the feeling that you are competent to take care of the same for benefit of yourself and fatherless children, and earnestly recommends that you deposit this money in a strong bank at interest, and that you use as little from month to month as you can get along with.[35]

When the checks, along with these instructions, were received, many recipients wrote the committee seeking clarification, and the committee in turn sent these letters to the Consulates for translation and reply.

In June, 1908, the Italian Consulate in Philadelphia set out its position with regard to the committee's procedure. Having argued earlier that the Consulate and the appropriate government offices would have been the appropriate offices to handle the monies, they were now being proved correct. Because the committee and their hired firm were unable to handle the investigations and the resulting correspondence, the Consulates were now being asked to handle the matter. In June the Consulate wrote a stinging letter to the committee criticizing the fact that they were being asked to make contacts and track down relatives while relief funds were being paid to a law firm to do the same thing.[36]

From the spring of 1908 through the next nine months, the committee met and authorized distributions until November, when they met and formally dissolved.

Ms. Byington, whose tenure lasted only a few weeks, had turned the work over to local staff and had returned to her previous endeavors. Frank P. Hill, who had acted as the committee's accountant on leave from the Citizens Dollar Savings Bank of Fairmont, handled the remainder of the correspondence and financial distribution, payments, and so on. The final distribution was made more than two years after the disaster. After extensive effort, eleven victims remained where neither family nor dependents could be identified.

In the end, Mrs. Mary Thala, widow of Jack and mother of five children, received $1,070.00. Mrs. Pearl Reed Wise, widow of Charles D. Wise, Camden's engineer, had two small children and received $543.00. Mrs. Caterina Veltri Bonasso, who has returned to S. Giovanni in Fioro, Italy, received $200.00 as the widow of Gionani Bonasso. Mrs. Maria G. D'Andrea, the widow of Victor whose brother-in-law was Father D'Andrea, had three children and received $722.00. On March 4, 1908, Maria D'Andrea gave birth to a baby girl who she named Victoria.[37]

Among the recipients, $1,244.00 went to Nina Willing, mother of six and widow of George. Mrs. Mary Urban, widow of Stanley, and her four children received $896.50. Peter Urban, because he survived, received nothing.

All four men who survived, because they had survived, received nothing. Of the four, only Orazio DePetris, who had returned to Italy received $200 because of the death of his son, Felice.

Mrs. Maria de Gaetano Abbate moved to Niagara Falls, New York—where her brother lived—with her four living children. Her payment was delayed and did not include any amount for the loss of her two sons. G. D. Caldara, the Italian Consulate, intervened and in the end she received $896.00.[38]

Among the survivors, Donato Dominico was injured in the explosion and unable to work; he was turned down for assistance by the Relief Committee since he had not been killed. In January, he went to H. C. DeShields, an attorney in Fairmont, for help. DeShields wrote Mr. Moore, the Mayor of Monongah, "the man Donato Domico was one of the miners who escaped death in the mines and he is injured and his wife is in need of shoes and necessities as well as himself. . . ." There is no record of what action Mayor Moore took.[39]

Anestis Stamboulis had missed the explosion because of illness. He went back into the mine, but left shortly thereafter when he moved to Jellico, Tennessee, and went to work in the recently opened Cross Mountain coal mine on December 9, 1911.

By this time, Stamboulis had changed his name to Sarbel. He was scheduled to work underground that December 9, but after the first group of miners had entered the mine, the second group was delayed because several rail cars were being brought into the mine.

At 7:20 an explosion ripped through the underground workings and 84 miners perished. Five miners survived by barricading themselves and were later rescued. Because of the delay, Sarbel had remained above ground and was spared.

He would later tell his children that he had cheated death twice, so he summarily quit the mines. He moved to Cincinnati, Ohio, raised seven children, and died from natural causes in Florida at the age of 80.

In addition to the victims of the initial explosion, three miners lost their lives in the rescue work, and their families were included in the distribution. One man, Joseph Newton, an African-American who was caught on the portal by the explosive force, received $100.00, which was mailed to his home in Gibson, North Carolina.

The committee's records identified 801 dependents from the disaster, 339 of who also were living in Europe, and 445 at Monongah. Seventeen African-American children were left fatherless. Of the 269 widows, 122 returned to their home countries, but most stayed in the United States, many making West Virginia their home for the rest of their days.

Catherine Davis's husband, G. L., died in the fearsome explosion, leaving his wife and eight children. For the next 29 years, until her death in 1936, Mrs. Davis carried a lump of coal four times a day from the mine to her home, a mile and one half, as a memorial to her husband.

After her death, a 300-ton mound was removed from her backyard, sold, and the proceeds donated to the Saint Barbara Nursing Home.[40]

Father Joseph D'Andrea continued at Our Lady of Pompeii Church until August 1914, when he left the Wheeling Diocese. Father Lekston remained at Saint Stanislaus parish until 1913 when he transferred to Springfield, Massachusetts.

Mary Urban, widow of Stanley and sister-in-law of Peter, and her four children received $820. But the committee, concerned that Mrs. Urban was not up to the task of handling the children's monies, placed the money in a trust, which they did in several instances.

But Mary Urban was not a woman to be trifled with. She and her husband had come from Czonolas near the town of Kolbuszowa, in the province of Galitzia, Austria, in what is now southwestern Poland. Mary was in her mid-thirties and a widowed mother of four children, two boys and two girls, all between the ages of 1 and 7 years. She was determined to gain control of the money and to see to it that it was placed in a bank with interest. She and her husband had money saved in a bank account and she began a spirited campaign to overcome the committee's decision.

First, she contacted Mr. Frank Hall, the committee auditor, who was steadfast in his refusal to overturn the decision. She then solicited assistance from Father Lekston, who sided with Mrs. Urban, but to no avail. Technically, under the committee rules, the only possible way to receive the lump sum was to convince the committee that she was taking her four children back to the old country, and when she made such an assertion, the committee demanded proof.

Not to be deterred, Mrs. Urban obtained from C. F. Zaruba & Co., Foreign Bankers and Ticket Agents of 320 Pike Street in Clarksburg a certification that she had purchased a steamship ticket for herself and her children. Finally, on January 5, 1909, the committee relented and gave Mrs. Urban a check for the balance of $620.00. Mrs. Urban remained in Monongah and raised her children in Monongah, as well as her grandchildren and great grandchildren who live in the community today.[41]

Mary Urban's typified the resilience and spirit of the immigrants and their families.

WHEELS OF JUSTICE

West Virginia corporate laws were so lenient that it became, to use the words of one commentator, the 'Mecca of Irresponsible Corporations.'

— "Trust and Industrial Corporations in the United States"

E. Von Halle, 1896

E. S. AMOS, the Marion County coroner, impaneled a jury in Monongah at 4:00 P.M. on Saturday, December 7, 1907, the day after the explosion. They were sworn in at the Monongah Mine offices and the inquisition officially began. Immediately, they walked across the river and went to the mine portals where they examined the mine cavities. Activity was still at a furious level as rescue workers and repair crews attempted to rebuild the ventilation systems. A short time later the jury adjourned, resuming on Monday with a viewing of the bodies as they were brought out of the mine. On Tuesday, they met and again adjourned until January 6 when they met in the main courtroom at the Marion County Court House in Fairmont.

The courthouse, completed in 1901 and restored in 2007, was an imposing four-story sandstone structure, one of the largest and most elaborate courthouses in West Virginia. The principal courtroom was the pride of the county, beautifully appointed with oak benches and chairs, capped by a stained-glass dome, windows, and a great gas chandelier. It could accommodate up to 300 spectators on the first floor and large balcony. Amos, the coroner and chairman of the jury, read out the instructions. The jury was charged with determining when, how, and by what means three identified miners—A. H. Morris, Charlie McCann, and John M. McGraw—and "about three hundred and fifty other persons came to their deaths."

The jury system, once considered the bedrock of guaranteed equal justice in the United States, was, during the first years of the twentieth century, showing signs of strain as an anti-immigrant bias swept the country. As a result of the changing population, especially with the influx of eastern and southern Europeans, fears of *mob politics* caused concern among the high-minded of society.

In recent years, such foreigners had been connected with the rise of labor unions and with the riots and strikes in the steel mills of nearby Pittsburgh and in the Pullman yards of Chicago. Criticized as being "frequently corruptible" in the cities, juries were seen to be "densely ignorant and stubbornly bigoted" against such immigrants.[1] In this instance, the jury in Marion County was picked in such a way that it contained neither immigrants nor any member of the affected group, nor persons whose interest would be sympathetic to miners.

The jurors were J. M. Jacobs, a member of the state legislature and secretary of the Board of Trade; W. E. Condnay, commissioner of the County Court; Festus Downs, former county commissioner; W. S. Hamilton, also a member of the Marion County Commission; George H. Richardson, formerly street commissioner of Fairmont; and A. S. Prichard. These men were associates of the Watson, Fleming, and Camden families. It could hardly be otherwise in a community the size of Fairmont, especially given the size and importance of the company. E. S. Amos, the jury foreman, was also an elected justice of the peace in Marion County and was politically connected with A. B. Fleming. Just ten months after chairing the Monongah jury on November 6, 1908, he was reelected as justice and wrote to Fleming:

I appreciate your friendliness in my late RACE for Justice more than words can express. I assure you that my judicial acts shall be conservative, always friendly to, and bearing in mind the business interests of Marion County, and should a crisis arise then I will gladly heed and thank you for your advice. Wishing you success, I am yours truly. MANY, MANY thanks.[2]

On Monday, January 6, the jury began hearing evidence, and it concluded its work one week later on Monday, January 13. Each witness was first sworn in and then questioned by the Marion County Prosecutor Scott C. Lowe, or the Director of the West Virginia Department of Mines James W. Paul. The Fairmont Coal Company was represented by counsel George W. Alexander, Charles Powell, and Harry Shaw. Alexander was a partner in the Fleming Law Firm and had been assigned by Fleming to monitor matters at the mine on a full-time basis from the moment the explosion occurred. As such he was more thoroughly familiar with the disaster than virtually anyone in the courtroom. Paul was familiar with the Fairmont Coal Company, having worked at the No. 6 and No. 8 mines before the accident and having sought employment with the Fairmont Coal Company as recently as 1901. In answer to Paul's employment request for a position as an engineer with the Fairmont Coal Company, Fleming wrote,

A few days ago I had a talk with Mr. W. B. Brooks relative to filling the position of chief engineer for the Fairmont Coal Co. and he said at his first opportunity he would take up the matter with the other officials of the company.[3]

In what would today be entirely unacceptable, company lawyers representing the coal company, potentially a guilty party, sat with the grand jury, were permitted to hear all testimony, and were even allowed to question and cross-examine witnesses. Coroner Amos initially described the process of attempting to identify the victims:

As soon as the bodies were brought from the mines to the morgue I saw the bodies taken from the stretcher onto the table and then personally supervised the undressing of them so that if possible we might be able to find some means of identification of them. If anything was found to indicate who the man was I made a record in the book as to who he was, and if no marks of identification were found I again inspected the body after it was cleaned up to try to identify it if possible.

Amos also described his actions in recording the victims:

We kept two books; I kept the most of this one myself. Someone assisted me of course. . . . [W]e tried to get the identification and any articles found, and money. We gave people all the chance that we could to identify their friends. Some were so mutilated that they couldn't identify them, and those were not held very long but were taken to the cemetery.[4]

The Fairmont Coal Company payroll clerk, George S. Gibbon, sat alongside Coroner Amos and kept a parallel set of books. He also helped identify the victims as his position made him most familiar with them. Gibbon testified first and told of the system that was used to help identify the victims.

Next, doctors who conducted autopsies testified as to the cause of death of several of the miners. Dr. F. W. Hill testified that he had rushed to Monongah from Fairmont and volunteered to help with victims, but that all but one was

dead. Hill testified that "they had come to their deaths by an explosion—
by violence—probably due to explosion or other causes." Dr. Hill went on,
"Some died from asphyxiation, some were badly mutilated, others were not."
He further stated that he had seen deterioration of the skin as evidence of
burning. Hill had also worked with some of the rescuers when they were
overcome by gas or lack of air and oxygen, but they had been resuscitated.[5]

Following Dr. Hill came the most dramatic testimony, the four miners who
had escaped the explosion. The first to testify was Orazio DePetris who had
come to Monongah in 1889, but had gone home to Italy for four years. He had
just returned and gone to work in No. 8 in June, 1906. He went into the mine
with his brother Angelo, as had his son Felice. At 5:30 A.M., they had waited for
the fire boss to come out and open the door. While they were waiting, his son
Felice came by with a motor and went into the mine ahead of Orazio.

Shortly after he began his testimony, apparently due to his lack of
English, an interpreter, Joe Berardelli was sworn in. DePetris continued
to testify that he and three others had gone to second right south, working
in room No. 15, but then they moved to left south face and headed off the
south main. He had told the pit boss that the four wanted to move to work
in a starting room, which would allow them better production possibilities.
Shortly after, they had moved to another room. They made a cut, shot the
coal, loaded a car, and the explosion occurred. He felt the explosion and
immediately saw smoke. The force of the air knocked all the cap lamps and
all other lighting dark, throwing the entire mine into pitch black. After recovering from the blasts, Orazio and others started walking back toward the
main entry feeling their way in the pitch black. Shortly, they were forced
back by the density of the smoke. "We couldn't walk anymore on ahead
and came back," DePetris said.[6]

Desperate, they reversed direction and went back fifty or sixty yards. The
smoke was hot and now pouring into the rooms where they were crawling.

During the fifteen minutes or so they called to one another while searching for an escape. There were three other men were working in the same room as Orazio—Angelo on one side and Leonardo Dominico and his father Dan on the other. Paul, the West Virginia Chief Inspector, then questioned whether he had noticed any change in the ventilation prior to the explosion; he said he had not. On continued questioning, Orazio described the scene. All the men had lost their caps and cap lamps. Their coats had been blown away and, with them, the matches Orazio had in his coat pocket. There was smoke all around and only the four men escaped. They encountered no one else during their escape.

After lunch, two other physicians testified, and early that afternoon, Leonardo Dominico was called to the stand. A lad of 15, Leonardo had worked in No. 8 mine since it had opened about three years earlier. He lived on Hill No. 3 and had resided in Monongah all his life. He had gone to work the morning of the explosion around 5:30 A.M. and testified that he found the mine gates open and no fire boss present. He originally went to the second right of the first south, but changed, with the others, to the third left again on the south side.

His foreman, Peter Kerns, had come to him that morning to see where they were working and to check on gas. Leonardo didn't see the explosion, but it knocked him down; he felt the shock and heard tremendous noise. Leonardo also lost his coat and his cap light had been blown out. As he struggled to get up after the first explosion, a second explosion knocked him down again. With the three other miners, he struggled to follow the rails out of the mine but was forced back because the smoke was so thick.

Dan Dominico was then sworn in to testify. Because his English was so poor, Joe Berardelli was again sworn. Dan had lived in Monongah seventeen or eighteen years and worked at the No. 8 mine. His testimony was brief. He was working with his son, Leonardo, when the explosion occurred and had suffered injuries. He did not see the explosion but was thrown down by the "jar" of the blast. His left arm and left ear were injured in the fall.[7]

Next, Angelo DePetris testified, through Berardelli's translation, that he had lived in Monongah eighteen or nineteen years and also worked at No. 8. He had only been in No. 8 one and a half months. He testified that the four had put off one shot, and he was picking the coal down from the roof at the moment of the explosion. The force threw him down, knocking off his cap and lamp. Trying to return to the entry, they were often forced back by the smoke. As they were struggling toward an exit, DePetris testified that he saw light "at the opening or hole the sun was shining through and the smoke and sun and light made a light that looked like fire."[8] He and the others raced to the toad hole and began to claw their way out of the opening. The hole was at the face of the first south section and put them just above the interurban line facing towards the Pentos or the Middleton sections of Monongah.

The four walked over to the No. 8 mine portal where the crowds had gathered. As news of their escape spread, the widows and families were encouraged and heartened.[9]

Later the same day, Peter Urban, the fifth survivor and only man rescued, was called to the stand. To provide Polish translation, William Vokolek was sworn in as interpreter. Urban testified:

All I know we went to work that morning and we had no cars; so we started to dig coal and then we went in eight; then at the time while we were eating there was a noise, or report; then I told my brother we better run—something had happened. He says: "Oh, what happened? I don't think anything happened," and took a pick and goes to the face and started to work. Then we started to run; then I don't remember nothing. I don't know where I came or what became of me.

After some confusion he continued, answering the question, "Where were you when you first became conscious of your surroundings, after the explosion?" "When I came to," Urban said, "had my mind together, I recognized I was at home." Urban, in dramatic testimony, said he had encountered gas and witnessed a methane pop and fire underground three days before the explosion, in which a horse had been burned and died:

Chief Inspector Paul: "But before this explosion occurred, do you know of any [gas exploding]?"

Answer from Urban: "There was before this once. It killed a horse. Three days before that it killed a horse."[10]

At this point, the Fairmont Coal Company attorney, Alexander, alarmed that this testimony might implicate the company in its past conduct and would establish the presence of methane gas, forcefully cross-examined Urban in an effort to discredit the story of an earlier fire.

Urban, who was clearly still stunned from the experience, was taken aback, but stood his ground in testifying that a horse was burned and died and was buried. Urban testified that he knew where the horse was buried, and Alexander wanted the grand jury to examine the location.[11] Alexander next attempted to belittle Urban and question his competence; such efforts did not go down well with some of the observers in the courtroom. The official representative from the Italian Consulate, G. D. Caldara, stormed out in protest of Alexander's aggressive attacks on Peter Urban.

On Monday, January 13, just one week after the jury began its deliberations, it concluded with the testimony of John W. Paul, director of the West Virginia Department of Mines. Paul admitted that some years earlier he had been connected with these mines and the Monongah Coal & Coke

Company, Camden's original company, which had been absorbed by the Fairmont Coal Company prior to his appointment to the position of the West Virginia Department of Mines. During this period in West Virginia, the appointment of the director was made by the governor, but was based solely upon the recommendation of the mine operators. Paul then testified that he had arrived at the mine disaster site at noon on Sunday, December 8, and that he had entered No. 6 at about 2:30 that afternoon.

In his thoughtful statement, Paul identified three significant contributing causes of the explosion and issues, which, if addressed, would make the Monongah mines as well as mines throughout the United States safer. His conclusion was that the explosion was more than likely caused by blown-out or overcharged shot, but that he could not rule out that the runaway train of coal cars was the cause rather than simply a remarkable coincidence. He conceded that each of the experts from the three European countries of Belgium, France, and Germany had concluded that the trip of cars was the cause of the explosion.

And most significantly, he concluded that coal dust, which had been allowed to accumulate in the mine entries and rooms, posed a more serious risk for explosion than had been recognized in the past. Paul concluded that the dust, both in the entries and in the rooms, had to be watered on a regular and continuous basis. This was a practice that the Fairmont Coal Company had adopted in some of its mines, but had not adopted at the Monongah mines. Paul's conclusions that the fine particles of coal dust alone could explode if ignited was contrary to the position that the company officials held, insisting that coal dust could only explode if ignited in a methane gas explosion. Paul pointed to the use of black powder, the practice at No. 6 and No. 8, as a source of unnecessary risk as there were alternative explosives on the market that were safer.

On Wednesday, January 15, 1908, the grand jury rendered its verdict and recommendations. The jury found that the miners

came to their deaths on the sixth day of December 1907 by means of an explosion in Monongah mines number six and eight, owned and operated by the Fairmont Coal Company, which was caused by either what is known as a blown-out shot or by ignition and explosion of powder in mine number eight.[12]

After citing the two conflicting theories, the runaway car or the improperly fired shot, as the possible proximate cause of the initial explosion, the jury drew their critical conclusion as to the culpability of the mine operator.

We further find from the evidence that the trace of gas in these mines were slight, and not considered dangerous, and dust which was created was removed or kept watered down as far as was deemed practical and that in operating these mines the company complied with the mining laws of the State.[13]

With this terse statement, which contradicted testimony by Director Paul and others, the jury completely exonerated any official or owner of the company of any responsibility for the explosions. Since the Marion County Grand Jury was the only judicial body with authority to address the question of civil or criminal liability or responsibility, their conclusions determined the mine company was completely without liability.

Given the magnitude of the explosions and the ferocity the forces created, such findings, particularly as they relate to dust, are difficult to explain. Even if the source of the initial explosion was unknown, the strength of the following explosions makes the finding that the dust was adequately removed or watered down particularly implausible. The two principal types of explosions in coal mines involve methane gas and coal dust. Coal dust explosions are by far the more ferocious, creating energy at levels ten or more times than that of methane. All indications at Monongah were that coal dust was the fuel that explained both the force and the color of the smoke.[14]

The conclusion the Monongah jury reached contrasts sharply with the grand jury conclusion after the Naomi explosion. The grand jury reviewing the Naomi explosion, a disaster which occurred in western Pennsylvania just sixty miles north of Fairmont and within days of the Monongah disaster, was strongly critical of the mine owners and management. There, the Belle Vernon jury addressed the United Coal Company role in the Naomi mine disaster. The jury admonished the mine operator to take aggressive actions to prevent similar occurrences in the future, including the recommendation that the use of open lamps be abolished.[15]

But the Marion County findings also precluded any civil liability since, at the time, the West Virginia mining law had no administrative or criminal penalty provisions. By default the case would have been considered under the tort law in civil court and the jury finding exonerating the company made this virtually impossible.

No federal mine safety and health laws existed, and since no other entity except the West Virginia state legislature had the authority to pursue the matter, the Marion County coroner's jury was the final word. Although committees appointed by the West Virginia legislature held several hearings, surprisingly, neither the State Department of Mines nor the legislature committees issued a final report.

However, having exonerated the company and its owners and officials, given the magnitude of the disaster, the grand jury felt compelled to make several recommendations.

As there are many other unsolved problems connected with mine explosions in the United States, we recommend that Congress make an appropriation for the establishment of a Bureau of Investigation and information to aid in the study of the various conditions under which explosions occur, and as to how they may be prevented. We also recommend the more general use of safety or flameless powders which we believe would tend towards greater safety in coal mining and that the firing and handling of explosives used in coal mines be placed in the hands of experienced and competent persons, and also that clay, or some noncombustible matter, be used in tamping.

And finally, turning to the state agencies, the grand jury concluded, "Owing to the fact that there are over six thousand persons now employed in West Virginia, we further recommend that four (4) additional District Mine Inspectors and two (2) Inspectors-at-large be appointed."[16] The recommendations for the creation of a federal bureau to study problems suggest that such an alternative would be less burdensome and cheaper than a new rule requiring certification of shot firers and, therefore, might be favored by the mine owners. An investigative body without the authority to cite or penalize the mine operator was far preferable to a beefed-up state enforcement authority with increased regulatory powers. Requirements to increase the use of water to remove the dust or make it inert, as well as mandates for using improved explosives, were to be traded for further experimentation and testing, an important task but not regulatory in nature, even though such requirements were recognized in Europe and acknowledged and recognized among many of the mining states in the United States, including Pennsylvania and Ohio. For some, the grand jury finding was a great cause for relief. Camden wrote to Fleming on January 17 from his winter quarters at the Hotel Royal Palm:

I see in this mornings papers that the Coroner's Jury has fully exonerated the Fairmont Co from all blame in the Monongah accident and in all respects rendered a very sensible and satisfactory finding—I am sincerely glad of this and feel greatly relieved, I regard the verdict of the utmost importance, and don't see how any of the unfortunate sufferers can seek redress or try to give the Co trouble.[17]

Fleming wrote back, pleased with the outcome of the grand jury and the confidence he had in the overall outcome, as well as to explain his position concerning voluntary compensation of the victims' families, a position he favored and which Camden had opposed. Camden replied on January 23rd:

I have no doubt you have had an anxious and worrying strain since the accident, but I was in hopes it was about over without aftermath—that is that there would be no effort to make the Company liable by suit—I followed the testimony as far as I could in the investigation and so far as I could see there was nothing to fix any neglect or responsibility on the Co—The experts disagree in their theories as to the cause of the accident, and none seem to have fixed or certain ideas as to the cause, and agree that the Co complied with the mining laws, and that the mines were in excellent shape—

Camden, however, continued his opposition against voluntary compensation to the victim's families:

The point is will it justify you to spend too much in compromises—won't it cause everyone to expect too much, and to take it for granted that you admit the company's responsibility for the accident would it not be cheaper and safer to keep a stiff upper lip and fight it out—than to do anything more than charity requires—of course I am only suggesting without knowing much about the real situation, and only desire to call your attention to this view that if you are too liberal in paying and compromising that you yourself are admitting your responsibility . . . I know that there are always a lot of jackals lying around to encourage trouble and to profit by it and it is hard to tell how best to avoid them—But it looks from this distance that it would be very difficult if not impossible to make final recovery against the Co. and that it might be better to keep that stand. I want you to consider however that I am only writing a friendly letter and giving my own notions in an offhanded way. Knowing your judgment is better than mine.

Camden then turned to the widows still occupying the company houses:

I should judge that the occupancy of the houses by the families of the unfortunate miners, would be a hard problem to deal with—and will be embarrassing, when it doesn't solve itself—[18]

In the early 1900s, families of miners who died in a mine accident or disaster had nothing in the way of economic protection and little legal recourse following a mine disaster. This was especially true in West Virginia where the coal interest was entwined with every facet of the state's political, economic, social, and legal systems. State workers' compensation statutes had not yet been adopted in any state, including West Virginia; in fact, it was not until one year later, in 1908, that the federal government adopted the first and quite limited workers' compensation system in the nation, which provided compensation for men killed or injured while working in hazardous occupations for the federal government.

The legal recourse after a miner was injured or killed was therefore to establish that the mine operator was negligent in the operation of the mine or in the event that led to the miner's death or injury during employment. But mine operators and other employers had successfully argued before the courts that their liability was also limited by the actions of the employee. The assumption of risk by the employee, the employee's contributory negligence, and the fellow servant doctrine were the trinity of standard defenses, which successfully protected employers from liability, and they were frequently used in mining death cases.

A few years earlier, the Fairmont Coal Company had been the subject of the first lawsuit in West Virginia growing out of a mine accident. In that case, a miner had been injured at the Gaston Mine in Fairmont and had sued, alleging that the company had violated West Virginia mining laws and had been negligent. At trial, the jury ruled for the miner and awarded him a substantial sum of money. However, upon appeal to the State Supreme Court, the company prevailed completely when the upper court threw out the case.

The Monongah mines fell within the Marion County District Court jurisdiction. The part owner and company's general counsel, A. B. Fleming, was very familiar with that court, having served as judge on the court years before, as well as with the judges on the Supreme Court of Appeals. In part, on December 2, 1907, just four days before the explosion, he had received correspondence from Ira E. Robinson, a member of the Supreme Court of Appeals of West Virginia. Apparently, Fleming had sent Robinson stock certificates. Robinson wrote,

I am indeed very sorry that I overlooked putting my signature to the assignment of one of the certificates of the Clarksburg Fuel Company, a Consolidation Coal and Fairmont Coal Company partner stock. I have signed the certificate which you returned to me, and have mailed the same to the auditor of the Fairmont Coal Company in the envelope which you enclosed.[19]

In total, five legal cases were filed against the company, one of which Fleming took seriously. Four were filed within West Virginia that did not proceed forward and may have been dismissed. The fifth case was a suit against the Camden interests by Ohio attorney, Leon Wise. Leon was the brother of Charles Wise, the mining engineer who Camden employed as a surveyor to record the removal of the coal underground. Charles was hired to protect Camden's interests since Camden still owned the coal, and the mines were leased to the Consolidation & Fairmont Coal Co. The survey was to determine the amount of royalties to be paid on the amount of coal mined, and to ensure that the mining company was removing as much coal as possible from the seam. Coal not mined was rendered valueless since re-mining in most instances was impossible.

Leon Wise had written Fleming and Camden on behalf of Charles's widow and two young sons, requesting that payment be made to the widow. Senator Camden, having already expressed his opposition to voluntary or, for that matter, involuntary cooperation, had passed away shortly after the mine disaster, and his son declined to meet the widow's request. However, according to the correspondence, after much delay and cajoling by Watson and Fleming, the younger Camden consented to pay part of the settlement.

The most serious legal challenge was filed on September 10, 1908, by Cipriano Ianiery on behalf of his son Gennaro Ianiery, who was killed in the disaster. The suit was filed in King's County New York Superior Court by Attorney R. Louis Lapetina of Brooklyn, New York. The suit alleged that Gennaro's death was a result of the company's negligence and that the 22 year old was a resident of New York.

Because the Fairmont Coal Company maintained offices in New York City, a suit could be brought in New York since courts would have jurisdiction. The amount of the demand was for $10,000. Fleming immediately hired the firm of Davies, Stone & Auerbach, one of the premier firms in New York City, to represent the company. A. B. Fleming was concerned that the New York suit could be a problem: first, because it would be expensive to defend, and second, because public opinion in New York would be against the company. He wrote to Senior Partner Julien T. Davies:

It is certainly very important to us to prevent the bringing of any suits away from this State. We are willing to fight any suits here, but it will be very expensive to take as many witnesses as we will need to New York. Here the sympathy and sentiment would be with us, while in New York it would be against us.

He continued,

This is a very important case, and if they succeed in it, other suits may be brought. I hope therefore, you will take the matter up and leave no stone unturned to throw it out of court for want of jurisdiction.[20]

But, to complicate matters the Fairmont Coal Company had failed to renew its registration with the state of New York, and thus lacked a designated person upon whom service of process might be made in New York. This failure could not only result in a fine, but more significantly, if this issue became public, the company would be seen as flaunting the laws of New York.

Attorney Davies, on behalf of the company argued that the deceased was an alien and was killed in West Virginia and therefore a suit could not be brought in New York. But since the victim's father had alleged that his son was a resident of New York, Fleming pressed to establish that, in fact, the son was a resident of West Virginia.

The company records showed the victim on the payroll as Jenoea Yaniero, also called Nick Yaniero but that his real name was Gennaro or Lenora Ianiery. Fleming also produced a record from the Marion County District Court that $56.95 in wages had been due him at the time of the explosion. In Marion County, an administrator had been appointed for every person without family or an heir, and the wages owed the victims were paid to these administrators. In this instance, the administrator, Earl Morgan, had paid the victim's landlady the back rent which she claimed had been owed.

But in order to deal with the most pressing issue, that of establishing Ianiery's residency in West Virginia, Fleming recruited Ralph Loss who was on the staff of the ostensibly independent Relief Committee that had been set up to help the wives and families of the victims. Loss was chosen because he also had the confidence of some of the immigrant families. Fleming asked Loss to obtain information regarding Ianiery's residence from some of his fellow Italians. On October 2, 1908, Fleming wrote to the New York lawyers reporting that he had information which would support the fact that Ianiery had lived and established residency in Marion County: "I have some more information, obtained for me by a representative of the Relief Committee. It would have been impossible to have obtained this information in any other way."

Fleming, it seemed, was faced with the collective code of silence.

The man who obtained it for us procured it from two Italians, Nicole D'Alessandro and Donoto Cesmarrio. Loss had first written out a statement for each man in Italian, but they refused to sign it written in Italian. He then wrote it in English, read it to them, and they signed it.

Fleming continued:

He says he is quite sure that we cannot procure their testimony and that they would not be willing to help the company against a fellow countryman. They would be afraid of being killed if they did. It seems to me, therefore, about our only hope is to give you such information as will enable you to draw the facts from the administrator. If it is impossible to do this, perhaps it would be worth the experiment to try to take the depositions of those two Italians here, but our people think that they would pick up and move away rather than give the depositions.[21]

In December, whether as a result of the obtained statements or other jurisdictional concerns, the victim's lawyer, I. Louis Lapatina, offered to compromise for $500. Fleming, not wishing to establish a precedent, counter-offered $150, the same amount that the company had paid each family and suggested that a compromise could be worked out on the amount of the attorney fees. The matter settled in Washington by the Royal Counsel of Italy, Legal Bureau, F. Fana Forni, for the smallest amount.

Finally, a significant claim that did not result in a lawsuit being filed was raised from the Italian embassy in Washington by the Royal Counsel of Italy, F. Fana Forni. Forni, through his attorney, had raised the issue of compensation from the Fairmont Coal Company for the families in Italy equal to that paid by the company to the widows and families in the United States. Initially, Fleming and Watson resisted, but after a period of time, they entered negotiations with the Italian Royal Counsel. Settlement was reached on January 29, 1909. The company agreed to pay $25,000 to the counsel for 68 families of married victims and 52 unmarried victims.[22]

THE NUMBER

"The presumption is that he was in the mine on that day."
— George S. Gibbons, Payroll Clerk, Fairmont Coal Company

500 Miners are Buried Alive by a Double Explosion 425 are killed
Fairmont, WV., Dec. 6 – An explosion of coal dust in mines No. 6 and 8 of the
Consolidation Coal Company of Baltimore, located on opposite sides of the
Monongahela River at Monongah, six miles from here this morning, resulted
in what from present reports is indicated to be the worst disaster in the history
of the coal mining industry of America.
— "Zanesville Signal," Friday Evening, December 6, 1907
Four o'clock Edition

THE December 8, 1907, *New York Times* article on the disaster read,

LOSS IN MINES MAY REACH 564

It was stated to-night by General Manager Leo L. Malone of the mines that 478 actual miners were checked off as entering the mines yesterday morning. This number,

it was further stated, did not include fully 100 trapper boys, mule drivers, pumpers and boys who are not under the check system.

The article went on to quote the company's official statement, which was in sharp contrast with Malone's statement: "There were 406 men employed at No. 6 and 8. Fifteen are located and known to be safe. We have hopes that of the 391 whose names are given below, a number were not at work."[1]

Even as the mine rescue efforts were beginning, the question arose of how many men and boys were trapped under the ground. At Monongah, like virtually every other mine in the country, there was no adequate system for keeping track of the number of miners underground. The principal means of identifying miners was a duplicate brass or tin tag system, which, in theory, registered each miner present in the mine. As the miner entered the mine, one tag was placed on a board with numbered hooks and the other was put in the miner's pocket. The first tag was to be carried on his person and used as a means of identification in the event of a mine disaster or accident. The second tag hung on the board showing that the miner was in the mine. The numbering system did not include men and boys who were brought in as subcontractors for the miners who were being paid per ton of coal loaded out, and as Malone said, "many were off the books." This system was by no means fail-safe, and in this case it was rendered completely useless when the explosion rocketed out of the No. 8, ripping a cavity in the earth nearly 100 feet across. The explosion blew everything in its path to bits, including both boards containing tags for nearly all the miners inside both mines, as the No. 8 portal was the entrance used by the majority of the miners in both mines.

A second factor that blurred the question of the number of miners underground was the employment system itself. At Monongah, two methods of employment were in place; first was the hiring of miners as independent contractors. The miner entered into a contract with the mine operator. The

operator allowed the miner to have access to the coal underground and provided rail cars to carry the mined coal from underground, while the miner
was responsible for the tools and necessary equipment including picks, shovels, black powder, timbers, drills, or anything needed during the mining process. The miner *drilled and shot* or dislodged the coal from the seam, loaded
it on a horse or mule drawn cart, and later transferred the cart to the underground rail system. When the loaded car reached the surface, it was weighed
by a company weighman and the miner was paid according to the amount
of coal he had mined. These were the men who hired others as unofficial
subcontractors to increase production.

Under the second employment system, *workmen* or *laborers*, titles distinct
from *miner*, worked on an hourly or daily basis. This system was used for
men or boys who performed support or backup work for the company, such
as preparing the mine tunnels or other internal or external workings of the
mine. For example, trapper boys opened and closed the doors, which controlled the mine ventilation trapping the air. Other jobs included *pumpers*
and *mule drivers*. As these men were not actually mining the coal, they were
paid a hourly wages.

As mentioned above, miners frequently brought with them brothers, sons,
nephews, or employed helpers. These boys or men were not on the company
payroll or records and were paid by the miners themselves, in effect working
as subcontractors. For many boys and men, the experience in the unofficial or
off-the-books positions served as on-the-job training, preparing them for even-
tual hire as miners. The practice of having subcontract miners off the books
was common throughout the mining industry, including in West Virginia, and
was practiced at No. 6 and No. 8. President Watson, Superintendent Gaskill,
and Payroll Clerk Gibbons each admitted that the practice existed at the
Monongah mines. Although it is difficult to believe, Watson asserted after the

disaster that it had occurred in only one instance when the body of a miner and his son who was not on the payroll were located and positively identified.

Watson's assertion conflicted with the sworn testimony of the company payroll clerk, George Gibbons, who also suggested that only one man was working off the books—for a reason different from Watson's. During his testimony at the inquest, Chief Inspector Paul asked, "Do you have any information as to whether or not bodies of men were found in either mine who were not supposed to be employed there?"

"Well that is according to what you mean," Gibbons replied.

"Did you find there were bodies of men who had worked on the coke yard, or in some outside capacity?"

"And gone in the mine without us taking a record?"

"Yes?"

"As far as I know there has only been one such case. That was not a coke man but a Polish boy."[2]

Prosecuting Attorney Lowe next asked, "The system employed in these mines is for the men you account for through your office to have certain numbers?"

"Yes, sir," Gibbons answered.

"And each man who was regularly employed had a certain number under which he worked?" Lowe asked.

"Yes, sir, the diggers did."

"As a matter of fact some of these men did what is called contract work?"

"Yes, sir," Gibbons said.

"And it is possible that several men in that way would be working under one check."

"Yes, but still their names would appear on the payroll for they would receive their pay through the contractor. I don't have their names. In this case, the man had gone in to help another one, without any record."

Gibbons' answers affirmed that the practice of helpers working off the payroll existed and that men and boys were in the mine without being listed. Gibbons then volunteered that there was a record of such persons but he didn't have it with him. No such record was produced nor asked for during the remainder of the hearings.[3]

Additional victims not on the books show the limited value of the records to produce an accurate account of the number underground. For example, Gibbons agreed that a man from Fairmont had gone into the mine seeking employment and died in the explosion and that person was not on his records.

But Gibbons's testimony also sheds doubt about the adequacy of the payroll records, especially as to whether new or recent hires would be recorded for the day that they started. Prosecutor Lowe presented him with a note written by John McGraw, a mine superintendent. The note read: "No 8 Petro Frediaro, Bessilo Pillea, o.k. Morris 56 coal (signed) Jno. McGraw." On December 12, 1907, R. T. Cunningham sent to Watson a list with morgue numbers. Bossilo Pillelo and Petro Frediro are listed with the note "Italians were in No. 8 Selecting a place to work. Chief Paul found their order copy x of mine laws." Neither name is found in the Monongah Mine Relief Committee report or record. Gibbons described the hiring process:

A man comes in and is questioned by the assistant superintendent as to where he has worked. If his replies are satisfactory he is given a slip of paper like this. He presents this paper to the mine boss under whom he wishes to work, and the mine boss gives him a room and fixes the price of coal, and gives this paper back. He brings this (the signed paper) to the office and goes to work.

Neither McGraw nor these two men survived, and thus the paperwork never got to the payroll office.[4] The *Pittsburgh Dispatch* reported that one company official had said that a number of new employees had started to work the Friday of the explosion.[5] But just as significant as this information was the fact that many bodies brought intact to the surface had no tags in the pockets. The Associated Press story for Friday afternoon reported:

The most conservative reports place the number of men entombed by the explosion at 300 and nearly all estimates, including those of most of the coal company officials place the number at least 500. Some estimates place the number even higher.[6]

Miner's bodies without tin tags would indicate either the presence of men and boys working off the payroll or that the tag system had been ignored. Gibbons testified that only "the diggers had a certain number under which he worked."[7]

An estimated number of miners killed could also be determined by a review of the number of men at work during periods leading up to the explosion. J. C. Gaskill, during his testimony on January 10, 1908, put into the official transcript of the hearing two records of the mine foreman for No. 8 and No. 6 for October 30, 1907. Mine No. 6, the larger of the two, showed 224 men employed on the day shift and No. 8 employed 145 men working on the day shift, totaling 369. The 369 miners were actually on the payroll just over one month before the explosion. If that number had stayed constant, coupled with the miners working off the books, the number of victims is substantially higher than officially recorded.

On Saturday morning, December 7, the *Baltimore Sun* and other papers reported that the two mines regularly employed 1000 men in two shifts according to mine management. Beyond these figures the company officials did not attempt to give estimates. The paper further reported that the general opinion in Monongah was that the number of dead and imprisoned will exceed 450 "as more than half of the total work force worked during the day."[8]

But the company officials in the best position to know supported the proposition that well over 400 were on the books as working at the time of the accident. Lee Malone, who had rushed to the scene and was in charge of the rescue efforts at midnight Friday, issued the following statement: "There is now no question whatever that the list of dead will reach 400 and possibly 425."[9]

A. J. Ruckman, the superintendent of the Monongah mines, testified with intimate knowledge of the mines that prior to the explosion, "Including all I should estimate the number as near 185 to 190 in each mine," or between 370 and 380 miners regularly at work in the mines. Ruckman made no mention of those working off the books.[10]

But by Saturday afternoon, Vice President Watson and Vice President Jere Wheelwright began an effort to downplay the number of miners killed. President Watson produced a list of 391 names of the men on the payroll. This number of course did not count the boys and men who were working off the payroll. President Watson said that several miners had been located, having not shown up for work Friday morning, and thus his official count could be reduced to 354. In fact, four miners originally identified as among the victims were discovered alive. Pat McDonald was injured outside No. 6, but was hospitalized and not dead as originally thought, while Ross Marka, Mari Bagineallo, and Anebra Spaw had been in nearby towns the morning of December 6, 1907.[11] Watson was certain that the number was even less than that because of the many absentees. According to one news article,

Among those who were absent Friday morning were eight members of the Who's Who Club of Wahoo (a neighborhood of Monongah), a social organization who at their monthly meeting Thursday night before the explosion had: "disposed of large quantities of the amber fluid, red liquor and refreshments of all varieties. The eight men who were spared were now digging graves for their coworkers.[12]

Later that Saturday, Watson dramatically revised the number of victims downward when he estimated that no more than 328 fatalities had occurred. Then on Sunday, without support or explanation, he asserted that the figure was impossible to know. How he drew that early conclusion, especially as the recovery had just begun and, indeed, had been stopped because of the danger of explosion, is difficult to understand. When confronted with the question of how many men or boys were working as miners' helpers for their fathers, brothers, or friends, Watson stated, "After careful investigation, I found that this was true only in the case of John P. Bazile, whose nephew worked under the same check. . ."

This statement was made on Saturday, a scant 24 hours after the explosion, and was characterized as describing the number of miners who had gone into these two shifts to work.

Watson's statement the evening of the accident contrasted sharply with the statement by Malone, the general manager, who said, "The day previous, 400 miners had gone into these two shifts to work. It was this fact which led the officers here to believe that fully this number were entombed in the wrecked drifts."

Malone, as general superintendent, was in a better position than President Watson to know how many were actually at work, and his statement was made immediately after the accident, not later when other considerations were possible. In addition, another source who had accurate information on the number at work was Superintendent Gaskill, who was quoted in the *Baltimore Sun* for December 7, 1907, immediately following the accident: "Mr. Lichtenstein had a talk with Superintendent Gaskill, of the mines, who stated that he had no hopes that any of the men escaped. He said there were from 425 to 550 men in the two mines. In the number were a corps of mining engineers, and these too, it is thought, were lost."

L. Lee Lichtenstein of Cumberland was in Fairmont at the time of the explosion. He is quoted as saying:

The explosion shook Fairmont about eight miles from Monongah, as if by earthquake. There was a rumbling noise, houses rocked to and fro, people rushed wildly to the street, and it was 15 minutes before it was known what had occurred.

An interurban streetcar had passed the mouth of the mines when the explosion had occurred. Had it been 30 seconds later, it would have been swept away by the explosion.[13]

Gaskill, along with Malone, was in a position to have firsthand knowledge of the actual population of the mine on a day-to-day basis and their comments were contemporaneous with the accident, not days later. Watson, who by all accounts was not involved in the day-to-day operations of the mines, was now attempting to lower the estimate, even more than he had first cited. To support this lower number, other more credible officials were needed.

On Sunday, Lester Emmitt Trader and his brother had been called back from their father's home in McKeesport to the mine by Frank Haas. Haas "called up and said he wants us to get back there. Frank and I couldn't leave the company that way. I went back and they gave me a job in the auditor's office in Clairmont.[14] Victor told Trader that in return for being given an office and a job in the accounting department, he would be quoted as the official spokesperson for the company. In his 1972 interview, Trader described the scene when he met with Frank Haas, David Victor, his mother's brother—Jere Wheelwright, and other officials at the mine company office. From the Monday night press release issued by the company for publication on Tuesday:

The Company still hopes the death list will not reach the figures they submitted to the press Sunday. They do not think the figures will total more than 260, and this is based on statements made today by Fire Boss Trader of No. 6 mine, he says he thinks there were not more than 110 men working in that mine, whereas the previous estimates placed the number at 174.[15]

As fire boss, Trader would have had little knowledge of the number of miners at work. It was not part of his job, and he would not come into contact with that information since his work hours would have placed him at the mine when the offices were closed. The circumstances that Lester Trader describes suggest an effort to manipulate the reports of the number killed or to cover up the real number. He had never before been a spokesman for the company and would never again be spokesman, and in fact he had never worked in an office that would have had access to the records.[16]

On December 8, the *Pittsburgh Dispatch* printed a list entitled "Known Dead at Monongah." 389 names are listed. While no source for the list is given, the only possibility is the company,[17] and the next edition added 19 more names for a total of 408.[18]

Almost immediately questions were raised as to the accuracy of this new lower count. Especially because several miners who lived out of town would have to be seen so that the list could be completed accurately. While most miners lived in and around Monongah, many lived some distance away in Fairmont or Clarksburg and surrounding communities and on remote farms, traveling by foot or on the interurban to work. Several such names are not included in the official list. Even some miners whose bodies were recovered, embalmed, and transported to their homes were not listed in the official record. On Monday, December 9, the *Pittsburgh Dispatch* reported that Fred Rogers, aged 26, was killed in the Monongah explosion and was buried at Fairchance near Uniontown, Pennsylvania. The Rogers family had been decimated by mine accidents—both Fred's father and brother had been killed in earlier accidents, and his mother died shortly after. A third son was seriously injured in a mine accident, and the implication is that the mother died when she received news of his injury. Fred Rogers is not included in the Relief Committees list, the Company list, or the Coroner's list.[19]

But by Monday and Tuesday the question arose as to whether all of the bodies that were in the mine would be recovered.

The *Baltimore Sun* reported some of the victims would never be seen:

Some of the experts who have entered the mine now state very strongly that they do not believe it to be possible to recover all of the bodies. They give as a reason for this that some of them were undoubtedly buried under tons of dirt and refuse, and that it will take many months at least to thoroughly search these sepulchers so suddenly created by the explosion.[20]

But the pressing question was the number. The *Pittsburgh Dispatch* reported,

There is still a great deal of difference of opinion as to how many men have lost their lives in the awful catastrophe, the officials of the mining company still aver that their list is near correct. This list numbers 406, of which several, it has been shown were not in the mine at the time of the disaster. This is offset by the fact that a number of men who received checks and entered the mines employed others as helpers. The coal company has no record of these helpers, as their names were not on the payroll. In many instances such cases have come to light. It is stated positively that some of the miners had as many as half a dozen of these helpers.[21]

And in contrast to the Trader quote:

One fire boss interviewed by me this evening stated positively that 436 checks had been issued on the morning of the explosion. In addition he insists there were a large number of boys employed in the mines.[22]

A. B. Fleming's private correspondence supports the higher number of fatalities cited by the *Pittsburgh Dispatch*. In a letter he wrote on December 13, 1907, to *Dispatch* reporter Goshorn, he states,

The reports of the Monongah Disaster published in your paper have been, so far as I have observed, accurate and fair, as the facts appeared. I have not seen in your paper the usual exaggerations as to the numbers who lost their lives, or as to the suffering for food and clothing. We appreciate the fair treatment which your paper has given us.[23]

Then on December 12, State Inspector Paul notified West Virginia Governor Dawson that the company payroll clerk estimated that 390 were killed. On that day, the *Baltimore Sun* also raised questions about the adequacy of the payroll records in determining the total number of victims. In addition, it confirmed that many more than one person was found working off the payroll:

A number of the bodies brought out today did not bear the brass checks used in the company's system of records and accounts of a majority of its employees, thus substantiating the statements of Monday that a large number of men and boys in the mines were not included in the checking rolls upon which estimates of the dead were largely based.[24]

In response to this growing controversy about the numbers killed, the *Sun* article continued, "This has also almost dispelled the hope expressed by mining officials the last few days that the number of dead has been over estimated. There is reason to believe tonight that the number will not fall far short of 500."[25]

But as the days wore on, Watson continued to lower the estimate of the number of victims: "President Watson of the Fairmont Coal Company is of the opinion that the number of dead will not be over 300," even though other officials were reporting that as many as 100 were not located and probably would not be found.[26] This statement was despite the fact that on the same day, R. T. Cunningham provided a list from the morgue with names of 340 dead miners who had been identified to C. W. Watson. Shortly after the explosions, Watson assigned Cunningham, the company auditor, the task of canvassing the town and nearby areas to attempt to determine the death count. In addition to the canvass, the post office in Monongah was reviewing its mail to attempt to use unclaimed mail as a source for names of victims.[27]

Throughout the effort, the Fairmont Coal Company officials received widespread acclaim from the media for their openness and accessibility. Watson and the other company senior officials stayed at the mine through the recovery. Watson and his secretary, C. N. Bennett, and Jere H. Wheelwright and his secretary, J. R. Buckingham, took shifts working as intermediaries with the media, "unlike some other companies' attempts to keep the reporters at bay." According to the *Baltimore Sun*, "From the beginning, both Messrs. Watson and Wheelwright said they wanted the newspapermen to get all the information necessary to keep the public posted regarding the conditions of the mines."[28] On December 12, President Watson reported the findings of the canvass conducted by Cunningham: "After a careful census of the community we can say positively that the death list does not exceed 338."[29]

Cunningham had sent out five parties of two men each, with one person in charge and one interpreter. For four or five days they visited every house on the company map and attempted to develop a record of all who were missing. The check included searching for boarders. They checked their findings against the company record books for rentals, and so on, as well as payroll records. Upon completing the check of the town, they went "around the country" and with the help of the Post Office, "ran down the names of any who were reported missing four or five miles out. . . ." Cunningham's first count was a list of 338 miners.[30]

But Cunningham had to revise this original total several times, as reported in the press initially, because the teams had missed one boarding house:

The death list was increased today by the census takers in the town of Monongah to 344. The list submitted by the Fairmont Coal Company of 338 was increased this afternoon by the investigators, who discovered that one company house in which six men lived was now unoccupied. The men kept bachelor quarters and all went into the mines on the fateful morning.[31]

Cunningham later testified that they identified 347 names when completed, but since completion three names had been added, including one man who was in the mine looking for work and two others. George Gibbons had testified earlier that Cunningham had told him over the phone that the list was 348 but the Polish priest had called him and given him the names of 4 or 5 who had been left off.[32] Gibbons then testified to what must be the most startling fact of the inquest: The number of bodies found was exactly the same as the number Cunningham's revised list contained. This happenstance is difficult if not impossible to accept, given the violence of the explosions, the state of some of the bodies, the presence of many men working off the books, and the fact that Watson, Fleming, and Malone all on separate occasions acknowledged additional victims.

Cunningham further testified that they had also checked this record against morgue records. The two records, according to Cunningham, did not match up because of the differences in the spelling of the "foreigners" names. When asked whether he would put his list in the record of the hearing he replied, "If required." That list as it appears in the transcript contains 323 names, not the 347 Cunningham cites in his testimony. The list is divided by mines and is described as a "list of men who lost their lives in mine No. 6 and No. 8." Two issues are significant with regard to the list. First is the disparity between the number of names Cunningham testifies are on the list (352) and the count on the list as published in the official transcript (323). Such errors might be more understandable in an extralegal setting, but the list is an official entry entitled, "Exhibit Cunningham No. 1."[33] Also significant is how the Cunningham list is described:

The annexed list shows from the best information obtainable from house to house census and information from all other sources a correct list of men reported to have lost their lives in the disaster at Monongah mines, No. 6 and No. 8, December 6th.

At the date of his testimony, Cunningham testified that "The list now shows 352. At the time it was finished, it was 347. I have added three men who have been reported since."

Cunningham was asked, "The scope of the work was sufficient to ascertain the number of men in the mine? That was the object?"

He answered, "That was the object, and we did everything we could, everything we knew to do."

The list showed no count of miners whose bodies were recovered but not identified, which, in theory, should have been reflected in Cunningham's survey. Nor does the list provide any names of miners whose bodies were not recovered, which also should have been done since the original intent was for a census "taken of those persons who were supposed to be in the mines on the morning of this explosion."[34] The number of unknown or unidentified bodies is at various times given at 70 or 80. The official number 362 does not include any unknown, if it did, the death total would reach 432 or 442. Father Everett Briggs, who founded St. Barbara's Nursing Home in 1961, argued that the unknowns were excluded and estimated the number killed at above 500.[35]

Over the course of the recovery effort, company officials, specifically Wheelwright and Watson, began to remark that perhaps every body would be recovered.[36] The evidence and every independent expert, as well as other company officials, disputed that assertion. Numerous officials were quoted as saying that as many as 100 bodies could have been either destroyed or trapped under massive falls and unrecoverable. A comparison of the various lists of victims does not help clear up the issue of the accurate number of men killed in the explosion. The Coroner's Report listed 360 bodies, including 71 who were unidentified.

The Coroner's list includes the number of unknown bodies found and buried. The absence of any unknown bodies from the Cunningham list is understandable as Cunningham's survey was an attempt to identify who was in the two mines by surveying the wives, families, and landlords. The Relief Committee report does not shed much light on the questions of the total number killed because even though it was not published until March 1, 1910, more than two and a half years later, it comes to the conclusion that 358 were killed, two fewer than shown on the Coroner's Report dated January 15, 1908. As noted previously, the Coroner's Report records the existence of 71 unknown bodies. Because of the Marion County Department of Health Order, the 71 bodies were buried within hours. Those 71 unidentified bodies would be in addition to the 340 named bodies in the December 12 company list provided to Watson,[37] bringing the total to 411.

But the question of the accuracy of the count and the Cunningham list is raised in a pointed way when the company payroll clerk was recalled to the stand. He was questioned by William Vokolek, who was the Polish translator. Vokolek began by asking whether Gibbons knew certain individuals: "Do you know, to the best of your recollection, whether Michael Keresti was working in the mine that day?"

"I don't know about Michael Keresti," Gibbons said, "but I know about Mike Keresti."

"You have a recollection that he was employed there?"

"Yes, in No 6."

"About the time of the explosion?"

"Yes, sir. . ."

Then Vokolek asked, "To the best of your recollection, was there any report handed down to you that this Mike Keresti was in the mine on the day of the explosion?"

Gibbons answered in what was to become the operative language: "The presumption is that he was in the mine on that day."

After listing four other names and having Mr. Gibbons testify that the presumption was that each was in the mine at the time of the explosion, Vokolek asked, "And a good many others were killed in the mine who were not identified?"

"Yes, sir."

"And these men might be presumed to be among those not identified?"

"Yes, sir."

Coroner Amos followed with a question. "You wrote me a note about Franciszk Soyer. In the face of that note I made a death certificate and sent it to Chicago. They required something more. Can you testify as to whether that man was supposed to be in the mine and killed?"

"His relatives report him missing. They further say that he went in the mine that morning and that he has not returned. The presumption is that he is dead."[38]

Gibbons was admitting that the system was only guesswork; the identification process had completely broken down. They had to presume that the persons missing in the community were among the unidentified dead.

He also testified that the census was flawed as evidenced by the fact that Cunningham revised the total several times when the Polish priest, Father Lestoka, identified additional miners. Cunningham had a list of names from interviews with surveyors. The coroner's list, as well as the list of the company, was of bodies recovered, some identified and some not. It appears that Cunningham merged his list with the coroner's list and simply assigned names to the unidentified bodies. But in an exchange that further undercut the accuracy of the account, Gibbons testified that there were bodies found in both mines of men who were not supposed to be employed.[39]

What translator Vokolek appears to be pointing out is that in the end, the 71 unidentified bodies were assigned names from either the Cunningham Survey list or if the authorities were notified of a person missing by relatives, they would assign unidentified bodies with these names, presuming, as Gibbons suggests, that they were in the mine at the time of the explosions.

David Victor, the chief safety inspector for the Fairmont Coal Company, testified late on the afternoon of January 8, 1908. Shortly after beginning, he was referred to a map of the mine that showed the location of the bodies and was asked about the ventilation. He replied by identifying each section where men were assigned to work and how many bodies were found in each section.

The first and second butt headings, first south face, is ventilated by the general intake air of the mine. The third right off first south was supplied with 16,700 cubic feet of air, four miners working and seven bodies found; second right supplied with 20,400 cubic feet of air per minute, sixteen miners working, sixteen bodies found; first right split 9,700 cubic feet of air, fifteen miners working and nineteen bodies found; first right split on Second North heading 12,600 cubic feet of air, seven miners working, five bodies found. . . .[40]

In total, Victor reports that the map shows 243 miners working and 301 bodies found in the actual working rooms of the mine. The 58 additional bodies could be presumed to be boys and men working off the books. This map is of limited value as it was common practice as we have seen with the survivors to move from section to section during the shift itself. Further, these figures do not include the miners in the entry ways, general maintenance workers, mechanics, drivers, and the multitude of others necessary to make the mine operate, simply those digging the coal room by room.[41] But if the number of miners was not known with certainty, the number of animals was: Ben Koon, stable boss for No. 8, testified there were 10 horses and 6 mules in his mine on the morning of December 6, and all perished.[42] In both mines, 35 mules died in the disaster.[43] Further evidence challenging the official count is the fact that certain names do not appear on any list but are reported in the news media. In the *Pittsburgh Dispatch* of December 14, 1907, a death notice announced that David James, Jr., 25, the son of Mr. and Mrs. David James, Sr., of Arnold, was one of the victims of the Monongah mine disaster.[44] James's name does not appear on the Coroner's list, the Relief Committee's list, or the list of the miners buried at the Monongah Graveyard.

By December 14, the spokesmen for Consolidation and Fairmont Coal companies were now arguing that a much smaller number were killed:

The coal company officials will not admit that there is more than 344 lives lost but, fearing there may be some mistakes, a verification of the house to house canvass, in which their figures were shown is again being made.[45]

Indeed, some miners thought to have died were found alive.

As each of the lists was prepared for a different purpose, it is understandable that the numbers would be different. The company officials were anxious to bring the matter to a close and simply reconciled the Cunningham list and the names on the Coroner's list.

The fact that the Cunningham list nearly matched the Coroner's list in total number almost certainly resulted from simply assigning names from the Cunningham list to the unknown bodies listed by the coroner, much as the cross examination of Gibbons implies.

The violence and ferocity of the explosions without doubt destroyed a number of miner's bodies entirely, and as the newspapers reported and Trader indicates in his 1950s interview, bodies and parts of bodies were being found even as the recovery wrapped up. The *Pittsburgh Dispatch* reported on December 13 that 338 bodies had been recovered, and on December 14, 1907,

The work of recovering the dead is progressing as rapidly as can be expected. Six bodies were taken today from under heavy falls of slate. All were unrecognizable. Heads and limbs were severed from the trunks. One head was discovered several hundred feet from what was supposed to be its trunk.[46]

Without question, given the ferocity of the two explosions and the fires and roof- and ribfalls that occurred immediately thereafter, as well as the rapid cleanup and return to production, it is probable that a good number of bodies were never recovered.

In the immediate days following the explosions, virtually every reporter included quotes from the company officials and experts on the numbers of bodies that would never be found either because they were entirely destroyed, lost under roof falls, or so badly dismembered or burned as be unrecognizable.[47] As the coverage drew to a close, these matters were little mentioned, perhaps again in an effort to protect the feelings of the families.

Father Everett Briggs came to Monongah in 1952 to serve as parish priest. He became very interested in the disaster and its victims as a result of listening to the people of the parishes and the town. Through the years he has collected information on the accident and especially its victims. By working through local interviews and graveyard records, he has asserted that over 500 men died that day.

The only independent effort to calculate the number of victims was conducted by the Catholic priests, Father D'Andrea and Father Lestoka. As soon as he learned of the disaster, Father D'Andrea canvassed the parishioners and the Italian community and found that 300 Italians had died. The Polish priest, Father Lestoka reported 110 Polish miners dead,[48] making the priests' total 48 more than the official company record.

In addition to the number killed in the explosion, five 'Americans' who were engaged in rescue and recovery work died from exposure.

The number of victims at Monongah will never be known with certainty. Clearly it is above 400, more likely above 550. The official number, 362, without question undercounts the dead. Watson, Haas, and Wheelwright began as early as Saturday morning, the day after the disaster, to talk down the total killed.

Watson contradicted Malone's estimate virtually upon his arrival at the mine from Parkersburg; he speculated that the number would not exceed 300, then said it would not exceed 235, a fact that those directly involved in running the mine disputed.

He also said that by Monday the company had completed a thorough investigation of the practice of taking underground men and boys not on the payroll and had concluded that, with a single exception, it was not done in the Monongah mines. No record of such an investigation has ever been found nor was it ever mentioned again. In any case, an investigation like that could not have been completed by the time Watson was reported to have made the statement. Bodies were only beginning to be brought out of the mine, and a complete investigation would not have been possible because most sections of the mine had not yet been recovered.

But most telling was the way Trader was used to publicly assert a lower number to the media in return for a promotion. Trader could be challenged as having a faulty memory were it not for the fact that the article in which he was told he would be quoted appeared in the morning papers almost precisely as he described it, which argues for the accuracy of his recollection.

In addition, individual victims were not counted, although the company officials, including Watson and Fleming, were aware of their existence. One employee of the B&O, which serviced the mine and could have been looking at the production system, is mentioned in the correspondence between Watson and Fleming and never added to the tally. Fleming, on his private telegraph line, wired Jere Wheelwright on December 26, 1907, asking him to get from the B&O a release of the employee who was killed in the disaster.[49] His name was not added to the list.

Both the Fairmont and Pittsburgh newspapers mentioned the death of an insurance salesman who was in the mine selling insurance when it exploded. Again his name does not appear on the official list, nor does the name of the Fairmont man who was underground seeking employment at the time of the explosion.

Trader, in his later interviews, speaks of bodies being found months and years later as does the news media.[50] The list does not include the names of the two new hires that John McGraw signed on just before the explosion. One individual miner whose death notice appeared in the Uniontown obituaries is omitted from the official record. By actual count, there are thirteen individuals who were killed and independently identified but omitted from any of the lists and the total of 362, so there were at least 375 victims.

The factor that accounts for the largest number of missing victims is the practice of taking sons and relatives into the mines as off-the-record helpers. Both Gibbons and Watson said that it happened only once. The two instances each man mentioned were different and therefore there are at least two. However, Gibbons' denial in his sworn testimony and Watson's throughout the investigation stretch credibility past the breaking point.

With more than 500 miners daily in both mines, a conservative estimate would suggest that at least 10 percent—and most likely higher—would employ underground helpers who would not be on any roll. This would have meant a minimum of 50 additional victims and, possibly, according to Malone and Gaskill, more like 100. Supporting the fact that such workers were in the mine was the recovery of significant numbers of bodies without brass identity tags. This would have meant that there were a large number of off-the-payroll workers. The failure to find the bodies was not unusual given the intensity of the explosions and fires. The forces that were unleashed would also have been sufficient to bury bodies under tons of debris. In addition, the use of lye by the recovery teams to aid in the rapid disintegration of the mules and horses likely affected the human bodies adjacent to or underneath the animals as well. Fifty would be a conservative estimate of the number of bodies never recovered from the underground.

It could be argued that the widows and families of the victims would have come forward and complained if their loved ones were not counted, especially if there was a potential for economic recovery. However, this may not have been the case because many miners were single or had no family in this country. Wives were at a terrible disadvantage because of the language, lack of access to information, and a common fear of deportation as they were still strangers in a strange land.

Father Francesco Pelliccia, Arch Priest, wrote to the Monongah Mine Relief Committee from Duruniadel Sannio on January 21, 1908. He provided the names of individuals who he had identified in his village who were killed in the explosion and had not been identified for relief: Farcse Giovanni, Zeoli Sabastino, De-Maria Sebastiano, and D'uva Giuseppe. The names were not added to any list. Indeed, what recourse would a parent, spouse, or priest have in this instance in a foreign country, 3,000 miles away?[51]

Finally, accurate totals of victims of man-made or natural disasters were not common in the first decade of the twentieth century. The April 18, 1906, San Francisco earthquake estimate of 3,000 dead has been considered by many as a gross underestimation.

The official number of 362 was clearly a count of located bodies, identified victims that were matched with names from the company survey. Thirteen others were recorded in newspaper accounts or as visitors, railroad men, and so on, making the total 375.[52] In addition, Victor testified that the recovery crews identified 301 bodies in the working rooms where only 243 miners had been assigned. The difference of 58 bodies would likely have been boys and men working off the books, thus likely bringing the total to 433. Using a conservative estimate, the approximately 50 bodies that were never recovered results in a total of 488. There were two men who were first in a position to know and were also asked immediately about the disaster. Lee Malone and Mine Superintendent Gaskill both, independently of one another, stated that the number was in excess of 500 and as high as 550 or 578.

Finally, the only independent surveys by the parish priests of Italian and Austro-Hungarian members of the two immigrant churches was 410.[53] When added to the 'Americans', both black (11) and white (74), and the Turks (5) the total comes to 500, so it is reasonable to conclude that the disaster at the Monongah mines certainly claimed in excess of 500 lives and probably more than 550 men.

"AN END TO THIS HUGE
LOSS AND WASTE"

It is of the utmost importance that a Bureau of Mines be established in accordance with the pending bill to reduce the loss of life in mines and the waste of mineral resources and to investigate the methods and substitutes for prolonging the duration of our mineral supplies.

—President Theodore Roosevelt in a special message to Congress

January 22, 1909

On December 10, 1907, the *Fairmont West Virginian* reported that the Verdi Brass Band of Monongah, having suffered the loss of so many of its members in the disaster, was disbanding and Professor Verdi was returning to Italy.[1]

On October 9, 1926, almost 19 years after surviving the disaster, Peter Urban was killed by a fall of coal in the same Monongah mine where he had been rescued. Five daughters and two sons survived him. The funeral mass was held at the St. Stanislaus church in Monongah.[2]

Before the Monongah disaster, modest efforts had been underway at the federal government level to study the causes of mine explosions. The

Technologic Branch of the Geological Survey, a division of the Department of Commerce, had begun a study in 1904, justified not on the grounds of the increasing death toll from coal production, but on the grounds of investigating fuel wastes. The Technologic Branch had grown out of a coal-testing exhibition at the 1900 Louisiana Purchase Exposition in St. Louis. That exhibit displayed the different properties and qualities of coal from states and foreign countries. The Branch was viewed first as a research position to assist and improve mineral extraction and utilization.

Holmes and others conceptualized the Technological Branch as a way to introduce advanced mining methods into the current, often backward, methods of mining coal.

During the months before the disaster at Monongah, Clarence Hall and Walter O. Snelling, both employees of the Technological Branch, had been working on a comparative report of accidents and disasters in the United States and abroad. Their report was a damning indictment of the United States mining industry. As they concluded, mining was without question the most dangerous occupation worldwide. In *Coal-Mine Accidents: Their Causes and Prevention: A Preliminary Statistical Report Bulletin 333*,[3] they describe in detail a frightening story of rapidly increasing accidents and explosions in the United States coal mining industry. This was especially notable because of the contrast with the decrease in the number of explosions and deaths in European mines over the same period of time.

The most dramatic finding was their conclusion that the American mining industry had the safest natural conditions in which to operate coal mining in the world. It is very doubtful whether natural conditions in any other country in the world are as favorable as in the United States for getting out coal with the minimum amount of danger to the workmen employed. Many of the conditions for United States mines presented "almost ideal conditions for mining." Yet during the five years that preceded Monongah, the United

States had the highest rate of deaths per ton of coal produced by any major producer. Mines in the United States killed an average of 3.39 miners per thousand employed each year, compared to 2.06 for Prussia, 1.28 for Great Britain, 1.00 for Belgium, and .91 for France. So, while the accident trend for the United States had increased during the five-year period, from 2.67 in 1885 to 3.40 in 1906, in every other country, deaths per ton of coal showed a substantial decrease. Also, the number of miners killed per ton produced in the United States varied greatly, increasing and decreasing from one year to the next, while in every other country the number continuously decreased. This fact is especially troubling because it points out that no systematic program was in place to control the accidents.

Moreover, the overall numbers of miners killed in the United States was increasing over time. In 1906, the number of miners killed reached 2,061, a record only to be surpassed in 1907 when the total reached a staggering 3,400. The conclusion reached was that death in the mines was out of control and growing.

Joseph A. Holmes had written an introduction to the report that attempted to explain the reasons why the American mines were so much more dangerous than anywhere else. This increase has been due in part to the lack of proper and enforceable mining regulations, and in part to the lack of reliable information concerning the explosives used and the conditions under which they could be used safely. These factors were partially due to rapidly increasing number of miners and the collection of coal from deeper in the earth, farther from the entrance, where good ventilation is more difficult and dangerous accumulations of explosive gas are more frequent.

The release of the report came just days after the Monongah disaster, and because of that calamity, as well as accidents at the Darr Mine in Pennsylvania and the mine in Yolande, Alabama, this obscure report gained prominence. According to p. 28 of *Historical Summary of Mine Disasters in the United*

States, Vol. I, Coal Mines—1810–1958, put out by the U. S. Department of Labor Mine Safety and Health Administration, 239 miners died in an explosion at the Darr Mine in Jacobs Creek, Pennsylvania, on December 19, 1907. On December 16, 1907, 57 miners died in an explosion at the Yolande Mine in Alabama. Newspaper editorial pages and magazines throughout the country quoted it at length. As a result, a shift began in the public's opinion, which came to believe that the loss of life should no longer be considered a part of the cost of doing business in the expanding economy. Critics could now point out that the rationale the mining industry had used for years— that mining was simply inherently dangerous—was wrong. If disasters were preventable in Europe where mining conditions were known to be far worse than the prime conditions in United States mines, then the industry should do a better job of preventing them. The report concludes, "These mine accidents may be reduced to less than one-third their present number."

Immediately following the disaster, Governor Dawson called a special session of the West Virginia legislature in Charleston, the state capital, for January. Many of the West Virginia coal operators were extremely concerned that Governor Dawson and the legislature would react to public opinion and adopt more stringent requirements for mine safety. J. C. Kinley, an operator from neighboring eastern Ohio, described the situation:

I believe that Governor Dawson is very fair and will honestly try to do what he can to promote the best interest of the coal industry in West Virginia. This being the case . . . there will be considerable pressure brought upon him . . . to consider mine legislation.[4]

In 1907, the regulation of safety and health risks in mines was the jurisdiction of the state, with no federal involvement. As a result, a patchwork of legislation existed that reflected, among other factors, the relative political influence of the mining industry in particular states and whether there were bal-anced interests of labor organizations and industry. Ohio and Pennsylvania, for example, had more comprehensive employment laws than most states. Where, on the other hand, the economy—as well as the political landscape—was dominated by a single industry like the coal industry and where the labor interests were underrepresented, the imbalance worked against comprehen-sive employment laws and safety regulations, as was the case in West Virginia. G. H. Caperton, then a secretary to a group of southern West Virginia coal operators, wrote to Fleming:

It appears that the Governor in his call for a special meeting of the Legislature will incorperate further mining laws in his call. Our committee feels there is to much law now, making the matter of mining a burden and that no further laws could be enacted to help out the situation."[5]

J. C. McKinley, president of the J. C. McKinley Coal Company of Wheeling, also wrote Fleming fearing that the legislature would adopt "radi-cal legislation" similar to that which existed in adjacent coal mining states; he particularly feared that Ohio legislature would go even further as a result of the disaster to adopt statutes which would be "drastic and burdensome if not prohibitive."[6]

A year before the Monongah disaster, the West Virginia Legislature had established a Joint Select Committee to investigate the causes of the Stuart mine explosions in 1907. The committee heard testimony in February of 1907 concerning the Stuart disaster, then when news of the Monongah acci-dent spread, the committee held its first meeting on the evening of December 16, 1907, at the Waldo Hotel in Clarksburg. The chairman, the Honorable Thomas Garland, was joined by R. F. Kidd on behalf of the Senate and Mrs. J. H. Strickling, M. K. Duty, and A. J. Mitchell on the part of the House. Next, the committee attended the hearings held before the coroner, E. S. Amos, and the Marion County Grand Jury in Fairmont. The committee stayed through three days of testimony on the 7th, 8th, and 9th and ordered a transcript for the rest of the hearing. On the afternoon of the 9th, the committee held a meeting at the Manley Hotel in Fairmont at which Messrs. Powell and Watson from the Fairmont Coal Company were present. Testimony was taken from one witness, George Harrison, chief inspector of mines of the State of Ohio.

On January 23 in the Finance Committee room of the West Virginia Capitol, the select committee reconvened. During the next several days, the committee heard from a number of witnesses beginning with John W. Paul, as well as each of the West Virginia mines' eight inspectors who were questioned about their experience and thoughts as to the accident causes. Other mining experts were called, as was A. B. Fleming who testified on the evening of January 24 at the Ruffner Hotel in Charleston.

Ex-Governor Fleming was asked what changes had been made in the methods of mining since the explosion. Fleming testified:

I will preface by saying that the explosion was so much of a surprise to us and so great a shock that the company was ready to do anything to minimize the danger to their other mines and in Monongah No. 6 and No. 8 whenever they should be ready to start. Conferences were held as to what could be done, or what experiments could be undertaken which would not likely increase the danger, and the object of which was to decrease the danger in the mines. We therefore, as an experiment, started very soon to require all holes drilled into the coal to be tamped with clay or some non-combustible matter, and I think in all our mines that practically has been pursued since shortly after the explosion at Monongah. We also concluded to try the employment of shot firers in the older and larger mines and inaugurated that system of firing in what is known as the Shaft, New England and Gaston plants, and later when we start No. 6 and No. 8 we will also have shot firers there—at least unless the experiment should prove unsatisfactory, which it has not done so far. We also, in the mines named, are using masurite, which has so far seemed to be successful. [Masurite is flameless/smokeless explosive powder as opposed to the cheaper and flame producing black powder.] This time we have also been using shot firers and the new powder has not been sufficient to fully test the same, especially as to the cost. However, we have adopted that powder and the use of shot firers. We did not consider the cost if it could be determined that it minimized the danger in the mines.[7]

Fleming further testified that they were now requiring the miners to block the coal and prohibiting shooting off the solid. Undercutting the coal had to be done before the explosions were set off, so the explosion would not to come out the drilled hole, creating a potential for igniting fires or explosions. The committee asked Fleming if the company ever compensated the miners for *blocking* (placing roof support timbers topped with blocks of wood to secure in place). He answered, "We do not pay anything for blocking, we make it a part of the miners' duty, we simply require them to block the coal." Admitting that this was more work for the miner at no increase in pay, Fleming testified that miners should do it because it was better and less dangerous, but he had heard no complaints because the mines were only running three days a week and "when work is slack of course you would hear no complaints about blocking or anything else, because there are plenty of men to do the work and more than enough."

After less than 10 questions, all of which dealt with changes and powder, Fleming was excused.[8]

In his public testimony and privately, Fleming signaled that he was in favor of significant changes in the West Virginia mining law. In a confidential letter to J. C. McKinley on January 3, 1908 he wrote,

My own opinion is that the mines should be classified by some competent authority and those dangers from dust or gas should be operated with greater care and necessarily with greater expense than those not so dangerous. Any mine using coal mining machines might be termed a dusty mine. In such mines and in mines generating gas in dangerous quantities, I think only Flynn's Powder should be used and shots fired only by experienced shot firers. The holes should not be tamped with coal or combustible matter. I might name some other safeguards.[9]

Fleming had accurately analyzed the safety problems in the mining industry, especially in West Virginia and the Fairmont Coal Company mines. Fleming had, in fact, gone as far as preparing a bill that he had arranged to have introduced into the West Virginia legislature by Joseph H. McDermott. McDermott had been in charge of the investigation on behalf of the State government.[10]

Now, however, despite the catastrophic loss of life, his fellow West Virginia coal operators raised stiff opposition to Fleming's position. William A. Ohley, a fellow West Virginia operator, wrote on January 15 that he hoped Fleming had changed his mind after discussion with fellow operators. He continued, "I have talked to a number of operators here and they are unanimous in the opinion that such a requirement in the law would do positive harm rather than good, and they will bitterly oppose any proposition of that kind." More significantly, Ohley reported that

I have learned through a confidential source which I regard as entirely reliable, that the Governor does not regard this as an opportune time for any new mining legislation and that he would favor making no change in the present law at the extra session, unless it might be something along the lines of strengthening the inspection department of the State. He will oppose any radical coal legislation.[11]

On January 28, 1908, mine No. 8 reopened. Scores of applications were received daily by A. J. Ruckman. Mine No. 6 reopened February 5, 1908.[12]

The company changed two practices: flameless powder was to be used to reduce the risk of blown-out shots and the method of watering the coal dust was modified—the dust in the rooms would be watered as well as in the entries.

The operators' grave concerns that the West Virginia legislature would enact more stringent legislation in response to public pressure were misplaced. The West Virginia Board of Trade set up a committee whose job it was to minimize the effects of the legislative actions. The preparations were apparently successful.

In its final report on the Monongah disaster, the Board of Trustees and the Legislative Committee concluded,

It was conceded that this explosion was a dust explosion, yet no one has been able to give all the elements that may be present to create a dust explosion. This reference to the Monongah mines and to the conditions that were thought to exist there at that time are especially made for the purpose of impressing upon the legislature the fact that the legislature cannot reach the causes or provide a remedy which will prevent future explosions, until the cause is known, this must be the result of future study and experiment.[13]

This conclusion would fit neatly with the argument developed and suggested by the grand jury that the federal government needed to conduct scientific research into the causes and prevention of the explosions. It also adopted the clearly erroneous position—which had already been rejected in Europe and among most prominent engineers in the United States—that a coal dust explosion could not occur without the presence of a methane gas explosion.

With this report the legislature lapsed into inaction. No new statutes were adopted during 1908. The West Virginia legislature did not act to improve mine safety and health laws, and for decades, the West Virginia statute continued to be far less stringent than the law in its neighboring states of Pennsylvania and Ohio. Many considered the code in West Virginia the weakest in the nation.[14]

Fleming was even rebuffed by his fellow operators in his commitment to adopt a legislative or regulatory requirement to mandate certified shot firers. In fact, as a reaction to the anti-immigrant blame theory, the West Virginia legislature took up a bill that would have placed limits or restrictions on the importation and use of immigrant labor. However, the mine operators successfully opposed the bill and the practice continued.

While Fleming was attempting to address legislative issues and his own feelings regarding responsibility, Clarence Watson was in White Plains, New York, at Muldoon's Hotel on a vacation. On February 1, 1908, he telegraphed Fleming: "Legislature or nothing else should stop you from coming here for two or three weeks wire at once so that I can get your room, I will guarantee five years more life."[15] Shortly, Fleming abandoned his efforts and joined Watson for a couple of weeks at Muldoon's. Muldoon's was a Hygenic Institute, operated by William Muldoon, a wrestler who had wrestled with and beaten John L. Sullivan, the champion prize fighter. His institute was for men who had "made fools of themselves for so long they had forgotten the art of living."

In 1894, Nellie Bly, the famous journalist, while taking the cure at a nearby female institution, had broken the gender barrier and stayed at Muldoon's. She reported that the mansion with its opulent interiors had cost $100,000.00 to convert.[16]

Camden was in Parkersburg at the time of the explosion and according to his excellent biographer, Festus D. Summers, "felt the full force of the catastrophe." In a letter to his son he wrote "he was too unnerved to attend to any business . . . worried and distressed to death about the great Monongah accident." In April, he returned to Baltimore where he died on the 25th day.[17]

In 1909, Lee L. Malone, then 48 years of age, suffered a series of strokes; after lengthy treatment at the Johns Hopkins Hospital in Baltimore, he returned home and died on July 29, 1909. His funeral drew a large crowd of well-wishers, and the eulogy touched on his exceptional career as a mining engineer and businessman. The *Fairmont Times*, in an editorial, concluded that his death was in large part a result of the sadness and pain that he felt as a result of the Monongah disaster.[18]

The publication by the Technologic Branch two weeks after the disaster undercut the United States operators' argument that the United States mines were as safe as their counterparts overseas. Indeed, the comparative statistics and analysis of safety and health practices between Ohio, Pennsylvania, Illinois, and West Virginia, reflected badly on the West Virginia operators. They were concerned that action at the state level might bring about regulatory change, forcing them to the level that the neighboring states were operating under. The less stringent standards in West Virginia were in fact an economic advantage to the West Virginia operators and gave them an edge over their competitors in Pennsylvania and Ohio. However, concerns about possible legislation on the national level prompted the West Virginia operators to act:

In view of the recent explosions, resulting from which legislation affecting the interests of every mine in the state is sure to follow and in view of the fact that some such legislation may be inimical to the true interests of labor and capital, we think it advisable that the principal mining interests of the State should meet.[19]

On January 8, 1907, the West Virginia coal operators convened a meeting in Washington, DC, at the National Metropolitan Bank Building near the

B&O train station. Fleming, who initially had resisted attending, was present as were several operators from Pennsylvania. Joseph A. Holmes and others from the federal government were also in attendance.[20] William N. Page, president of the Soup Creek Collier Co., Fayette County, West Virginia, urged the group to seek the involvement of the federal government: "A single individual can accomplish nothing. We stand today in the position of a sick man, and we have the Legislature and Congress as doctors. They want to prescribe medicine when they have not diagnosed the disease."

For Page, this represented a change of heart. On December 14, 1907, he had written Fleming expressing reservations about one of the federal experts who was at the site of the Monongah disaster: "I saw Mr. Hall, the Government expert, the day he left here [Washington, DC]. And as you know by this time, he is an expert on explosives, but knows little or nothing about mines, or the practical problems of mining."[21]

The group adopted three official resolutions: first, supporting congressional appropriations for research into the causes of mine disasters; second, a resolution stating that presently the causes of such disaster was unknown; and third, "that the United States Government should take the necessary steps to determine the causes before any attempt is made to apply legislative remedies."[22] The next morning, still in Washington, DC, the West Virginia operators met alone without state and federal government representatives and formed the West Virginia Mining Association as a way to have a more effective role in West Virginia coal-related issues, a position hard to explain since they were so dominant up until that time.

In early 1907, President Theodore Roosevelt created the *National Conservation Commission*, a joint federal and state effort to address the issue of mineral resources exploitation in the country. Primarily concerned that the nation's mineral resources were being depleted by wasteful extraction operations and methods, which removed only the cream of the reserves and made almost all of the remainder unmineable, the commission was concerned, as a secondary matter, with the human cost of mineral production.

President Roosevelt, at the opening of the White House conference, said,

We know now that our mineral resources once exhausted are gone forever, and that the needless waste of them costs us hundreds of human lives and nearly $300,000,000 a year. Therefore, let us undertake without delay the investigation necessary before our people will be in position, through state action or otherwise to put an end to this huge loss and waste, and conserve both our mineral resources and the lives of the men who take them from the earth.[23]

In May, 1908, a conference of governors was convened with Gifford Pinchot of the Interior Department as Chair of the Executive Committee. In attendance were 44 state governors, some 500 experts and numerous federal officials. The commission divided into sections, focusing on lands, forests, waters, and minerals. Joseph A. Holmes was serving as secretary of the minerals section, as well as a member of the executive committee. Among other findings, the commission proposed the first inventory of natural resources in the country, and encouraged the establishment of a conservation commission in each state. In his transmittal of the report to Congress, President Roosevelt described the consumption and waste of our mineral resources as reaching nearly one million dollars each working day, but issued his strongest denunciation for the death level among mines:

The loss of life in the mines is appalling. The larger part of these losses of life and property can be avoided. It is of the utmost importance that a Bureau of Mines be established in accordance with the pending bill to reduce the loss of life in mines and the waste of mineral resources.[24]

Within the mining community nationwide, the western metal mine operators were the most in favor of a Bureau of Mines. Their interest was for a governmental entity that would help underwrite the cost of the exploration and mapping, as well as development of improved mining methods. This was especially true as applied to the vast portions of land owned by the federal government. As a model, they viewed the Department of Agriculture's roll in assisting the farming community. The interest in safety and health research was, if present at all, a secondary factor.

In January of 1909 on Capitol Hill, as a result of the publicity surrounding Monongah and the other mining disasters, momentum for a bureau of mines was building, and the Second Session of the 60th Congress was opening. Six separate bills were introduced calling for the creation of a Bureau of Mines. In March of 1908, A. B. Fleming testified before the Committee on Mines and Mining, pointing out that recent accidents

have stirred up the people wonderfully. Not only operators and miners, but all people, and the talk and the desire is for a department of mines and mining as we have always understood it in connection with the Interior Department. That has been discussed a great deal of late, and I have not heard of any person but is in favor of it.

I am interested. I am a director in the Fairmont Coal Company, which operated the two mines, Monongah 6 and 8, which blew up on the 6th of December, in which accident there were 356 people killed; the most deplorable accident, I believe, of which we have any record except the one in France a year or two ago. I think it is appropriate, as we understood it, belonging to the Fairmont Coal Company, out of the 30 we had.

Fleming was then asked if he had discovered what had been the cause of the explosion. Fleming answered,

No, sir; that is what impressed upon us forcibly the importance of such a bureau as you are discovering here and contemplating creating.[25]

Fleming further testified,

This is a matter that should be taken hold of by the Federal Government and not left to the State and the operators.[26]

Finally, Fleming stated,

If these explosions are going to continue, we will have to go out of business. We cannot stand it, another explosion as we had would kill us.[27]

Following Monongah, the need for a bureau now became a national cause with more than 1,000 newspapers around the country calling for some form of federal action to prevent mine accidents.[28] Representative Kendall commented, "It is a matter for congratulation that the conscience of the country is at last awakening and that the human impulses of our people are finally aroused."[29]

On April 6, 1908, the House Committee reported out HR 20883 and recommended passage. On May 21, 1908, the full House passed the bill: 222 *yays*, 29 *nays*, 7 *present* votes, and 129 not voting. The bill was sent to the Senate where it ran into opposition from Senator Henry M. Teller of Colorado, among others.

His stated opposition was fourfold: 1) that the states were the proper authorities; 2) that the federal government lacked jurisdiction and authority to regulate; 3) that work was already being done by the Commerce Department's Technologic Branch; and 4) that the establishment of such a bureau would be too costly.

Underlying these concerns was a constitutional argument that the federal government had not until this time become involved in any way in the protection of workers and the strongly held opinion that such protection was a matter solely within each state's jurisdiction. Conservatives and industrialists had continued to hold to the proposition that despite the continued carnage, mining companies should not have government interfering in their affairs. Child labor and food safety were also issues before the Congress but faced stiff opposition as a result of the opposition to the federal government's involvement in the workplace. Philosophically, the question was whether capitalism would be allowed to continue to operate in an unfettered manner or would the national government deal with a national scandal. This debate stalled the Bureau of Mine's progress, until the following year, 1910, when the proponents of the bureau were able to overcome the opposition. Holmes was instrumental in keeping the issue on the forefront, arguing for an Organic Act that would create a bureau with a wide grant of authority as opposed to one that was limited to only investigations of explosions and not other types of events such as fires.

Proposals to establish a bureau of mines had been introduced as early as 1865 and had been supported by the western mining interests, notably the metal interests. As mentioned, these efforts were directed at providing assistance for the mining companies in developing minerals. With the impetus of Monongah, Naomi, Darr, and Yolande, the concept of a bureau had been transformed into both a minerals development agency as well as one that would conduct research and investigations into safety, notably prevention of disastrous explosions.

By December, 1909, Senator Teller had retired from the Senate. Perhaps even more significant was the fact that a month earlier, a mine fire had occurred in northwestern Illinois at the Cherry Mine on November 13, 1909 — over 259 lives were lost.[30]

On Saturday afternoon, a fire had started underground in the stables when dry baled hay was accidentally ignited, suffocating the miners underground. The second largest coal mine disaster, the Cherry Mine fire, provided forceful argument that the agencies' investigative authority should be broad and not limited simply to explosions, as some had argued. Again, the public was outraged at the failure of the mine operators and the state agencies to protect the miners. In the spring of 1910, the United States Senate, after the Committee on Mines and Mining bowed to certain mine operators, agreed to amend the bill to explicitly exclude any intent to grant the bureau powers of inspection or supervision, and passed the bill out of committee. The bill passed the Senate on May 2, 1910, and The Organic Act creating the United States Bureau of Mines was signed into law by President Howard A. Taft on May 16, 1910.

The bureau established a system of investigation for mine disasters involving fires and began to publish investigative reports, information circulars, and other materials that were distributed throughout the mining community across the country. Thus the bureau advanced knowledge of disaster prevention methods, and the application of that knowledge in mines gained acceptance. The bureau also developed and shared information across state lines about safety practices and methods for improving safety.

To support their efforts, the bureau conducted a series of tests on the various types of explosives and rated their safety levels, resulting in a gradual phasing out of the least safe products, such as black powder. This testing led to the development of approval and certification requirements for any newly introduced underground mining equipment, the first such requirement for any industry in the United States and one that exists to this day.

Ventilation was studied, and recommendations were made for improving methods of removing methane and other explosive gases. In addition, the bureau established a series of mine rescue stations throughout the country with teams located at strategic intervals, allowing rapid access to mines where accidents occurred. The teams developed expertise in fighting fires and using mine rescue equipment that was first imported from European countries and later developed and manufactured in the United States. Further, in an innovative scheme, Holmes purchased eleven railroad cars, fitted them out for mine rescue efforts, and utilized them in rescue efforts for the next fifty years. But during the periods when the cars were not needed for mine rescue, they were taken into the coal camps and used as classrooms for teaching miners, as well as mine supervisors, the lessons of mine safety and health.

In what was perhaps the most remarkably original program, the bureau developed educational and training materials, and then, acting through state and local governments and associations, began the long process of educating and training both miners and supervisors in every aspect of mining safety and health.[31]

In July, 1915, Joseph Holmes died at the age of 56 from exhaustion while visiting mining locations in the west while he was still director of the bureau. Almost immediately, a nongovernmental association, the Holmes Safety Association, was established in his name; it was made up of industry, labor, and government officials who provided education and training to the new immigrants as well as mine operators. Pictures taken of the bureau and the Holmes Association classes show newly arrived immigrants, men in ill-fitting suits, intently studying the best methods of setting off explosives and removing methane gases.[32]

But in order to spread the gospel of safety to the local level, the bureau also established a program at each mine for miners, companies, and unions. The "Safety First" slogan, which was the program's slogan, would become the most wide spread industrial safety slogan ever used. After first being adopted in the mining community, it spread through railroad and steel industries and finally to all American industries.

Lastly, and although gradual, the most significant development that grew out of the Monongah disaster was the fact that the issue of protecting workers' safety and health in the workplace began to be accepted as a part of the mining industry process, and safety practices began to evolve.

A basic philosophical shift had occurred, first among the general public and then among the mining industry. Death, especially on a large scale, was preventable and therefore wrong. Those companies that operated mines where such disasters occurred were criticized and scorned in favor of those mines that were comparatively safer. In part because of such criticism, some companies, such as United States Steel and Bethlehem Steel, adopted company-wide programs that incorporated safety practices in all parts of their mines and steel mills. Unfortunately, progress was uneven. The Consolidation Coal Company and the Fairmont Coal Company were not as progressive, and its miners continued to experience high risk and disaster for decades.

Nor should the improvements be overstated. Carnage in the mines continued: during each of the next ten years, thousands more miners died. Disasters caused by disregarding known methods of prevention, the use of improper equipment, and explosives improperly loaded, occurred with remarkable regularity. Immigrants and 'Americans' continued to die by the thousands, and despite the passage of The Organic Act of 1911 by Congress, it was not until 1937 that the United States Supreme Court in a landmark ruling, NLRD v. Jones & Laughlin Steel Corp., abandoned the legal fiction that held that mining was a local undertaking and not subject to federal jurisdiction as part of the flow of interstate commerce; mining was therefore subject to protection under the Commerce Clause, thus overcoming the objection that mining could not be regulated by the federal government.

Indeed, the health conditions in coal mines grew worse in the decades after 1910. With the increased use of mechanized equipment, so much coal dust was created in the mining cycle that, during the 1940s, '50s, and '60s, black lung reached epidemic proportions among the miners. Unfortunately, the majority of the mine operators of the United States again refused to recognize coal dust as the culprit, some arguing that such dust was actually good for your lungs by acting as a filter similar to charcoal filters, and followed the patterns established during the 1900s explosion delay and debate.

Black lung, or coal worker's pneumoconiosis (CWP), was not recognized in the United States as an occupational disease until 1960, while its existence was accepted and efforts to prevent exposures adopted throughout Europe in the 1930s.

Over the next five decades, there were five rewrites of the original 1910 organic mining law, yet progress in improving accidents and illness was slow and difficult.

Shortly after Monongah, and nearly simultaneous with the mine safety reforms and inspired by the mining example, safety movements in other industries took hold. Safety movements in the railroad and steel industries gained popularity, and improvements in safety also came about in mills and factories, but certainly not in time to prevent the Triangle Shirt Waste Factory fire and other tragic occurrences; still, progress was being made. Child labor laws and food safety statutes were also adopted during this period.

But concurrent with the safety movement, and in part resulting from its limited success, the union movement gained ascendancy in both mining and industrial settings at large. Beginning with John Mitchell who had led the Monongah miners in earlier efforts to organize, unionization increased during the next decade frequently focusing attention on safety and health issues. By the 1930s, under the leadership of John L. Lewis, the United Mine Workers of America grew to be the single largest union in the country and it spawned the United Steelworkers and the United Rubber Workers, among others.

Yet despite the presence of the bureau and the unions, voluntary, if not legally required, efforts by the mine operators and state-by-state enforcement of safety and health laws proved inadequate and miners continued to die by the thousands.

On November 20, 1968, the Farmington Mine, a mine not five miles from the Monongah mine in the same Pittsburgh seam owned by the same company, Consolidation Coal Company, exploded, trapping seventy-eight miners. It was regulated inadequately by the same West Virginia law and West Virginia Department of Mines, and the U.S. Bureau of Mines. During the next few days, nine separate explosions ripped through the underground maze, the forces so strong that huge caverns were created. Finally, across the country, the public's reaction also exploded. Bitterness toward the mining industry both in the coal fields and nationwide was rampant, and it reached an all time high. The industry, although politically potent, no longer dominated the national scene. Despite the UMWA's corrupt leader, Tony Boyle, and his conciliatory comments about the Consolidation Coal Company being a good, safe company, and despite state and federal officials alternatively blaming God, the miners, or Mother Nature for the explosions, Congress acted and wrote the strongest law ever to be adopted before or since to regulate safety and health in the mines in the United States and abroad, The Federal Coal Mine Safety and Health Act of 1969.

Yet, despite remarkable progress since 1969, as both fatal and nonfatal accident totals and rates dropped dramatically, miners continued to die. As the century came to a close, the lowest numbers of miners were killed in the nation's mines. Thirty-five coal miners perished in 1999. In the year 2000, thirty were killed, and in 2001 and 2003 another thirty deaths occurred. In the area of health, black lung continues to plague miners, albeit a lesser number, and silicosis cripples and kills men, and now a few women, who work in the mines.

Death still stalks the mines, though with less frequency or regularity. Large disasters are rare. The bureau's disaster definition adopted in the early years that five deaths constituted a disaster was relegated to the past. But near misses, mine fires, and explosions continue to occur.

In 1995, the United States Congress abolished the United States Bureau of Mines. Years before, it had been stripped of its enforcement responsibilities, which had been transferred to a separate enforcement unit within the Department of the Interior and from there to Mine Safety and Health Administration in the United States Department of Labor. During the last two decades, the Bureau of Mines was exclusively a research agency. On February 3, 1996, the last director, Rhea Graham, closed the last office, transferred its functions to other government entities, and ended its illustrious history.

But miners and their families, whether newly immigrated and lacking in knowledge and language skills, or 'Americans,' proved an irresistible force for Monongah, the bureau, the union, and industry in the long march of history. By any objective analysis, this poorly educated, ill-equipped gaggle, often compromised, frequently corrupted, spied upon, isolated geographically, in guarded coal camps, brutalized on the job, killed by the thousands, injured by the tens of thousands, and plagued by horrible diseases, fought back. They joined and refused to join together in unions, divided by ethnic and color lines, but kept demanding justice, fairness, and a safe place to work. These men, women, and children proved indomitable.

On January 2, 2006, an explosion ripped through the Sago Mine in Upshur County, West Virginia, about sixty miles south of Monongah. Twelve miners died: eleven had survived the blast, but were trapped and died later of carbon monoxide poisoning. Later that same month in Logan County at the Aracoma Alma Mine, a belt fire claimed the lives of two miners. In May 2006, five miners were killed in an explosion at the Darby Mine in Harlan County, Kentucky. Along with several single deaths, the death toll for 2006 was forty-six, the highest toll in five years.

It is too soon to suggest there is an upward trend in mine fatalities and explosions, but the three events are too many to ignore. Investigations into the cause of Sago strongly suggest that lightning was the probable cause, and at Aracoma Alma, irresponsible safety practices were the cause of the deaths. What has to be said is that the rescue efforts were not successful and the equipment provided to miners to ensure their escape was inadequate. The brass tag identification system in use at Monongah was still in use at Sago. The telephone system, the only means of communication, was developed in the 1930s and 1940s. Updated versions have been employed, but no new technology has been adopted by the mining industry in the past twenty-five years.

THE CONSCIENCE OF A NATION

"Glück auf."

> —*German miner's greeting, which translates*
> *roughly to "Good luck"*

IN MONONGAH, there is no question that the runaway mine cars that struck the mine's ventilation system and the subsequent shock to the air, were factors contributing to the disaster. The disruption of the normal flow of air, the sparks generated in the base of the No. 6 mine entry, the displacement of the methane gas, and most significantly, the massive amounts of coal dust caused by the wreck did, as the Ohio and European investigation teams concluded, contribute to the explosion.

There is objective evidence from the underground investigations following the explosions of shots in both mines that some were improperly fired or were only partially successful in knocking down the coal. The level of burned dust and charcoal in those locations indicated that they could have been the locations of the initial explosions.

In the end, the precise cause or causes of the explosion may never be known, and in many ways, it is of little significance. The sciences of mine and industrial safety have concluded, in this country and elsewhere, that disaster prevention is about reducing or eliminating the sources of ignitions, reducing or eliminating the amount of combustible material, and finally, reducing or eliminating the number of persons who are killed or injured. Accidents are rarely the result of a single cause or factor. In the Monongah mines, the large amounts of highly explosive coal dust—a risk that was recognized in mining circles in the United States and in Europe—contributed to the magnitude and the strength of the explosion. Although the Fairmont and Consolidation engineers continued to argue that coal dust would not explode without a methane explosion, the great majority of engineers in the U.S. and abroad at the time had argued that it could. Soon, experiments by the Bureau of Mines would show that coal dust in the presence of an ignition source would explode on its own. Using open helmet lights, safety lamps, and black powder; shooting on the solid; failing to employ certified shot firers; and allowing pick miners, whether foreign or domestic, to shoot down their own coal faces were all factors that contributed to increased potential for ignition and an explosion.

The Monongah mines systematically acted contrary to each of the basic principles of disaster prevention. First and foremost, the mines were connected by a heavy wooden door, thus doubling the number of potential victims. It was well known in mining circles that such connections could be lethal in the event of a disaster. Several states, including Ohio, had by that point outlawed such practices. West Virginia had had the issue taken before its mine panel in years preceding the disaster. Camden and the Consolidation Coal and Fairmont Coal officials were fully aware that such legislation was pending and that many of the state's coal companies had been working for years to prevent adoption of such a prohibition.

Second, in the three years before Monongah exploded, leading U.S. and European mining engineers had propounded the risk of dust explosions and the need to remove the dust or to render it inert with water. Even though such practices were common and were adopted in other Consolidation/Fairmont mines, they were not practiced at Monongah. What watering that was done was so inadequate that even those doing the watering recognized the futility of their actions. Then, the introduction of electric cutting machines and rail motors increased the amount of dust and no stepped-up prevention schemes were introduced. Dust removal was virtually nonexistent and depended on the individual miner; given the economics of the mining process, it's no wonder dust removal efforts were rare. Individual miners were not paid to remove the dust, which slowed them down, nor were they paid for dust loaded with the coal.

Third, the use of miners as shot firers, especially foreign and domestic untrained miners, meant an increase in improper shots with the potential for deadly consequences. Other states required certifications for shot firers, and the issue had been debated in West Virginia mining circles and in the West Virginia legislature. Consolidation and Fairmont officials, fully aware of the other states' requirements, joined with fellow West Virginia coal operators to argue against any regulations being adopted. Moreover, the use of black powder as the explosive agent, rather than other, more stable agents, increased the potential for explosions. Despite the knowledge that black powder increased the risk, it was used at Monongah, perhaps because it was cheaper than other methods.

Fourth, allowing the practice of shooting off the solid and not tamping shots was an industrial form of Russian roulette prohibited in neighboring states and foreign countries.

First Camden, and then the Watson-Fleming interests, had spent large sums of money and energy to develop the production capacity of the mines in the most up-to-date manner. From the standpoint of production efficiency, the mines were models. From the vantage point of labor relations and safety and health, they were almost medieval. Camden and other mine operators, along with investigators, had all recognized that connecting mines was a risky and potentially catastrophic practice. They knew that the introduction of mechanical equipment increased the amounts of dust created, which everyone knew was dangerous, yet watering and dust removal systems at Monongah were below the standards adopted at other company mines in the areas. Watson, Fleming, and the others knew that introducing electricity and mechanical transportation increased the risk of accidents. Yet the mine operators were willing to take the chance—accept the risk—because each decision improved the economic efficiency of the mines. Few immigrant miners were aware of the doubly dangerous effects of connecting mines, the increased risk of an explosion resulting from mechanical cutting and haulage, or the hazards of not introducing watering systems in the rooms. The miners did not control the decisions concerning their own risks, and efforts at unionization had been brutally beaten back. Still, it was they who would pay the price for all the risks that the Consolidation and Fairmont company officials took. It was they who would suffer the consequences of the decision to connect the mines. It was they who would pay for all of the other decisions that increased the likelihood of disaster. And pay dearly they did.

But their deaths, stirring as they did the conscience of a nation, led to the first halting steps of a mine safety movement: passage of the embryonic Organic Mine Safety Act of 1910 and the beginning of a slow but steady change in the way America treated its miners.

POSTSCRIPT

IN 1950, Father Everett Briggs, pastor of the Catholic Churches in Monongah, broke ground for the St. Barbara Nursing Home, high on the hill above the town. St. Barbara is revered throughout Europe as the protector and patron saint of miners. A large block of coal dug in the Monongah mine was placed in the yard in front of the Home as a memorial to all those who had lost their lives in the 1907 tragedy. Father Briggs died December 20, 2006.

In 1961, Mines No. 6 and 8, which had been renamed the Monongah No. 63 mine, closed for good, the coal resources exhausted.

The Farmington Mine disaster, which happened on November 21, 1968, proved to be the mine safety bookend to Monongah, and led to the passage of the Federal Coal Miner Safety and Health Act of 1969, the strongest occupational health and safety law in the United States and perhaps the world. Following the passage of the law, many in the mining industry began to consider safety a part of doing business.

Consolidation Coal Company changed after Farmington. The company philosophically altered the way it conducted its mining operations, although accidents and fatalities still happen in their mines.

Even today, 100 years after the Monongah disaster, some mine operators have not made safety paramount.

On January 2, 2006, the Sago mine outside of Buckhannon, West Virginia, exploded. One man was killed instantly and twelve were trapped inside. They barricaded themselves deep in the mine, awaiting rescue. Some 40 hours later, rescuers found eleven dead and miner Randall McCoy barely alive. Sixteen days later, the Aracoma Alma mine in Logan County, West Virginia, caught fire and two men perished.

A few months after that, in May of 2006, the Darby mine in Harlan County, Kentucky, exploded and five more miners died. Just over a year later, the Crandall Canyon mine outside of Huntington, Utah, suffered a *coal bump*, which is a tame name for a violent release of rock and coal forced into the mine entry by pressure from the surrounding strata. The nation watched as a torturously slow rescue effort unfolded, days turning into weeks, only to have the mountain explode again, this time killing three rescue workers, including a federal inspector. Six more were injured. Finally, the rescue effort ceased, and the original six trapped miners were entombed beneath the mountain.

Death still stalks the mines of America.

There is a moment in the mines when the cage pulls even with the lip of the earth and the afternoon sunlight explodes into a crowded elevator car that had until then been barely lit by miner's headlamps. The miners have just finished a shift. In that moment—miners tired, work finished without mistake by men or company, Mother Nature having been kind—safety in that moment is assured and all is right with the world. The companionship, the shared risk, the common problems overcome: all these things and more can make mining for coal the most enviable profession in the world. The bitter sweetness of that moment has tragically been made possible only by so many deaths, injuries, and illnesses. That moment is more charged and frequent because of the over 500 men and boys who perished at Monongah and elsewhere since then.

Safe home.

NOTES

Chapter 1

1   Testimony transcript of Leonard taken at an inquisition held in Fairmont, Marion County, West Virginia, beginning January 6th and concluding January 15th before E. S. Ames, Marion County Coroner. In *Report of Hearing before the Joint Select Committee of the Legislature of West Virginia, 1909*. 269. [Hereafter, *Transcript*.]

2   Transcript, Fry, 274.

3   Transcript, Leonard, 269.

Chapter 2

1   Bruchey, *The Wealth of Nations*, 100.

2   Energy Information Administration, *Production Trends of Bituminous Coal & Lignite*.

3   Thrush, *A Dictionary of Mining Minerals & Related Terms*, 47.

4   Beachley, *History of the Consolidation Coal Company*, 1. [Hereafter, *Beachley*.]

5   Beachley, 17.

6   Beachley, 37

7   Hungerford, *The Story of the Baltimore & Ohio Railroad*, 240-259. [Hereafter, *Hungerford*.]

8   Marshall County Historical Society, *History of Marshall County*.

9   Hungerford, 264.

10   Hungerford, 259, 264

11 Thrush, *A Dictionary of Mining Minerals & Related Terms*, 976. [Hereafter, *Thrush*.]

12 Thrush, 828

13 Thrush, 700.

14 Thrush, 175.

15 Sisler, *Bituminous Coal Fields of Pennsylvania*, 201, 221-232.

16 Survey of Labor Statistics, Report of the Immigration Commission S. Doc. 633, 61st Congress, 2nd Session, 1910-1911, 9. [Hereafter, *Doc 633*.]

17 Doc 633, 11.

18 Doc 633, 12.

19 Lord, 3.

20 Okkonen, *Baseball Memories*, 13.

Chapter 3

1 Harper, *Days & Customs*, 306.

2 Transcript, Delasandro, 372.

3 Cupp, *Report on Monongah*, 12. [Hereafter, *Trader 1972 Interview*.]

4 Trader 1972 Interview, 12.

5 The West Virginia statute required, "[t]hat every mine owner or operator of a mine which produced dangerous quantities of gas to employ fire bosses who were citizens of West Virginia and had knowledge of fire damp and other dangerous gases as to be able to detect gases with flame safety lamps and have practical knowledge of ventilation of mines and at least three years' experience in mine generating gases."

6 Watchorn, 180.

7 Trader 1972 Interview, 12.

Chapter 4

1 Summers, *Johnson Newlon Camden*, 367.

2 Letters and Papers of Johnson Newlon Camden. Among the most important sources of this book, the collection contains nearly one hundred thousand items. Located at the West Virginia University Library, West Virginia and Regional Collection. [Hereafter, *Camden MSS*.]

3 Camden MSS, 371, 372.

4 Camden MSS, 380.

5 Summers, 375–377.

6 Summers, 46.

7   Summers, 175.

8   Camden MSS, Camden to O. H. Payne, June 9, 1875.

9   Summers, 167.

10   Summers, 134.

11   Summers, 174.

12   Summers, 366.

13   Summers, 377.

14   HCCC Beachley, 39.

15   Summers, 375–377.

16   Summers, 535.

17   *History of Marion County*, 20. [Hereafter, *Marion County*.]

18   "The Valley Coal Story," by James Otis Watson II, 1957, first appeared as article on page 6 of the *Fairmont Times* before being published as a 38-page booklet.

19   *Fairmont Times*, Ramsey, July 2, 1997, 12.

20   Marion County, 25.

21   Massay, *Legislators, Lobbyists & Loopholes*, 167. [Hereafter, *Massay*.]

Chapter 5

1   Summers, 381, 387.

2   Summers, 387.

3   Summers, report of Spilman to Camden, May 12, 1891, 387.

4   Summers, 389.

5   Titan, 291, 292.

6   Summers, 540.

7   Fairmont Coal Company records, Hagley Museum, Wilmington, Delaware.

8   HCCC Beachley, 35.

9   Summers, 540.

10   HCCC Beachley, 51-52.

11   Camden MSS, Correspondence with Clarence Watson, December, 1906 and January, 1907. A&M 7 General Correspondence Box 29.

12   HCCC Beachley, 40.

13   Massay, 95; HCCC Beachley, 52.

14   Massay, 81.

15   HCCC Beachley, 44.

16   Massay, 90.

Chapter 6

1   Core, *The Monongahela Story*, 4.

2   Leeper, 4.

3   Koon and Smith, *Marion County*, 71.

4   Summers, 381.

5   Summers, 366.

6   *Black's Law Dictionary*, 1146.

7   Summers, 369.

8   Summers, 381.

9   Chernow, *TITAN*, 167.

10 Koon and Smith, 72.

11 The first state police force in the United States was the Pennsylvania State Police Force. It was created in 1905 in the aftermath of the Great Anthracite Strike of 1902 when violence spread across county lines, and the mine operators prevailed upon the Pennsylvania Legislature to authorize the creation of the infamous Coal & Iron Police. The private army was paid by the operators to break strikes and terrorize the mining communities, especially newly arrived immigrants. *Pennsylvania State Police Historical, Educational, and Memorial Center.* www.psp.hemc.org/88k.

12 Transcript, 264.

13 Massay, 35-40.

14 Trader 1972 Interview, 9-12.

15 Leeper, 5.

16 Polk City Directory, Fairmont, 4-5.

17 Survey Book, Robert Cunningham. Cunningham conducted a survey following the December 6, 1907, disaster. Stanhage Book No. 1, WVU Regional Collection. Each survey team is identified by the last name of the lead member.

18 *Fairmont Free Press*, May 22, 1896, 1.

19 *The Fairmont Index* as quoted in Massay, 224.

20 *Fairmont Free Press*, November 28, 2001, 1.

21 *Fairmont Free Press*, October 26, 1999, 1.

22 The Bituminous Coal Miners and Coal Workers of Western Pennsylvania published a study of the western Pennsylvania mining town built around the same time. W. Jett Lauck, with the U.S. Immigration Commission, April, 1911, Vol. 26, 34-51. [Herafter, *Lauck.*]

23 Lauck, 367.

24 Massay, 200.

25 Massay, 198.

26 *Fairmont Free Press*, November 15, 2000, 1.

27 Leeper.

28 Lauck, 37, 48.

29 Letter from F. F. Lyon to Camden, June 6, 1890; Summers, 383.

30 Lauck, 39.

31   Lauck, 39.
32   *Fairmont Free Press*, December 12, 1907, 7.
33   Thrush, 974.
34   Massay, 219.
35   Lauck, 41.
36   Lauck, 41.
37   Neely, 2.
38   Massay, 222; Leeper, 6.
39   *McAteer Family History*, File No. 1. [Hereafter, *McAteer.*]
40   Fairmont Coal Company Detailed Statement of Cost of Producing Coal;
     September, 1909, author's records.
41   Monongah Mine Relief Committee Archives, pages in box no. 1. [Hereafter,
     Relief.]
42   Underground mines use one of three techniques to reach the coal: *shaft, slope,*
     or *draft*. A *shaft mine* utilizes a shaft driven vertically into the ground until it
     intersects with a coal seam. A *slope mine* utilizes opening driven at an angle to
     intersect with the coal seam. A *draft mine* utilizes a horizontal passage to the
     coal seam. Thrush, 350, 993, 1029.
43   Transcript, Smyth, 340.
44   Thrush, 919.
45   Transcript, Truckman, 278.
46   Transcript, R. S. Larue, 473.
47   The Congregation of Missionaries of St. Charles Borromeo was founded
     in 1888 specifically to assist Italian immigrants "to ensure as far as possible
     their moral, civil, and economic welfare by providing priests for immigrants."
     Catholic Encyclopedia, www.catholicforum.com/saint/s/ned06594.htm.
     Anniversary Year 50, 1907-1957, 9.
48   *Fairmont Free Press*, May 21, 1901, 1.
49   Miss Loss later married Ralph Wells of Fairmont. Author interview with David
     Wells.
50   Catholic Churches of Monongah, *Anniversary Year 50, 1907-1957*. 39-page
     booklet by Father F. Briggs, 1957, 10.
51   Catholic Churches of Monongah, 6.
52   Camden MSS, H. G. Bowles to J. N. Camden, December 29, 1929. Reverend
     Daniel O'Conner was pastor of St. Anthony's Church in Monongah.
53   *Fairmont Times*, November 27, 1907, 2.
54   *Fairmont Free Press*, February 4, 1997, 3.
55   *Fairmont Free Press*, February 16, 1997, 1.
56   Massay, 209.

57   Marion County, 2.

58   Pierce, 2003 Calendar, WV; Division of Culture and History, State Historic
     Preservation Office.

59   Marion County, 93.

60   Neely, 7.

Chapter 7

1   1906 Department of Agriculture yearbook, 524.

2   Lauck, 35.

3   Massay, 226.

4   Massay, 226; Lauck, 35.

5   Massay, 238.

6   Hungerford Vol. II, p. 78, *Polish Arrivals at the Port of Baltimore 1880-1884*,
     compiled by Jeanne Davis-White: History Press, Baltimore, MD, 1.

7   Lauck, 35.

8   Lauck, 36.

9   Lauck, 36; Lockard, 89.

10   Transcript, O. DePetris, 240.

11   Alsatia ship manifest records, Ellis Island immigration records, New York City
     Public Library immigration records.

12   Transcript, Dan Dominico, 245, 247; Transcript, O. DePetris, 371; Transcript,
     Urban, 265.

13   Transcript, Dan Dominico, 245, 247; Transcript, O. DePetris, 371; Transcript,
     Urban, 265.

14   Byers, Randolph, and Tenney, *In the Mountain State*, 5–12.

15   Transcript, Urban, 265.

16   Davis-White, 1.

17   HCCC Beachley, 60.

18   Gallagher, 92.

19   Flannery, unpublished manuscript.

20   McAteer.

21   Email correspondence with Robert Sarbell, grandson of A. Stamboulis. In
     author's possession.

22   Baldwin, 180.

23   *New York Times*, July 6, 1906, 16.

24   Baer, George F., President of Philadelphia & Reading Railway Company in an
     open letter to the press, August, 1902. History at OSU, Multimedia Historians.

25   *The Great Strike: Perspectives on the 1902 Anthracite Coal Strike*, proceedings
     from the Centennial Symposium, October, 2002, Canal History and
     Technology.

Chapter 8

1   Summers, 383.
2   Summers, 384.
3   B. D. Spilman to Camden, May 20, 1891.
4   Summers, 463.
5   Summers, 395.
6   Summers, 463.
7   Massay, 224.
8   Massay, 225.
9   *Fairmont Free Press*, October 17, 1897, 1.
10   *Fairmont Free Press*, July 5, 1897, 1; as presented in Massay, 224.
11   Jones, *Autobiography of Mother Jones*, 12.
12   Green, *Only a Miner*, 242-244.
13   Summers, 535.
14   John Mitchell Papers, 293. [Hereafter, *Mitchell Papers.*]
15   Mitchell Papers, 294.
16   Massay, 193.
17   Massay, 194.
18   Mitchell Papers, 295.
19   Jones, 44.
20   Aretas Brooks Fleming Papers, Box A40. [Hereafter, *Fleming MSS.*]
21   Jones, 49.
22   Massay, 193.
23   Fox, 90.
24   This and preceding two quotations are from Decision of Judge John J. Jackson, U.S. District Court, July 24, 1902, Parkersburg, West Virginia.
25   Guaranty Trust Company of New York v. Haggarty et al., 116 US 515 (1902).

Chapter 9

1   Blind Alfred Reed copyrighted the song in 1928. Reed, a West Virginia preacher and songwriter, altered "The Dream of the Miner's Child," Green, 132.
2   Transcript, Leonard, 269.
3   Transcript, Victor, 390.
4   *Pittsburgh Dispatch*, December, 7, 1907, 1.
5   *Fairmont Times*, December 7, 1907, 1.
6   *Fairmont Free Press*, December 7, 1907, 1.
7   *Pittsburgh Dispatch*, December 7, 1907; Transcript, Victor, 341.
8   Transcript, Leonard, 269-270.
9   Transcript, Cardelli, 269, et seq.
10   Transcript, Cary Meredith, 255.

11   *Pittsburgh Dispatch*, December 7, 1907, 6.

12   Transcript, Stalnaker, 257.

13   *Pittsburgh Dispatch*, December 7, 1907, 1.

14   Transcript, Cardelli, 351.

15   Transcript, Stalnaker, 257.

16   Transcript, Cardelli, 351.

17   *Baltimore Sun*, December 7, 1907, 3.

18   Transcript, Curry, 257.

19   Transcript, Knight, 250.

20   This and previous quotation from Transcript, Peddicord, 260 et seq.

21   Transcript, Bice, 369.

22   Transcript, Urban, 264.

23   Transcript, Jenkins, 262.

24   Transcript, Ruchman, 277; Transcript, Dean, 349.

25   Transcript, Dean, 349.

26   Email correspondence with Robert Sabell, grandson of A. Stamboulis. In author's possession.

27   Letter to author from Steve and Andrea Leach, August, 2001. From research in Vienna.

Chapter 10

1   Transcript, Dan Dominico, 247, et seq.

2   Transcript, L. Dominico, 245, et seq.

3   Transcript, Don Dominico, 248, et seq.

4   Transcript, Ruchman, 246, 247.

5   Transcript, Ruchman, 1, 14.

6   West Virginia Coal Mining Institute Report of 1909, West Virginia Archives, Cultural Center, Charleston, West Virginia.

7   Watson, *The Coal Valley Story*, 15.

8   Transcript, Ruckman, 277; Transcript, Dean, 349.

9   Watson, 15.

10   Interview with Bonnie Fleming Reese, Eyewitness, Monongah, West Virginia in 1990.

11   *Pittsburgh Dispatch*, December 7, 1907, 6.

12   Transcript, Gaskill, 397; Transcript, Ruckman, 277; Transcript, Dean, 394.

13   Transcript, Trader, 307, et seq.

14   Transcript, Trader, 398; Trader 1972 Interview, 5.

15   "Explosions and Blast Injuries. A Preview for Clinicians." CDC Injury Prevention of HHS. Atlanta: The Center for Disease Controls, 2007. (Special thanks to Dr. Jeffrey D. Kellogg and Joni Bradly, R. N., of Shepherdstown, West Virginia)

16   Thrush, 300, 108, 1235.

17   Transcript, Dr. F. W. Hill, 238.

18   *Pittsburgh Dispatch*, December 8, 1907, 1.

19   *Pittsburgh Dispatch*, December 8, 1907, 1, 4.

20   Transcript, Urban, 265.

21   Transcript, Urban, 265. On October 9, 1926, almost 19 years after the Monongah mine disaster, Peter Urban was instantly killed by a fall of coal in the Monongah mine of Consolidation Coal Corporation. He was survived by five daughters and two sons. The funeral mass was held at the St. Stanislaus Church in Monongah. *Fairmont Times*, October 10, 1926; Death Certificate 14279.

22   *Greatest Coal Mine Disaster*, 226.

23   Transcript, Dr. Hill, 238, et seq.

24   *Fairmont Times*, December 8, 1907, 1.

25   *The Human Toll of the Coal Pit*, World's Work, Vol. 15 (February, 1908), 9930.

26   Relief, John Graham MSS. See footnote 256 below—Box 1.

27   *Baltimore Sun*, December 7, 1907, 1.

28   Camden MSS, Telegraph of C. W. Watson to J. N. Camden, December 7, 1907, 9:10 A.M.

29   *Pittsburgh Dispatch*, December 7, 1907.

30   *Zanesville Signal*, December 13, 1907, 5.

31   *Baltimore Sun*, December 7, 1907, 3.

32   *Pittsburgh Dispatch*, December 9, 1907, 1.

33   Transcript, Cunningham, 463.

Chapter 11

1   Transcript, Amos, 238.

2   The Bank was a Watson-related business.

3   Transcript, LaRue, 473.

4   Transcript, Dr. Hill, 238; *Pittsburgh Post Dispatch*, December 4, 1907, 1.

5   *Pittsburgh Dispatch*, December 7, 1907, 1.

6   *Fairmont Times*, December 8, 1907, 1.

7   *The Explosion at Monongah Number Six & Monongah Number Eight of the Fairmont Coal Company*, F. N. Haas, December 6, 1907. First published as a proceeding of the Fairmont Coal Company.

8   *Fairmont Times*, December 8, 1907, 1.

9   *Baltimore Sun*, December 10, 1907, 1.

10   *Baltimore Sun*, December 10, 1907, 1.

11   *Baltimore Sun*, December 10, 1907, 1.

12   *Baltimore Sun*, December 10, 1907, 1.
13   *Baltimore Sun*, December 9, 1907, 2.
14   This and previous three quotations from Kellogg, 1315-1316.
15   Relief, Case No. 2- and Case No. 3+1.
16   Kellogg, 1318.
17   Kellogg, 1314.
18   Notes and files of John G. Smyth, December 27, 1907, West Virginia University Archives. Smyth A&M No. 2. [Hereafter, *Smyth Archives.*]
19   Smyth Archives, No. 527.
20   *Baltimore Sun*, December 9, 1907, 2.
21   *Pittsburgh Dispatch*, December 13, 1907, 8.
22   *Baltimore Sun*, December 10, 1907, 1.
23   *Fairmont Times*, December 11, 1907, 1.
24   Relief, Case 4; *Pittsburgh Dispatch*, December 13, 1907, 8.
25   Relief, Case No. 5.
26   *Pittsburgh Dispatch*, December 13, 1907, 8.
27   *Pittsburgh Dispatch*, December 14, 1907, 3.

Chapter 12

1   Transcript, Trader, 13.
2   *Pittsburgh Dispatch*, December 7, 1907.
3   *Pittsburgh Dispatch*, December 7, 1907.
4   *Fairmont Times*, December 24, 1907, 1.
5   Transcript, 423, 424.
6   Transcript, Payne, 447.
7   Transcript, Ohio inspector, 355.
8   This and the previous five quotations taken from Harrison's testimony: Transcript, Harrison, 354.
9   Transcript, Harrison, Ohio Investigation Team Report, 356-360.
10   This and the previous eight quotations taken from Harrison's testimony: Transcript, Harrison, 354.
11   Roy as quoted in Watchhorn, *Cost of Coal*, 183.
12   *Fairmont Times*, December 12, 1907, 2.
13   Transcript, Paul, 511.
14   Transcript, Parsons, 453.
15   *Explosion at Monongah Mines*, 1. [Hereafter, *Haas Report.*]
16   The report that was produced as a paper to be given to the West Virginia Mining Engineers Association annual meeting has two other curious aspects. First, the author, Frank Haas, changed his name to Frank Hass between the time of his testimony in January, 1908, and the time the report was issued in

January, 1909; second, this Consolidation Coal Company report inexplicably became the report that was found in the West Virginia Department of Mines files and given as the official report to the author by the Director of the West Virginia Department of Mines, Walter Miller. See *Historical Summary of Mine Disasters*, Vol. 1, 27.

Chapter 13

1   Byington, 17.
2   Charles L. Magee, Secretary *Baltimore Sun*, December 9, 1907, 2.
3   History of Carnegie Hero Fund Commission, http://trfn.clpgh.orgcarnegiehero/ history.html. Accessed May, 2007. [Hereafter, *Hero Fund*.]
4   Carnegie Hero Fund had two gold medals struck to commemorate the loss of these two rescuers: "In commemoration of the acts of heroism displayed by Mr. Selwyn M. Taylor and Mr. Daniel Tyler. . ."
5   Monongah Mine Relief Committee Report, 175. [Hereafter, *Relief Report.*]
6   Relief Report, 174.
7   Relief Report, 176.
8   Relief, letter from Wilmot to Cunningham, February 10, 1909.
9   American Red Cross Archives, M. Byington correspondence with R. Cunningham.
10   Relief, Box 2.
11   Transcript, Coroner's Jury, 484.
12   Red Cross Archives, Correspondence of Mabel T. Boardman.
13   Fleming MSS, A&M 40 Box 36
14   *Pittsburgh Dispatch*, December 14, 1907, 6.
15   MSS A&M 40 Box 30, Camden to Fleming, January, 1908.
16   Letter from Bishop J. Donahue to Mabel T. Boardman, January 22, 1908.
17   Fleming MSS, A 40 Box, Correspondence, January 1908.
18   Fleming MSS, A&M 40 Box 36A, Correspondence, January 1908.
19   Fleming MSS, Box 36B, Correspondence, January 1908.
20   Red Cross Archives, Correspondence Mabel T. Boardman.
21   Fleming MSS, Box 36B, Correspondence, January 1908.
22   Byington, 15.
23   Fleming MSS Box 36A, Correspondence, February 1908.
24   Charles L. Magee, Secretary *Baltimore Sun*, December 9, 1907, 2.
25   Hero Fund. Accessed May 2007.
26   This quotation and information in the previous three paragraphs from Hero Fund. Accessed May 2007.
27   Red Cross Archives, Correspondence of Mabel T. Boardman.

28   American Red Cross National Headquarters, Hazel Baugh Records Center and
      Archives, Historical Resource Department, Folder No. 230, Sub. No. 967.
29   Relief Report, 175.
30   Relief Report, 176.
31   Relief, Case No. 6.
32   Elliott, History of the American National Red Cross, 174.
33   Relief, Case No. 7.
34   On January 28, 1908, the Monongah Mine Relief Committee reported that 145
      families and 1000 children were left without means of support. *Fairmont Times*,
      January 29, 1909.
35   This and the previous two quotations from Relief.
36   Relief, Byington, 17.
37   Relief, Byington, 17.
38   *A History of the Diocese of Wheeling-Charleston*, 30.
39   Byington, AM 1733, Letter DeSheilds, H.C. to Moore, Mayor of Monongah,
      Chairman of the first Relief Committee, January 6, 1908.
40   Relief, Byington, 18.
41   Relief, Case 334.

Chapter 14

1   Jackson, 61.
2   Jackson, 62.
3   Relief, Case No. 4.
4   This and previous quote from Relief, No. 12.
5   Transcript, Hill, 293.
6   Transcript, DePetris, 241.
7   Transcript, Dominico, 247.
8   Transcript, DePetris, 249.
9   Transcript, Dominico, 246.
10   Transcript, Urban, 266.
11   Transcript, Urban, 267.
12   Transcript, Jury Findings, p. 488.
13   Transcript, Jury Findings, p. 489.
14   Jackson, 65.
15   The Austro-Hungarian Consulate officials were located in Clarksburg,
     Bartholomew de Peche, and Charleston, West Virginia, Dr. Michael de
     Staraszewski, the Consulate officer initially cooperated with the Monongah
     Mine Relief Committee but became disturbed when the Committee hired
     the law firm Kneuth, Nached & Kuhne to distribute the forms and the money.
     Relief, Box 1.

16 This and previous quote from Transcript, Jury, 489.

17 Relief, Case No. 2.

18 This and previous three quotes from Relief, File No. 74.

19 Relief, Case No. 3.

20 Fleming MSS, Box 36A, Correspondence for Fleming to Daives, October 1907.

21 Fleming MSS, Box 36A, Correspondence from Fleming to Davies, October 1907.

22 Fleming MSS, Forni, Royal Counsel D'Italia.

Chapter 15

1 *New York Times*, December 8, 1907, 16.

2 Testimony transcript, Gibbon, 396.

3 Testimony transcript, Gibbon.

4 *Pittsburgh Dispatch*, December 7, 1907, 1.

5 *Pittsburgh Dispatch* reported, "The list of victims will reach at least 380, this number having been checked by the officials of the company late tonight in the mines when the explosion occurred." December 7, 1907, 1.

6 *Zanesville Signal*, December 7, 1907, 1; *Pittsburgh Dispatch*, December 7, 1907.

7 Transcript, Gibbons, 396.

8 *Baltimore Sun*, December, 1907.

9 *Pittsburgh Dispatch*, December 8, 1907, 1, in Goshorn, 1.

10 Transcript, Ruckman, 288.

11 *Pittsburgh Dispatch*, December 9, 1907, 1.

12 *Pittsburgh Dispatch*, December 12, 1907, 2.

13 *Baltimore Sun*, December 7, 1907, 2.

14 Trader Interview, 3.

15 *Pittsburgh Dispatch*, December 10, 1907, 8.

16 Trader interview, *Baltimore Sun*, December 12, 1907.

17 *Pittsburgh Dispatch*, December 8, 1907, 4.

18 *Pittsburgh Dispatch*, December 9, 1907, 3.

19 *Pittsburgh Dispatch*, December 11, 1907, 7.

20 *Baltimore Sun*, December 12, 1907, 1.

21 *Pittsburgh Dispatch*, December 9, 1907, 1.

22 *Pittsburgh Dispatch*, December 9, 1907, 1.

23 Fleming A&M 40, Box 36A.

24 *Baltimore Sun*, December 12, 1907. 1.

25 *Baltimore Sun*, December 12, 1907. 1.

26 Relief, Letter of R. T. Cunningham to C. W. Watson, December 12, 1907.

27 *Pittsburgh Dispatch*, December 12, 1907, 2.

28 *Baltimore Sun*, December 12, 1907. p. 1.

29 *Pittsburgh Dispatch*, December 13, 1907, 8.

30 Transcript, Cunningham, 463.

31 Cunningham Correspondence, Relief Commission Correspondence, West Virginia University Collection.

32 Transcript, Gibbons, 394.

33 All quotations in this paragraph from Transcript, Cunningham, 464.

34 This and previous four quotations from Transcript, Cunningham, 464. In the Relief Committee, no Yanieros are listed, while according to R. Cunningham's letter to A. B. Fleming, there should have been two. Although it might be argued that the Relief Committee's spelling was different as there is a Gennaro Janiero. This, however, has to be rejected because the Administrator, Earl Morgan, did not appear on the company administration list.

35 Letter from Father Briggs to author, May 4, 2001.

36 *Pittsburgh Dispatch*, December 13, 1907, 8.

37 Relief, Cunningham to Watson, December 12, 1907.

38 Testimony transcript, Gibbons, 396.

39 This exchange from Transcript, Gibbons, 397.

40 Transcript, Victor, 342.

41 Transcript, Victor, 352. There were several miles of tunnels and 475 rooms in the mines.

42 Transcript, Koon, 352. There were several miles of tunnels and 475 rooms in the mines.

43 *Pittsburgh Dispatch*, December 8, 1907, 5

44 Patrick McDonald was terribly burned about the face and chest and thought dead, and was discovered at a local hospital. He just recovered consciousness and had been placed in the hospital, authorities thinking he was a foreigner. McDonald had been working outside mine No. 6 and was just about to re-enter the mine when the concussion hurled him over 100 feet under the bridge leading to the tipple. He had been the motorman on the runaway trip but was temporarily doing an outside job. Three other men who were thought to be victims but escaped were Ross Manha, Mari Bagineallo, and Andrew Spaw. The first two had gone to visit some friends in Clarksburg early in the morning of the explosion and did not notify their boarding bosses of their intentions. Spaw, thought to have been blown into the river at the entrance of No. 6, had been on a visit to Grafton. *Pittsburgh Dispatch*, December 9, 1907, 1.

45 *Pittsburgh Dispatch*, December 4, 1907, 3.

46 *Pittsburgh Dispatch*, 3.

47 "It is assumed by the mine experts that dozens of them were simply blown to atoms and there is not the slightest vestige of their remains that has not been obliterated entirely with the possible exception of small pieces of charred flesh and cuticle occasionally observed by rescuers during their passage through the

treacherous subterranean windings in their search for former comrades. It is considered very probable many of the corpses will never be revealed to their friends and relatives. This is particularly true where the explosion was most violent in the No. 8 mine." *Pittsburgh Dispatch*, December 8, 1907, 1.

48   *Pittsburgh Dispatch*, December 9, 1907.

49   Fleming, MSS Box 36A.

50   The *Fairmont Times* on January 28, 1908, notes that additional bodies were being found in January, one on January 25, 1908. The article also notes the number of recoveries was 359. *Fairmont Times*, January 28, 1908, 1.

51   Relief, Letter of Francesco Pelliccia, Arch Priest, January 21, 1908.

52   List of Dead.

53   *Pittsburgh Dispatch*, December 9, 1907, 8.

Chapter 16

1   *Fairmont West Virginian*, December, 10, 1907, 6.

2   *Fairmont Times*, October 10, 1926. Death Certificate 14729.

3   Coal Mine Accidents, U. S. Department of Commerce, 1907

4   Fleming MSS, A&M 40 Box 36.

5   Fleming MSS, Gr. 20.

6   Fleming MSS, Letter, January 2, 1908.

7   Transcript, Fleming, 569.

8   Transcript, Fleming, 570.

9   Fleming MSS, A&M 40 Box 36.

10   Fleming MSS, A&M 40, Box 36, Letter McDermott to Fleming.

11   Fleming MSS.

12   Fairmont Coal Company Records, Hagley Museum, Wilmington, Delaware.

13   Fleming MSS, A&M 40 Box 36.

14   Relief, File No. 74.

15   Fleming MSS, A&M 40 Box 36A Telegram.

16   Westchester, *Yesterday in White Plains*.

17   Summers, 569-570.

18   *Fairmont Times*, July 30, 1909, 1.

19   Fleming MSS, Box 36A, Correspondence, November 1908.

20   Fleming MSS, A&M 40 Box 36A.

21   This and previous quotation from Fleming MSS, Graebner, 18.

22   Graebner, 19.

23   National Conservation Commission Report.

24   Report of the National Conservation Commission, United States Senate, Document # 670, Washington, DC. 1909, 3.

25   This and previous quotation from Establishment of a Bureau of Mines, 16.

26   Establishment of a Bureau of Mines, 21.

27   Establishment of a Bureau of Mines, 23

28   US Congress, Senate Committee on Mines and Mining, establishing Bureau of Mines in Interior Department, Senate Report 695 to accompany HR 20883, 60th Congress 1st Sess. 198 Ser. 5219, 17.

29   Report of Hearing before the Committee on Mines and Mining, United States House of Representatives. March 9-30, 1909. Government Printing Office, 14.

30   Historical Summary of Mine Disasters, Vol. II, Mine Safety and Health Administration, 1998, 17.

31   Kirk, 34.

32   Powell, 1-161.

BIBLIOGRAPHY

PRIMARY SOURCES

Manuscripts

Aretas Brooks Fleming Papers. Morgantown, WV: West Virginia University Regional Collection, Wise Library.

Boardman, Mable Thorp. Suitland, Maryland: American Red Cross Correspondence. American Red Cross Archives, United States National Archives.

Consolidation Coal Company, Fairmont Coal Company Collection. Wilmington, DE: Hagley Museum and Library.

"Emmitt Lester Trader: Papers and Maps." Author's possession.

"History of Kathrine Flannery and Family." Unpublished manuscript. Author's possession, 1910.

Holmes, Joseph Austin. Southern History Collection #3866 (1859-1915). Chapel Hill, NC: Manuscripts Department, University of North Carolina Library.

J. C. Gaskill Papers. Morgantown, WV: West Virginia and Regional History Collection, West Virginia University Libraries.

John Mitchell Papers. Washington DC: Catholic University of America Library.

Johnson Newlon Camden Papers. Morgantown, WV: West Virginia University Regional Collection, Wise Library.

Kennedy, Mary Agnes. "History of Katherine Flannery and Cecilia and Philip Erwin, 1747 to 1900." Author's possession.

Leeper, Thomas M. "Who Has Lived about Monongah." In "Monongah," an unpublished manuscript in author's possession.

"McAteer Family History." Unpublished manuscript in author's possession.

Monongah Mines Relief Committee Archives. Morgantown, WV: West Virginia University Regional Collection, Wise Library.

Relief Committee Files. West Virginia Manuscript Collection. Correspondence, 1908 and 1909. Morgantown, WV: West Virginia University Regional Collection, Wise Library.

Dissertations

Massay, Glenn F. "Coal Consolidation: Profile of the Fairmont Field of Northern West Virginia, 1852-1903." Diss., West Virginia University, 1971. Morgantown, West Virginia: UMI, 1971.

Smith, Barbara E. "Digging Our Own Grave: Coal Miners and the Struggle Over Black Lung Disease." Diss., Brandeis University, 1981. Ann Arbor, MI: UMI, 1981.

Articles

Byington, Margaret F. "The Monongah Relief." *The American Red Cross Bulletin* (1909).

Davis-White, Jeanne. "Polish Arrivals at the Port of Baltimore 1880-1884." Baltimore: History Press.

Forbes, Edger Allen. "The Human Toll of the Coal Pit." *World's Work* (February 1908): 9929.

Hubbard, Joseph. "The Tragedy of the Mines." *Atlantic* (January 1911).

Kellogg, Paul U. "Monongah." *Charities and the Commons* (4 January 1908): 1313.

"Review of Coal Mine Accidents, Their Causes and Prevention." *The Nation*, Vol. 86 (1 February 1908).

Stowe, Lyman Beecher. "To the Rescue." *Outlook* (25 September 1909).

Taylor, Graham. "A Mine Test for Civilization." *Charities*, Vol. 19 (1 February 1908): 297.

Watchhorn, Robert. "The Cost of Human Life." *Outlook* (22 May 1907).

Watson, Sylvestus. "The Coal Valley Story." *Fairmont Times* (1957).

Government Documents

Code of West Virginia, The. Wheeling and Charleston: State of West Virginia, 1883-1908.

Dawson, Governor Wm. M. O. *Biennial Message*. Legislature of West Virginia: Charleston, 1907.

First Annual Reports of BOM. Joseph D. Holmes, Director. Washington, DC: Department of Interior, 1911.

Hearings Before the Committee on Mines and Mining, United States House of Representatives, to Consider the Question of the Establishment of a Bureau of Mines, Washington, DC: Government Printing Office, (9-30 March 1908).

Hill, Clarence, and Walter O. Snelling. *Coal Mine Accidents: Their Causes and Prevention*. Department of Commerce, U. S. Geological Survey. Washington, DC: Government Printing Office, 1907.

Historical Summary of Mine Disasters in the United States. Vol. 1. Washington, DC: U.S. Department of Labor, Mine Safety and Health Agency, 1998.

Kirk, William S. "History of the U. S. Bureau of Mines." In *Minerals Yearbook, 1997-1998*. United States Department of the Interior: Washington, DC.

Powell, Fred Wilber. *The Bureau of Mines, History, Activities and Organizations*. New York: D. Appleton Company, 1922.

The Prevention of Mine Explosions, Report and Recommendations. U.S. Geological Survey Bulletin, 369. Washington, DC: Government Printing Office, 1908.

"Production Trends of Bituminous Coal and Lignite, 1890-1981." Energy Information Administration, U.S. Dept. of Energy Fact Sheet. Washington, DC: Government Printing Office.

Report of Hearings before the Joint Select Committee of the Legislature of West Virginia, to Investigate the Cause of Mine Explosions within the State and to Recommend Remedial Legislation Relative Thereto, Together with the Preliminary and Final Reports. West Virginia Archives. Charleston, West Virginia.

Report on the National Conservation Commission. United States Senate Doc. 670. Washington, DC: Government Printing Office, (February 1909).

Rice, George S. *Explosibility of Coal Dust.* Department of Interior, Bureau of Mines. Washington, DC: Government Printing Office, 1911.

Yearbook of the Department of Agriculture, 1906. Washington DC: Government Printing Office, 1907

Conference Proceedings

"The Great Strike: Perspectives on the 1902 Anthracite Coal Strike." Proceedings from the Centennial Symposium, October, 2002, Canal History & Technology, National Canal Museum Store. URL: http://www.canals.org/store/The Great Strike-p120C17.apx. Accessed: May 27, 2007.

Proceedings of the West Virginia Coal Mining Institute of 1909. Charleston,
    WV: West Virginia Archives, West Virginia Division of Culture and
    History.

Music

Reed, Blind Alfred. "Monongah Mines No. 6 and No. 8, Explosion in the
    Fairmont Mines."
Sinnot, James. "The Monongah Disaster: A Song."

Newspaper Sources

Baltimore Sun. December 7, 1907-January 20, 1908.
Fairmont Free Press (Farmers Free Press). 1895-1907.
Fairmont Index. December 7, 1907-January 20, 1908.
Fairmont Times. 1900-1909.
New York Times. December 7, 1907-January 20, 1908.
Pittsburgh Dispatch. December 7, 1907-January 20, 1908.
Zainesville Signal. December 6–13, 1907.

Periodicals

Bailey, Keith R. "A Judicious Mixture: Negroes and Immigrants in the West
    Virginia Mines, 1880-1917." *West Virginia History*, Vol. XXXIV, No. 2,
    January 1973: 141.
Barkley, Frederick A. "Immigration and Ethnicity in West Virginia, A Review
    of Literature." *West Virginia History, Critical Essays on Literature*. Ronald
    L. Lewis and John C. Hennen, Jr., Eds.
"The Greatest Coal Mine Disaster in Our History." In *The American Review
    of Reviews*, Vol. 37 (February 1908).
"Human Toll of the Coal Pit." *World's Work*, Vol. 15. February, 1908.
Koon, Thomas. "The First Fathers Day." *Goldenseal* (Summer, 2000).

Lauck, W. Jett. "The Bituminous Coal Miner and Coke Worker of Western Pennsylvania." *The Survey* (1 April 1911).

Massay, Glenn F. "Legislators, Lobbyist, & Loopholes: Coal Mining Legislation in West Virginia, 1875-1901." *West Virginia History Journal.*

Mitchell, Guy Elliott. "Overcoming Coal-Mine Disasters." *Review of Reviews* (May 1909).

Stafford, Sam. "America's Worse Mine Disasters." *Holmes Safety Association Bulletin* (April 1999).

Author Interviews

Cupp, William. "Report on Monongah." Unpublished interview of Lester E. Trader by U. S. Bureau of Mines Employee on September, 1972. Author's possession.

Reese, Bonnie Fleming. Eyewitness, Monongah, West Virginia in 1990.

Wells, David. Interview with the author in Fairmont, WV, in July of 2001.

Other

Byers, Judy R., John H. Randolph, and Noel W. Tenney. "In the Mountain State: A West Virginia Folklore and Cultural Studies Curriculum." West Virginia Humanities Council, 1994.

"Explosions and Blast Injuries. A Preview for Clinicians." CDC Injury Prevention of HHS. Atlanta: The Center for Disease Controls, 2007. (Special thanks to Dr. Jeffrey D. Kellogg and Joni Bradly, R. N., of Shepherdstown, West Virginia.)

Haas, Frank. "The Explosion at Monongah Mines, Fairmont Coal Company." Fairmont Coal Company Bulletin, No. 11. Fairmont, WV: Supplemental Annual Report of Operation, (20 December 1908).

History of the Carnegie Hero Fund Commission. URL: www.carnegiehero/history.html. Accessed: September 17, 1999.

Pierce, Susan M. "West Virginia County Courthouses, 2003 Calendar." Charleston, WV: Division of Culture and History, State Historic Preservation Office, January 2003.

SECONDARY SOURCES

Books

Agricola, Georgius. *De Re Metallica*. Trans. Herbert C. Hoover and Lou H. Hoover. New York: Dover Publications, Inc., 1950.

Bailey, Kenneth R. *Mountaineers Are Free: A History of the West Virginia National Guard*. St. Albans, WV: Harless Printing, 1978.

Baldwin, Leland D. *The Stream of American History*. Vol. 2. 2nd ed. New York: American Book Company, 1957.

Barger, Harold, and Sam H. Schurr. *The Mining Industries, 1899-1939: A Study of Output, Employment and Productivity*. Publications of the Natural Bureau of Economic Research, Inc. No. 43. New York: National Bureau of Economic Research, Inc., 1944. New York: Arno Press, 1975.

Bartlett, Melody, and Bill Grubb. *The Monongah Mine Disaster and Its Social Setting: A Collage of Newspaper Accounts*. Fairmont, WV: Fairmont State University Publication, 2001.

Beachley, Charles E. *History of the Consolidation Coal Company 1864-1934*. New York: Consolidation Coal Company, 1934.

Bernardo, Stephanie. *The Ethnic Almanac*. Garden City, NY: Doubleday & Company, Inc., 1981.

Black's Law Dictionary, 4th ed., revised. 1968. Saint Paul, MN: West Publishing Company.

Braithwaite, John. *To Punish or Persuade: Enforcement of Coal Mine Safety*. Albany, NY: State University of New York Press, 1985.

Brestensky, Dennis F., Evelyn A. Hovanec, and Albert N. Skomra. *Patch/ Work Voices: The Culture and Lore of a Mining People.* Pittsburgh, PA: University of Pittsburgh, Center for International Studies, 1978.

Bruchey, Stuart. *The Wealth of Nations.* New York: Harper & Row, 1988.

Callahan, James M. *History of West Virginia, Old and New in One Volume.* Chicago: The American Historical Society, Inc., 1923.

Chernow, Ron. *The House of Morgan: An American Banking Dynasty and the Rise of Modern Finance.* New York: Simon & Schuster, 1990.

_____. *TITAN: The Life of John D. Rockefeller, Sr.* New York: Random House, Inc., 1998.

Conley, Phil. *History of the West Virginia Coal Industry.* Charleston, WV: Charleston Printing Co., 1960.

Core, Earl. *The Monongahela Story.* Parsons, WV: McClain Printing Company, 1974.

Daughen, Joseph R., and Peter Binzen. *The Wreck of the Penn Central.* Boston: Little, Brown & Co., Inc., 1973.

Dillon, Lacy A. *They Died in the Darkness.* Parsons, WV: McClain Printing Company, 1976.

Dix, Keith. *What's a Coal Miner to Do?* Pittsburgh, PA: University of Pittsburgh Press, 1988.

_____. *Work Relations in the Coal Industry: The Hand-Loading Era, 1880-1930.* West Virginia University Bulletin, Series 78, No. 7-2. Morgantown, WV: Institute for Labor Studies, West Virginia University, 1978.

Du Pont: The Autobiography of an American Enterprise. Wilmington, DE: E. I. Du Pont De Nemours & Co., 1952.

Egan, Rt. Rev. Msgr. Martin J. *Historical and Pictorial Review of St. Peter's Parish*, Fairmont, W. VA. 1873-1948 Diamond Jubilee. 1948.

Fones-Wolf, Kenneth, and Ronald L. Lewis. *Transnational West Virginia.* Morgantown, WV: West Virginia University Press, 2002.

Fox, Maier B. *United We Stand: The United Mine Workers of America 1890-1990*. United Mine Workers of America, 1990.

Freese, Barbara. *Coal: A Human History*. Cambridge: Perseus Publishing, 2003.

Gallagher, Thomas. *Paddy's Lament, Ireland 1846-1847 Prelude to Hatred*. San Diego: A Harvest Book, Harcourt, Brale & Co.

Graebner, William. *Coal-Mining Safety in the Progressive Period*. Lexington, KY: The University Press of Kentucky, 1976.

Green, Archie. *Only a Miner: Studies in Recorded Coal-Mining Songs*. University of Illinois Press, 1972.

Harper, Reverend Howard V. *Days & Customs of All Faiths*. New York: D. D. Fleet Publishing Co.

History of the Diocese of Wheeling-Charleston. Wheeling–Charleston Diocese: Charleston, West Virginia, 2005.

History of Marshall County, West Virginia. Moundsville, WV: Marshall County Historical Society, 1984.

History of the Monongah Mines Relief Fund. Fairmont, WV: Monongah Mines Relief Committee Trustees, 1910.

Hull, Arthur M., Ed., and Sydney A. Hale, Assoc. Ed. *Coal Men of America*. Chicago: The Retail Coalman, Inc., 1918.

Humphrey, H. B. *Historical Summary of Coal-Mine Explosions in the United States, 1810-1958*. Bureau of Mines, Bulletin 586. Washington, DC: Government Printing Office, 1960.

Hungerford, Edward. *The Story of the Baltimore & Ohio Railroad 1827-1927*. 2 Vols. New York: G. P. Putnam's Sons, 1928.

Husband, Joseph. *A Year in a Coal Mine*. New York: Houghton Mifflin Co., 1911.

Jackson, Carlton. *The Dreadful Month*. Bowling Green, OH: Bowling Green State University Popular Press, 1982.

Jones, Elliot. *The Trust Problems in the United States*. New York, 1927.

Jones, Mary H. *The Autobiography of Mother Jones*. 3rd ed. Chicago: Charles H. Kerr Publishing Co., 1976.

Koon, Thomas J., and Oce Smith. *Marion County West Virginia: A Pictorial History*. Virginia Beach: The Donning Company Publishers, 1995.

Korson, George. *Black Rock: Mining Folklore of the Pennsylvania Dutch*. Baltimore: The Johns Hopkins Press, 1960.

Lewis, John L. *Papers of John L. Lewis: Guide to a Microfilm Edition*. Madison, WI: The State Historical Society of Wisconsin, 1970.

Lewis, John L. *The Miners' Fight for American Standards*. Indianapolis: Bell Publishing Company, 1925.

Lewis, Ronald L. *Transforming the Appalachian Countryside: Railroads, Deforestation and Social Change in West Virginia*. Chapel Hill, NC: The University of North Carolina Press, 1998.

Lockhard, Duane. *Coal: A Memoir and Critique*. The University Press of Virginia, 1998.

Lord, Walter. *The Good Years: From 1900 to the First World War*. New York: Harper & Brothers, 1960.

Lukas, J. Anthony. *Big Trouble*. New York: Simon & Schuster, 1997.

Lunt, Richard D. *Law and Order vs. The Miners: WV 1906-1933*. Charleston, WV: Appalachian Editions, 1992.

Marion County Historical Society. *History of Marion County, West Virginia*. L.C. No. 85-52172. Marceline, MO: Walsworth Publishing Co., 1985.

Massay, Glenn F. *Legislators, Lobbyists & Loopholes: Coal Mining Legislation in West Virginia, 1875-1901*. West Virginia History, Vol. 32, 1971.

McAteer, J. Davitt. *Coal Mine Health and Safety: The Case of West Virginia*. Published in cooperation with the Center for Study of Responsive Law. New York: Praeger Publishers, 1973.

McCullough, David. *Mornings on Horseback*. New York: Simon and Schuster, 1981.

Meunier, Constantin. *Bergbau-Museum Bochum*. Germany: Bergbau-Museum, 1970.

Miller, Donald L., and Richard E. Sharpless. *The Kingdom of Coal: Work, Enterprise, and Ethnic Communities in the Mine Fields*. University of Pennsylvania Press, 1985.

Mining Explained in Simple Terms. Toronto: Northern Miner Press Limited, 1955.

Munn, Robert F. *The Coal Industry in America: A Bibliography and Guide to Studies*. Morgantown, WV: West Virginia University Library, 1965.

Neely, John C. *The Big Yellow Cars: A Nostalgic Look at a Remarkable Interurban Streetcar System*. John Champ Neely, 1987.

Okkonen, Marc. *Baseball Memories, 1900-1909, An Illustrated Chronicle of the Big Leagues' First Decade, All the Players, Managers, Cities & Ballparks*. Sterling Publishing Company, 1992.

Parkinson, George. *Guide to Coal Mining Collections in the United States*. Morgantown, WV: West Virginia University Library, 1978.

Paul, Wolfgang. *Mining Lore: An Illustrated Composition and Documentary Compilation with Emphasis on the Spirit and History of Mining/Memorial Edition*. Portland: Morris Printing Co., 1970.

Petersham, Maud, and Miska Petersham. *The Story Book of Coal*. Philadelphia: The John C. Winston Company, 1935.

Pohs, Henry A. *The Miner's Flame Light Book: The Story of a Man's Development of Underground Light*. Denver: Flame Publishing Company, 1995.

Powell, Wilber. *The Bureau of Mines, Its History, Activities and Organization*. New York: Institute of Government Research, D. Appleton & Company, 1922.

Reppetto, Thomas. *American Mafia: A History of Its Rise to Power*. New York: Henry Holt and Company, LLC, 2004.

Rosner, David, and Gerald Markowitz. *Deadly Dust: Silicosis and the Politics of Occupational Disease in Twentieth-Century America*. Princeton, NJ: Princeton University Press, 1991.

Shepherd, Robert. *Ancient Mining*. London: Elsevier Science Publishers, Ltd., 1993.

Sinclair, Upton. *King Coal, A Novel*. 1930. [Introduction by Dr. George Brandes].

Summers, Festus P. *Johnson Newlon Camden: A Study in Individualism*. New York: G. P. Putnam's Sons, 1937.

Tarbell, Ida M. *History of the Standard Oil Co*. New York: The MacMillion Company, 1933.

Thrush, Paul W., Ed. *A Dictionary of Mining, Mineral, and Related Terms*. U. S. Dept. the Interior, Bureau of Mines. Washington, DC: Government Printing Office, 1968.

Vecsey, George. *One Sunset a Week*. New York: E. P. Dutton & Co., Inc., 1974.

Von Halle, E. *Trust or Industrial Combinations and Coalitions in the United States*. New York, 1896.

Watson, Sylvestus. *The Coal Valley Story*. Fairmont, WV: Fairmont Publishing Co., 1957.

Whiteside, James. *Regulating Danger: The Struggle for Mine Safety in the Rocky Mountain Coal Industry*. Lincoln, NB: University of Nebraska Press, 1990.

Wilhelm, Jr., Gene. "Folk Settlements in the Blue Ridge Mountains." *Appalachian Journal* 5.2 (1978): 204-45.

Willey, William P. *An Inside View of the Formation of the State of West Virginia*. Wheeling: The News Publishing Company, 1901.

Williams, John Alexander. *Appalachia: A History*. New York: W.W. Norton & Company, 1984.

Williams, John Alexander. *West Virginia: A Bicentennial History*. New York: Norton & Company, 1976.

Williams, John Alexander. *West Virginia and the Captains of Industry*. Morgantown, WV: West Virginia University Foundation, 1976.

Workman, Michael E., Paul Salstrom, and Philip W. Ross. *Northern West Virginia Coal Fields: Historical Context*. The Institute for the History of Technology and Industrial Archaeology, Technical Report No. 10. Morgantown: West Virginia University, Eberly College Arts & Sciences, 1994.

Yesterday in White Plains, A Picture History of a Bygone Era. Hoffman Westchester Historical Society Library. Westchester County Historical Society.

INDIVIDUALS MENTIONED
IN MONONGAH

What follows is a list of the people mentioned in *Monongah*. Some of them are major players, others appear only briefly, but they were all a part of the events that surround the Monongah explosion.

Miners and Their Families

Abbnte, Carlo: miner who died in Monongah disaster, son of Maria de-Gaetana Abbnte

Abbnte, Francesco: miner who died in Monongah disaster, husband of Maria deGaetana Abbnte

Abbnte, Joseph: miner who died in Monongah disaster, son of Maria de-Gaetana Abbnte

Abbnte, Maria deGaetana: lost husband and two sons in Monongah disaster

Alexander, Joseph: owner of a watch found stopped at 10:42 after explosion

Beabilly, William: union organizer and leader of unrest along Pittsburgh, miner from Indiana

Bice, George: track layer in No. 8 with the same last name as the dying engineer

Bitonti, Jim: lived at house 232 in Brookdale

Bitonti, Juste: lived at house 232 in Brookdale

Cerdelli, Christiana: a 17-year-old woman who watched disaster from her home across the river from the mines

Colaneri, Felice: lived at house 232 in Brookdale

Colarusso, Carmela: lived at house 232 in Brookdale with husband, Dominac, and two children

Colarusso, Dominac: lived at house 232 in Brookdale with wife, Carmela, and two children

Colarusso, Giuseppe: lived at house 232 in Brookdale

Colasessano, Felice: lived at house 232 in Brookdale

D'Andrea, Maria Gattini: lived in Monongah with husband, Victor, and their three children

D'Andrea, Victor: Monongah miner, lived in Monongah with wife, Maria, and their three children

Daran, Andrew: immigrated to America in 1900 and worked at Monongah mines

Delasandro, Libberato: Italian immigrant miner who had been working No. 6 for 4 years, one of four who escaped

DePetris, Angelo: brother of Orazio or Crazio, one of four who escaped

DePetris, Crazio: possible alternative spelling of Orazio, one of four who escaped

DePetris, Orazio: brother of Angelo, one of four who escaped

DePetris, Felice: son of Orazio Depetris

DeWolfe, John S.: Name of the ship that sailed from Killala, Ireland, carried the Erwin family

Dominico, Dan: father of Leonardo Dominico and Don Dominico, both of whom joined the Depetris brothers and escaped

Dominico, Donato: son of Dan Dominico and miner who worked the Monongah mines

Dominico, Leonardo: son of Dan Dominico

Erwin, Cecily: daughter of Katherine Flannery and wife of Philip Erwin

Erwin, Mary Agnes: daughter of Philip and Cecily, married Michael Kennedy

Erwin, Philip: husband of Cecily Erwin, did contract work grading for the railroads

Flannery, Kathrine: a 55 year old widow who sailed from Killala, Ireland

Flannery, Kathrine: unmarried daughter of Kathrine

Giovanni, Farcse: miner who died in the explosion

Giuseppe, D'uva: miner who died in the explosion

Grace, Daniel: member of the union group

Gynia, Adolph: 17-year-old miner severely burned in the explosion

Hanyik, Marton: miner who died in the explosion, grandson of Anna Jagos

Hanyik, Paul: miner who died in the explosion, grandson of Anna Jagos

Hofaker, Charles B.: owner of gold watch found still running after explosion

Honaker, Charles: 15-year-old trapper who died in Monongah disaster

Jagos, Anna: widow of Paul Jagos and grandmother of Paul and Marton Hanyik

Jagos, Paul: miner who died in the explosion, husband of Anna

James, David, Jr.: miner who died in the explosion

Jenkins, Will: blacksmith at the No. 6 mine called by Frank Moon to shoe a horse in the mine

Kennedy, Ellen: daughter of Mary and Michael Kennedy's daughter, Ellen, married Daniel Thomas Purcell

Kennedy, Mary: wife of Michael

Kennedy, Michael: member of a family that emigrated from County Mayo and worked railroad construction, husband of Mary

Leonard, J. H.: oiler in No. 6 and one of the oldest men working in the mine

Lyle. Daniel A.: miner who worked at mine neighboring Monongah and died in rescue attempt

Mainella, Domenico: lived at house 232 in Brookdale

Martin, Sarah Ann: lived with her son Charlie on Hill No. 3 across the river from the portals, just above the stables.

McDonald, Pat: standing near No. 6 opening, had face lacerated in disaster

Moon, Frank: miner in the Monongah mines

Morris, Andy H.: Trader's fellow fire boss in No. 6

Newton, Joe: Negro who suffered a compound fracture and lost his right eye.

Nolan, Sam: lived at house 753

Mysella, Tony: boss at house 233 in Monongah

Poggiana, Joe: an Italian immigrant miner, union organizer alleged to be an anarchist

Purcell, Daniel Thomas: husband of Ellen Kennedy

Riccinto, Antonio: boarder at house 233 in Monongah

Riccinto, Dominic: single 19-year-old and boarder at house 233 in Monongah

Riccinto, Pasquale: boarder at house 233 in Monongah

Rosebeiq, Peter: another name for Peter Urban

Sabastino, Zeoli: miner who died in the explosion

Saltos, Michael: traveled from Greece with Anestis Stamboulis

Sari, George: miner who died in the explosion; left widow in Czeke, Hungary; cousin of Michael Sari

Sari, John: miner who died in the explosion; left widow in Czeke, Hungary; cousin of Michael Sari

Sari, Maria Szalaga: wife of Michael Sari

Sari, Mary: daughter of Michael and Maria Sari

Sari, Michael: miner who died in the explosion

Sari, Stephen: miner who died in the explosion; left widow in Czeke, Hungary; cousin of Michael Sari

Sebastiano, De-Maria: miner who died in the explosion

Snodgrass, G.: lived at house 753 with his wife and daughter

Snodgrass, Grace: lived at house 753 with her husband and daughter

Stambouli, Anestis: Greek immigrant miner working the No. 6

Sticke, Andy: miner who died in the explosion

Taylor, Selwyn M.: miner who worked at mine neighboring Monongah who died in rescue attempt

Tomko, Barbara: wife of John Tomko

Tomko, George: brother of John Tomko, also worked the No. 8

Tomko, John: initially survived the Monongah disaster, died as he was being brought out by rescue teams

Trader, Lester Emmitt: 22-year-old untrained assistant fire boss in the No. 6

Urban, Andy: son of Peter and Caroline

Urban, Anne: daughter of Peter and Caroline

Urban, Caroline: arrived in U. S. in 1891 and lived in Fairmont with her husband and three children

Urban, Joe: son of Stanley and Mary Urban

Urban, Kate: daughter of Stanley and Mary Urban

Urban, Mary: wife of Stanley Urban

Urban, Nelle: daughter of Stanley and Mary Urban

Urban, Peter: arrived in U. S. in 1891 and lived in Fairmont with his wife and three children

Urban, Stanley: brother of Peter, died in the mine disaster

Urban, Stanley: son of Peter and Caroline, nephew of Stanley

Zulu, Martin Bosner: miner who died in the explosion

Company Men and Money Men, Professionals and Politicians

Alexander, C. B.: initial incorporator of The Monongah Company

Alexander, George W.: lawyer representing Fairmont Coal Company

Amos, E. S.: Marion County coroner

Anderson, John: built a mill on Booth's Creek around 1818

Arnett, W. E.: Fairmont mayor

Baer, George F.: mining industry spokesman and one of the most prominent mine operators in the country of the day

Bailey, W. H.: former assistant general superintendent for Monongah Coal & Coke Company

Bartlett, C. R.: manager of the company store in Monongah as of 1894

Bice, William: engineer who died in Monongah disaster

Black, H. Crawford: Consolidation Coal manager

Bowles, H. G.: general superintendent of the Monongah Railroad

Brown, John: built mill near Fairmont in early 1800s

Burd, James: discoverer of the Pittsburgh seam

Bush, B. F.: president of Western Maryland Railroad

Byner, E. V.: West Virginia state mine inspector in charge of district in which Monongah Coal & Coke Company operated

Camden, Johnson N.: force behind founding of Monongah Coal & Coke Company and the Monongah Mines; U.S. Senator

Camden, Spriggs D.: initial incorporator of The Monongah Company, Standard Oil Executive

Caperton, G. H.: a secretary to a group of southern West Virginia coal operators

Carr, Dr. John D. M.: prominent physician and full-time resident of McLure House, Wheeling, West Virginia, for whom "Tupsey Waltz" was composed

Carr, Roseberry: rail systems superintendent who oversaw the joining of two B&O lines at Roseby's Rock

Clark. E. W.: on board of Monongah Coal & Coke Company and of the financial firm of E. W. Clark and Company of Philadelphia

Colton, S. W., Jr.: first president of Monongah Coal & Coke Company

Condnay, W. E.: commissioner of the County Court, juror for the Marion County Inquest

Cook, Dr. J. R.: Fairmont physician

Cunningham, Robert: company auditor who conducted a census after the explosion and creator of Cunningham List

Curry, Lee: stationary engineer for No. 8 mine

Dawson, William M. O.: West Virginia Governor

Dean, Charlie: surface foreman at the No. 6 and Leonard's boss

Dolin, Thomas: mine foreman at No. 6

Downs, Festus: former County Commissioner, juror for the Marion County Inquest

Duty, M. K.: member of state House of Representatives and on the Joint Select Committee to investigate the causes of the Stuart mine explosions in 1907

Elliott, C. D.: Federal Marshal

Fair, James G.: on the board of Monongah Coal & Coke Company and U.S. Senator of Nevada

Fickenger, J. A.: initial incorporator of The Monongah Company

Finley, William: Monongah town sergeant

Fleming, Alexander: one of the founders of Fairmont, sold a farm to J. O. Watson

Fleming, Aretas Brooks: founding member of Monongah Coal & Coke Company, lawyer and judge, J. O. Watson's son-in-law

Fleming, Benjamin: father of A. B. Fleming

Ford, Elizabeth: wife of N. Cochran

Frick, Henry: mining industry baron, Pittsburgh, worked for Andrew Carnegie

Fry, Ed: preparation plant engineer

Garland, Thomas: Chairman of the Joint Select Committee to investigate the causes of the Stuart mine explosions in 1907

Gaskill, J. C.: company superintendent with Monongah Coal & Coke Company

Gibbons, George: Monongah Coal & Coke Company payroll clerk

Goff, Nathan: Clarksburg Republican, candidate for Governor

Gorman, Anthem P.: invested in and was on the board of Monongah Coal & Coke Company

Gould, George Jay: Railroad owner whose proposed development of the Wabash Railroad to compete with the B&O and offer to buy the Fairmont Coal Company threatened the B&O and Consolidation plans to complete the first railroad from Baltimore to the Ohio River and merge with the Fairmont Coal Company.

Graham, Rhea: last director of the Bureau of Mines

Haas, Frank: asst. general manager of Monongah Coal & Coke Company

Hall, Clarence: nation's leading mine explosive expert

Hamilton, W. S.: member of the Marion County Commission, juror for the Marion County Inquest

Hanford, J. B.: mine operator and president of the West Virginia Coal Mining Institute

Hanna, Mark: mining industry baron, Cleveland, Ohio

Harkins, Charles W.: on the board of Monongah Coal & Coke Company and of Standard Oil of Cleveland, representing Rockefeller interests

Hass, Frank: name Frank Haas signed as the author of report

Hesse; H. V.: general superintendent of Consolidation Coal Company in Frostburg

Hill, Dr. F. W.: Fairmont physician

Hill, Frank P.: accountant for the Relief Committee

Holmes, Joseph A.: geologist from the Commerce Department, first Director of Bureau of Mines

Hood, Colonel William: Fairmont financier

Jackson, Elihu E.: invested in and was on the board of Monongah Coal & Coke Company and later became governor of West Virginia

Jackson, John Jay: Federal District Court Judge sympathetic to the Company

Jacobs, J. M.: a member of the state legislature and Secretary of the Board of Trade; juror for the Marion County Inquest

Jolleff, Sheriff M. A.: Marion County sheriff

Kerns, Peter: foreman at Monongah mines

Kidd, R. F.: member of the state Senate and on the Joint Select Committee to investigate the causes of the Stuart mine explosions in 1907

Knight, E. R.: tipple foreman at No. 6 mine

Lamb, Leonard: built mill near Fairmont in early 1800s; J. O. Watson's father-in-law

Lamb, Matilda: daughter of Leonard Lamb, who was prominent in iron industry, and wife of J. O. Watson

LaRue, R. S.: mine inspector for state of West Virginia, responsible for Monongah Mines No. 6 & 8

Limnion, Constantius: a Greek immigrant who was a recruiting agent for mining companies in West Virginia

Little, T. A.: a surveyor, hired by James Watkins in 1880 to lay out plots for Pleasantville

Lord, Charles K.: on the board of Monongah Coal & Coke Company, vice president of B&O, and initial incorporator of The Monongah Company

Loree, Leonor F.: B&O president

Lowe, Scott C.: prosecutor for the Marion County Inquest

Malone, Lee L.: general manager and man in charge of all company mines

Mayer, Charles F.: president, Monongah Coal & Coke Company

McDermott, Colonel Joseph H.: speaker of the West Virginia Legislature

McGraw, Pete: foreman at the Monongah mines

McKinley, J. C.: president of the J. C. McKinley Coal Company of Wheeling

McKinley, William: president of the United States who was shot by a disgruntled immigrant who had lost his government job.

Meredith, Carl: foreman for the No. 8 tipple

Mitchell, A. J.: member of state House of Representatives and on the Joint Select Committee to investigate the causes of the Stuart mine explosions in 1907

Moore, W. H.: mayor of Monongah

Morgan, J. P.: mine operator and tycoon

Neely, M. M.: colonel in charge of Company H of the First Infantry of the National Guard

Nugent, John: immigration commissioner for the state of West Virginia

Ohley, William A.: West Virginia coal operator

Page, William N.: president of the Soup Creek Collier Co.

Parsons, Frank E.: West Virginia mine inspector

Paul, James W.: director of West Virginia's Department of Mines and the state's chief inspector

Payne, Dr. Henry M.: professor of mining engineering from the West Virginia University School of Mines

Payne, O. H.: treasurer of Standard Oil

Peddicord, George E.: outside foreman at No. 8

Pierpont, Francis H.: opened first mine in Fairmont with J. O. Watson

Pinchot, Gifford: secretary of interior

Prichard, A. S.: juror for the Marion County Inquest

Reidy, Dr.: company doctor and former staff member of Baltimore City Hospital

Rockefeller, John D.: billionare founder of Standard Oil Company, which purchased through J.N. Camden controlling interest in West Virginia's oil production; was one of the initial investors in Camden's mining endeavors includeing the Monongah No. 6 and 8 mines; employed A.B. Fleming as West Virginia counsel

Roosevelt, Theodore: president of the United States during the Monongah mine explosion

Roy, Andrew: Ohio geologist and mine safety authority

Ruckman, A. J.: mine superintendent at No. 6

Sands, Joseph E.: Head cashier of First National Bank of Fairmont

Showalter, J. A.: early mayor and manager for Fairmont Coal

Sloan Jr., James: on the board of Monongah Coal & Coke Company and of Farmer's and Merchant's National Bank of Baltimore

Sloan, Bill: underground foreman at the No. 6

Smyth, John Graham: assistant chief engineer for Monongah Coal & Coke Company, in charge of underground recovery

Sovereign, J. S.: general master workman of the Knights of Labor

Sperrow, Samuel: on the board of Monongah Coal & Coke Company and of Drexel Morgan Company of New York

Spilman, Baldwin D.: named general manager of Monongah Coal & Coke Company by father-in-law J. N. Camden; son-in-law of C.K. Lord

Strickling, Mrs. J. H.: member of state House of Representatives and on the Joint Select Committee to investigate the causes of the Stuart mine explosions in 1907

Taylor, Selwyn M.: mining engineer from Pittsburgh

Thompson, D. S.: on the board of Monongah Coal & Coke Company and MCCC mine superintendent

Thompson, G. W.: on the board of Monongah Coal & Coke Company and brother-in-law of C. K. Lord

Thompson, William P.: on the board of Monongah Coal & Coke Company, Secretary of Standard Oil, and Camden's brother-in-law

Trumbauer, Horace: noted Philadelphia architect

Veach, Jacob: built mill near Fairmont in early 1800s

Vernon, Perry: foreman at the Monongah mines

Victor, David: early member of city council, Fairmont Coal supervisor, L. E. Trader's uncle

Vokolek, William: Polish translator for Marion County Inquest

Watkins, Ann: ran a millinery shop

Watkins, James: built mill near Fairmont in early 1800s

Watson, Caroline Margaret: daughter of J. O. Watson, married A. B. Fleming

Watson, Clarence Wayland: youngest son of J. O., became a senator and was put in charge of family business

Watson, James Edwin: son of J. O. Watson

Watson, James Greene: grandfather of J. O. Watson and one of first white settlers in Marion County

Watson, James Otis: invited by Camden to become part owner of Montana mines, 4 miles northeast of Fairmont

Watson, Minnie Lee Owings: wife of C. W. Watson

Watson, Sylvanus: son of J. O. Watson

Wheelwright, Jere H.: Consolidation Coal vice president

Wiltshire, F. W.: head of the Fairmont Coal Company's New York City office

Wise, Charles D.: chief engineer of the Monongah Coal Company whose body was found after the explosion

Clergy and Philanthropists

Boardman, Mable T.: head of the national office of the American Red Cross

Boutlou, Father Arsenius: pastor of St. Peter's in Fairmont

Burke, Henry: lived at house 753

Byington, Margaret F.: trained social worker, employee of the Red Cross

D'Andrea, Father Joseph: an Italian priest who assisted Italian immigrant families.

David, Rev. W. O.: pastor of the Monongah Presbyterian Church

Devine, Dr. Edward T.: editor of *Charities and the Commons* and General secretary of the Charity Organization Society of the City

Donahue, Bishop Patrick J.: Bishop of Wheeling Diocese, jurisdiction over Monongah, assisted priests and visited homes after explosion

Helmick, Reverend: ran a tent revival in 1890 that recruited about 15 converts

Kellogg, Paul U.: writer and staff member of Charity and the Commons, a New York City charitable organization

Lekston, Father Joseph: opened St. Stanislaus Church became its first pastor in 1904

Lorenzoni, Fr. Ricardo: first pastor to serve Monongah

Loss, Virginia: beautiful, young parishioner who raised funds to help build Our Lady of the Most Holy Rosary of the Vale of Pompeii

Labor

Burke, Tom: union organizer and leader of unrest along Pittsburgh seam

Debs, Eugene V.: president of the Railway Union

Evans, Chris: UMWA organizer

Gompers, Samuel: president of the American Federation of Labor

Haggerty, Thomas: strike commander and veteran of the western Pennsylvania efforts

Jones, Mary Harris ("Mother"): effective and tireless union organizer

Malone, J. D.: president of the Street Railway Union.

Mitchell, John: UMWA president

Rashover, Andrew: union organizer and leader of unrest along Pittsburgh seam

Ratchford, Michael D.: UMWA president

Silver, Joe: union organizer who helped form nucleus of the organizing committee

Wilson, Pete: union organizer and leader of unrest along Pittsburgh seam, from Illinois

Investigators and Inventors

Byers, Judy Prozzillo: currently heads up the West Virginia Folk Life Center at Fairmont State College

Caffarul, M. Jacques: Inq. Au Corps des mines and Director de la sation de Essails de Lieuim

Caffauel, Jacques: French mine safety government worker

Caldara, G. D.: Italian Consular

Clanny, Dr. William R.: British physician who first successfully demonstrated a flame safety lamp

Davy, Sir Humphrey: refined the first flame safety lamp

Dumaine, M.: French mining engineer; chief of French Government mining delegation, which investigated the Monongah mine disaster

Others

Carwell, John: early policeman

Cochran, Nathaniel: one of the first white settlers of Briar Town

Kelly, Michael: owned and operated early tavern catering to the Irish

Maruka, Ross: operated a store at 210 Company Row

Mason, Columbus: opened first saloon in Monongah

Marianni, Joseph W.: Royal Italian Consul

Moon, William H.: grocer providing alternative to company store

Muldoon, William: owner-operator of the Hygenic Institute

Salvait, C.: opened a grocery at 210 Company Row

Stalnaker, Hyre: carpenter working in the No. 8 shop

Talbot, William J.: grocer providing alternative to company store

Verdi, Professor Raymond: director of the Verdi Brass Band

REPRINT
OF THE MINES RELIEF
COMMITTEE REPORT

Report of the Monongah Mines Relief Committee.

The Disaster.

On the morning of December 6, 1907, there occurred at Monongah, West Virginia, in two of the mines of the Fairmont Coal Company, known as Monongah No. 6 and Monongah No. 8, a disastrous explosion, resulting in the death of every man within both mines, 358 in all, and of Wm. H. Bice, engineer, who was fatally injured in the wreckage of the power house in front of the opening of Mine No. 8. their names follow, classified by nationality:

Americans — 74

Carl Bice	Thomas Donlin
William H. Bice	Thomas Duffy
Henry Burk	Harry Evans
Robert Charlton	James Fletcher
Fred Cooper	Jahu Fluharty
Fay Cooper	Floyd Ford
William R. Cox	Thomas Gannon
G.L. Davis	John W. Halm

John Herman

E.V. Herndon

Patrick Highland

Lon Hinerman

C.B. Honaker

John Jones

Sam Kelley

Patrick Kerns

Thomas Killeen

Patrick Loughney

L.D. Layne

Adam Layne

Timothy Lyden

Patrick McDonough

John T. McGraw

Charles McKain

Henry Martin

Scott Martin

Albert Miller

James Moon

Frank Moon

L.L. Moore

Andy H. Morris

C. E. Morris

Cecil Morris

Marion Morris

John H. Mort

Charles D. Mort

Sam Noland

Homer Pyles

Hugh Reese

John Regulski

David Riggins

John Ringer

T. O. Ringler

Fred Rogers

David V. Santee

Harry Seese

Beth Severe

Jesse Severe

Frank Shroyer

Dennis Sloan

Scott Sloan

F. E. Snodgrass

George Snodgrass

Michael Soles

Leslie Spragg

Will Stealey

Sam Thompson

Harold Trader

William Walls

J. A. Watkins

Milroy Watkins

George Willey

Charles D. Wise

Americans (Colored) — 11

Charles Farmer

Richard Farmer

George Harris

Gilbert Joiner

Calvin Jonakin

Rippen McQueen

W. M. Perkins

John Preston

K. D. Ryalls

Jesse Watkins

Harry Young

Italians — 171

Carlo Abbate

Francesco Abbate

Giuseppe Abbate

Franceso Abbruzzino

Angelo Adducchio

Antonio Adducchio

Pasquale Adducchio

Domenico Pasquale Agostino

Biase Anciello

Celestino Anciello

Domenico Anciello

Paolo Anciello

Antonio Angiolillo

Angelo Bagnoli

Francesco Antonio Basile

Giovanni Basile

Salvatore Basile

Saverio Basile

Giuseppe Belcastro

Serafino Belcastro

Angelo Berardo

Celestine Berardo

Felice Berardo

Giacinto Berardo

Vincenzo Berardo

Antonio Bitonti

Rosario Bitonti

Giovanni Bonasso

Tommaso Borzonia

Adolfo Brandi

Vincenzo Cavallaro

Giovanni Ciambotiello

Liberato Ciambetiello

Nicola Ciambetiello

Domenico Cimino

Giuseppe Colarusso

Nicola Colaciello

Felice Colaneri

Andrea Colantuono

Francesco Colarusso

Giuseppe Colarsso

Felice Colasessano

Nicola Colitto

Antonio Conversi

Francesco Condino

Raffaele Cuoccio

Victor Davia

Antonio D'Alessandro

Giuseppe D'Alessandro

Pasquale D'Alessandro

Donato D'Amico

Michele D'Amico

Victor D'Andrea

Pasquale D'Ella

Giuseppe D'Uva

Michele D'Uva

Michele D'Onofrio

Pietre D'Onofrio

Antonio De Felice

Michele De Felice

Giuseppe De Maria

Sebastiano De Maria

Felice De Petris

Antonio De Prospero

Clemente Di Bartolomeo

Domenico Di Bartolomeo

Giovanni Di Jelsi

Giuseppe Di Marco

Umberto Di Marco

Angelo Di Maria

Michele Di Maria

Sebastiano Di Maria fu Michele

Luca Di Mario

Nicola Di Placito

Celestino Di Salvo

Domenico Di Salvo

Felice Di Salvo

Florangelo Di Salvo fu Pietro

Florangelo Di Salvo di Antonio

Gioccchino Di Salvo

Giuseppe Di Salvo di Fedele

Giuseppe Di Salvo di Antonio

Vincenzo Di Salvo

Vitale Di Salvo

Ruggero Di Sipio

Ventura Dosa

Armando Fallucco

Vincenzo Fasanelli

Giovanni Farese

Luigi Feola

Carmine Ferrara

Giuseppe Ferrara

Matteo Ferrara

Prospero Florentino

Antonio Foglio

Pietro Fratelacova

Antonio Fratino

Giuseppe Fusaro

Francesco Gaetani

Antonio Gallo

Vincenzo Glaeobini

Antonio Gioia

Pietro Gioia

Raffaele Girimonde

Francesco Guarascio

Domenico Guerra

Gennaro Janiero

Giuseppe Janiro

Pasquale La Vigna

Luigi Lelli

Giovambattista Leoneiri

Carmine Lerose

Francesco Lerose

Giovanni Lombardi

Salvatore Lopez

Francesco Loria

Domenico Mainella

Antonio Manzo

Domenico Manzo

Leonardo Manzo

Michele Manzo

Giuseppe Marinetti

Salvatore Marra

Domenico Mascia

Felice Masella

Michele Mastropietro

Carlo Meffe

Francesco Meffe

Michele Meffe

Cosmo Meo

Pietro Morsella

Giovanni Oliverio

Antonio Olivito

Antonio Pasquale

Louis Patch

Basilio Pellillo

Giacinto Pellillo

Thomas Perri

Saverio Pignanelli

Nicola Pirrocco

Berardino Prioletta

Francesco Prioletto

Pasquale Prioletta

Pietro Prioletta

Pietro Provenzale

Carmine Prozzillo

Antonio Riccinto di Domenico

Antonio Riccinto di Nicola

Domenico Riccinto

Pasquale Riccinto

Antonio Rinaldi

Giuseppe Rinaldi

Raffaele Rinaldi

Michele Rizzo

Luigi Scalese

Giuseppe Serafini

Antonio Siletta

Francesco Todero

Gennaro Urso

Leonardo Veltri

Domenico Vendetta

Francesco Vendetta

Antonio Vergalito

Pasquale Vergalito

Francesco Yacones

Giovanni Yacones

Pasquale Yannacone

Francesco Zampino

Carmine Zeoli

Francesco Zeoli (Barone)

Sebastiano Zeoli (Barone)

Austrians — 15

Wojciech Bassaman

Thomas Drwal

Ignac Gach

Felix Gaada

John Hainer

Anton Hervatin

George Krol

Stefan Noga

Frank Soja

Frank Swiatek

Jacob Traia

John Trusowicz

Anton Udovic

Stanislaus Urban

Johan Valencich

Hungarians — 52

Andrew Barany

George Barany

Michael Banyaczki

Joseph Begala

Michael Bilyo

Martin Bosner

Elek Busztin

Paul Cicvak

John Danko

Michael Danko

George Dankovcik

John Durectz

Michael Durkata

Michael Egri

Joseph Foltin

John Gemercsak

Michael Hamas

Wojcech Hanacsak

Marton Hanyik

Paul Hanyik

John Hornyak (Privracki)

Stefan Ignacsak

John Ihnat

Paul Jagos

Michael Kassic

Michael Kereszeti

Josef Kovacs

John Kresko

John Kristoftz

Frank Loh

Frank Loma

Andreas Marczin

Michael Osval

John Palinkas

George Porhoncsak

John Rehics

Michael Sabak

George Sari

John Sari

Michael Sari

Stephen Sari

Andrew Stih, Sr.

Andrew Stih, Jr.

George Stofira

Joseph Toth

George Tomko

John Tomko

Paul Varga

Michael Vataha

Georgius Zachorcak, Sr.

Georgius Zachorcak, Jr.

Michael Zubko

Russians — 31

Mike Bolinski

George Cikas

Frank Dutko

Andrew Cerak

John Goff

Paul Goff

Walenty Kedzlora

John Kowalike

Wadislaw Kowalsky

Frank Kreger

Frauziscek Krul

Joseph Kviatkovski

Ignaty Lipinsky

John Luba

John Martikonis

Peter Martikonis

Thomas Martikonis

Marcel Miechotka

Vasily Mikitfuk

Carlo Mylkowski

Victor Niwinski

Felix Pierzgalski

Peter Rossa

Thomas Siykowski

Andy Smuzewski

John Smuzewski

Thomas Sosnowka

Joe Stahnlski

Michael Stempen

Thomas Adelbert Stempen

Thomas Zilnis

Turkish Subjects — 5

Andy Kiriazes

Nick Kiriazes   Nick Saltos

Coss Leventy   Nick Sousta

In addition to the above, Maurice Beedle, Richard Beedle and John Neary, who were engaged in the rescue work, subsequently died in consequence, perhaps, of exposure; and the Committee in recognition of such work considered them as victims of the disaster. John Newton (colored), who was standing about fifty feet from the entrance of No. 8 mine, was the only man directly affected by the explosion who escaped with his life. He was injured by the force of the explosion, suffering the loss of his right eye and the middle finger on his right hand.

INDEX

DAVITT MCATEER is internationally recognized as an expert on mine and workplace health and safety. He worked with consumer advocate Ralph Nader to enact the landmark 1969 Federal Coal Mine Health and Safety Act. During the 1970s, he led the safety and health programs of the United Mine Workers of America and founded the Occupational Safety and Health Law Center. From 1994 to 2000, he served as Assistant Secretary for Mine Safety and Health at the US Department of Labor under President Bill Clinton.

Shortly after the terrorist attack on the World Trade Center in 2001, he was called on as an advisor to the recovery efforts at Ground Zero, consulting with union representatives of equipment operators and transportation workers.

Today Davitt McAteer is vice president of Wheeling Jesuit University, where he leads several centers that promote economic development, education, and mine safety. Among these is the Coal Impoundment Project, which works to stabilize or remove coal impoundments throughout Appalachia. He is a consultant to the university's Clifford M. Lewis Appalachian Institute, which addresses issues relevant to residents of the region.

In January 2006, West Virginia Governor Joe Manchin asked McAteer to conduct an independent investigation into the causes of the Sago Mine Disaster and the Aracoma Alma No. 1 mine fire. McAteer and his team produced reports that included recommendations to improve mine safety in West Virginia and across the nation. He also testified before Congress about the need for improvements in mine conditions, which resulted in passage of the Miner Act of 2006.

Davitt McAteer maintains a law office and lives in Shepherdstown, West Virginia, with his wife Kathryn.